HOME-BASED BUSINESS SERIES

HOW TO START A HOME-BASED SECRETARIAL SERVICES BUSINESS

3rd edition

by Jan Melnik

The Globe Pequot Press

Guilford, Connecticut

To Danny, Westy, and Stephen, my three little loves.
To Ron, with my love.

Copyright © 1994, 1997, 2000 by Jan Melnik

Cover and text design by Nancy Freeborn
Cover photographs: Top left and bottom right © EyeWire;
Top right © Image Club Graphics, INC.

Library of Congress Cataloging-in-Publication Data

Melnik, Jan.
    How to start a home-based secretarial services business / by Jan Melnik. — 3rd ed.
        p.   cm. — (Home-based business series)
    Includes bibliographical references and index.
    ISBN 0-7627-0515-9
    1. Secretaries.   2. Typewriting services.   3. Home-based businesses.
    I. Title.   II. Series.
    HF5547.5.M446   1999
    651.3'7'068—dc21   99-41011
                                                                                CIP

Manufactured in the United States of America
Third Edition/First Printing

CONTENTS

3 PLANNING / 41

ACKNOWLEDGMENTS

My sincere thanks and appreciation to:

Understanding clients, for their support and patience . . .

Julie Lynch, for the right connection . . .

Mike Urban, for the opportunity . . .

Wonderful ABSSI colleagues and friends, for their enthusiasm for this project and their willingness to share their stories over the years . . .

My editor of the early editions, Mace Lewis, for his encouragement and expertise as well as providing a wonderful "excuse" (along with Laurie!) to relive all those incredible "early twin" memories while we worked on this together . . .

Louise McGuire Kursmark, for helping me get my business off the ground in 1983 with her good advice, moral support, and deep friendship—and just always being there . . .

Nana and Grampa, for my entrepreneurial passion . . .

Mom, for insisting that I learn to type . . .

Dad, for my love of reading and my thirst for words . . .

My little boys, for their love, hugs, and inspiration . . .

Ron, just because!

INTRODUCTION

The beginning is the most important part of the work.

—Plato, *The Republic, Book 1* (c. 320 B.C.)

In creating, the only hard thing's to begin;
A grass-blade's no easier to make than an oak.

—James Russell Lowell, *A Fable for Critics* (1848)

As with so many things in life, particularly those things most worth doing, getting started and actually beginning can sometimes be the most challenging steps.

I always knew I would someday work for myself. For a number of years prior to starting my company, I'd experienced some margin of success as a freelance writer, with my byline appearing in local newspapers and magazines as well as several national publications. But it wasn't until 1982, when my roommate from college and dear friend Louise McGuire Kursmark decided to start *her* own business providing secretarial services, that I began to really contemplate owning my own business.

Lou had her first child in October of that year and determined that the sometimes inevitable return to the "corporate rat race" after her maternity leave ended was not for her. Instead, she started Secretarial Services Unlimited from her home in North Reading, Massachusetts. (She moved to Reading, Massachusetts, a few years later, renamed the business Best Impression on her tenth anniversary, and relocated once more to Cincinnati, Ohio, in 1995.) Because we'd always stayed in close contact, I watched every step of her business growth, and within a few months she was well on her way to success—clientele was becoming established, cash was coming in, it was looking good. I shared her initial excitement and realized the appeal this opportunity offered.

My own circumstances at that time were different from my friend's. I was on a "career fast track" with Digital Equipment Corporation (now Compaq) and working lots of hours. Still, I couldn't resist the appeal of channeling some of the energy I had into trying to make a go of an entrepreneurial venture. Two things happened to push me over the edge into the lifestyle I now have. In early 1983 my company announced an employee purchase program that would facilitate employee purchase of its new PC equipment at a 50 percent discount with attractive financing options also available. In addition, the district for which I worked was relocating to a new facility. Because this was during the booming 1980s, the relocation was accompanied by a plan to replace all of the office furnishings. I volunteered to assist some of my colleagues in organizing a giant corporate "tag sale" to dispose of all the "old" furniture (most of which was in excellent condition). For our efforts we received "pick of the litter" and could purchase at very favorable rates choice-quality furniture. (I discuss in chapter 3 the details of how I put together my physical office.)

Once I established a corner in my basement with my "new" furniture and DECmate computer system (with then state-of-the-art letter-quality printer), I was ready to launch a business venture by October 1983. Admittedly, this is not the conventional way of going into business. But I've learned from talking with many other service providers in this industry that certain pivotal circumstances often provide an underlying incentive to starting a company.

A colleague from work (who became my husband a few years later) volunteered to post notices about my "typing service" around the campus of the university where he was attending classes during the evening. This publicity resulted in my first client in November 1983 (for a lengthy term paper). This project, billed at my hourly rate of $10, grossed me $74 . . . and was my only revenue for the fiscal year ending 1983 (actually, just a six-week period of time). I started slowly, while continuing to work full-time hours by day. I made the wise decision in the spring of 1984 to install a business telephone line and also arranged for two Yellow Pages ads under Typing Service and Resumes. Interestingly, despite numerous technological changes, these continue to be my two strongest categories for pulling first-time clients today.

I handled a few more projects throughout the spring and summer of 1984, and finally the updated annual telephone directory carrying my ads was published in September 1984. Then the telephone began to ring . . . and it's fair to say it really hasn't stopped ringing since (except for the intervals around my two relocations that followed—from Connecticut to Boston in 1986, and back to Connecticut in 1988).

Throughout these early years I continued to maintain my full-time position at Digital (with a few promotions along the way). Relying on my answering machine to take calls during the business day, I would utilize my lunch hour to go to a pay phone and dial in with my remote playback device to obtain messages left in the morning—and quickly return those calls. I also met with clients at a McDonald's located near my office, conducting business in a booth. The minute I'd get home from work, I would check the answering machine again and return the afternoon calls. Thus, callers would have a gap of at most five or six hours between leaving a message and receiving a return call.

For the majority it was transparent that I was working full-time away from my home office during the day. Was this easy? Absolutely not. But it allowed me to start and build the business slowly, while still having the security and benefits of a full-time position. It was during this time that I was also able to avail myself of lots of relevant training programs in the areas of human resources, interviewing, and people development—all skills needed for my position by day (by then I'd been promoted into management), while at the same time rounding out my skill set for the work I ultimately wanted to do: providing resume consultation and interview training services as a component of my overall business.

It wasn't until my twins were born in 1987 that I determined my own personal objectives (staying home with my children) and plans for my business (taking it to full-time status) could be enacted in one fell swoop: I opted not to return to my corporate position after my maternity leave ended.

Because my decision to go full-time with my business coincided with a move back to my native Connecticut, I had my third (and hopefully final) opportunity to "restart" the business (as well as a third baby!). I enacted most of the advice I provide in this book to kick things off quickly. A *major* handicap: We moved in September 1988, missing publication of my advertising in the Yellow Pages by one full year. The first book I could get into was not distributed until September 1989. So, as you read through this text, keep in mind that while I began under what I consider to be a worst-case scenario for starting a secretarial service business (poor timing with publication of the Yellow Pages), there were still many inventive programs I implemented to jump-start the business successfully.

And it did happen quickly. The first few years back in Connecticut with newborn twins and a newly reborn business passed in nearly a blur. Thank goodness I shot a roll of film about every week for several years . . . and kept a good journal of my babies' progress! One year after the Yellow Pages advertising first appeared in September 1989, my revenues exceeded what I'd been earning in "the real world." I'd achieved my preliminary goal: staying home with my babies while making decent money. The business has only continued to grow, experiencing outstanding growth each year since hitting that important first-year threshold.

About the only things I miss from the corporate world are the daily in-person contacts one has with numerous colleagues and the opportunities for travel. A relatively small trade-off, in my opinion. I relish my independence, love the widely diversified and interesting projects I handle, thoroughly enjoy my wonderful clients, and am thrilled with the financial rewards.

On the personal side—I'm a lot more available to my family than I would be under any other working scenario. I have complete flexibility with regard to taking the time my family or I need for everything from childbirth, vacation, and an hour out in the garden to caring for the three kids when they all had chicken pox, scheduling the time I needed to write this book, and fitting in daily swimming lessons for two-week intervals throughout the summer. With advance planning, tight scheduling, and excellent client communications, anything is possible with this business. No employer I know would be nearly as accommodating, yet I sustain 100 percent productivity and solid profitability. Adding in the sheer pleasure that comes from providing top-notch services that please clients and knowing you're doing excellent work that you truly love—what, I ask you, could be better?

Since writing the first edition of this book back in the summer of 1993, I'm happy to report little has changed (in terms of my overall satisfaction and happiness with my business to date)—and everything has changed! What do I mean by this seemingly contradictory paradox? Well, I changed my business name from Comprehensive Services Plus to Absolute Advantage in 1996 (my thirteenth year in business, ten of those years as Comprehensive Services Plus after the first three years as Professional Services Plus), but I still operate from the office built in 1989 adjacent to my home in Durham, Connecticut. After several experiments with part-time employees, I discovered that I really do like handling every aspect of my business myself (the work *and* the administrative responsibilities); therefore, despite the company's growth, I still do it all myself (by choice). I no longer worry about juggling babies' feedings and nap schedules around client appointments and project deadlines, but instead try to balance my volunteering in my three sons' elementary classrooms with field trips, conflicting Little League schedules, piano lessons, and just time to be a family!

The two things I reported six years ago as "missing" from my world as an entrepreneur have been obviated by the very fact that my business has grown, along with my children. First, I'm now able to travel (from both a financial standpoint *and* from the position of feeling more comfortable in leaving my children at home with their dad for four to five days at a time, two or three times a year, while I attend professional conferences).

Second, I'm able to more effectively network with clients, colleagues, and prospects. I finally joined the chamber of commerce in 1994 and can actually attend a few of its meetings each year (something that was impossible when I had three little babies to tend to and meetings were typically held at 7:30 A.M. or between 5:00 and 7:00 in the evening). I'm also able to schedule a luncheon appointment with a client every so often. (My youngest boy is now in fourth grade; my twins are in sixth grade.) Scheduling clients isn't the gymnastic exercise it was for years when the kids were small; I'm now able to concentrate the overwhelming majority of my client appointments during the hours when my boys are in school, meeting with clients during the evenings or weekends strictly by exception. These appointments I try to combine on just one Saturday and one or two evenings *per month* (a far cry from my start-up years of being able to meet with clients *only* during the evenings and on weekends). Some things are easier . . . and some things are more challenging.

Compared to when I first began my business, technology has vastly improved the way in which business is transacted in the professional office support services industry. On-line communications, fax machines, modems, electronic mail, and cellular digital phones all greatly facilitate the exchange of information and communications between my office and my clients, my service vendors (typically printers), and my colleagues. Our shrinking global marketplace coupled with the acceptance and prevalence of the Internet has created new opportunities for business across every sector of the marketplace—including secretarial services. Many of these business opportunities were unheard of just five years ago. When I think back to how I'd use that remote playback device to "capture" my answering machine messages, I truly realize how much easier it's become to "do business." At the same time, the technological wizardry available can be staggering—and keeping on top of it all has become a part-time effort in itself. (My solution? I subscribe to several excellent periodicals [see information in Appendix], which I organize and store on my bookshelves for detailed research *when* I know I'm actually in the market for a new printer, computer system, database management program—you name it! This way, I don't expend valuable time each month perusing articles I don't yet need—but will someday.)

Also, when I consider how rich my network of colleagues is now (compared to my first five years in business, when Louise Kursmark was my one and only resource . . . she's still my first line of defense in networking!), I realize just how far I've grown as a professional. In the past decade, I've presented major programs at professional conferences around the country (both in the secretarial services and resume-writing fields). I am a regular radio show guest on a program broadcast nationwide dispensing career and job search information to listeners and callers from around the country. I've done a few television appearances and discovered that I really enjoy being in the public eye. These experiences have bolstered my self-confidence, enhanced my speaking ability, (I love to talk and enjoy sharing information and have found I truly do love public speaking), and really broadened my background not only as a business owner but also as an author and publisher. I've found one axiom that continues to bear true as I enter my seventeenth year in business: There is no limit to the amount of information you can continue learning, no matter how experienced you become. I learn as much from folks brand-new to this profession as I do from some of the very most "seasoned" of my dear colleagues.

A new millennium provides each of us with opportunities to conquer many exciting new frontiers. Home-based entrepreneurs have never been more accepted than they are today. There are no barriers to "where" you can do business. In fact, I'll postulate that the typical secretarial service of 2002 will resemble one of 1982 in very few ways—from an operational perspective. But some things will never—should never—go out of vogue: excellence in quality, customer service orientation, added value, and delivery of services that *exceed* client expectations. These are all values I hold near and dear and attempt to embrace every day of my working life.

When I look back on how my business operated in 1983 . . . the major growth points it began to attain in the late 1980s . . . the entire decade of the '90s . . . and how it looks today, I'm struck by the myriad changes—most of which I never anticipated. Yet they're all positive in every way! Technology, to be sure, has been responsible for sweeping operational trends in our industry. Client demands and needs—many times in response to technological nuances—have a major affect on our businesses. Being responsive, flexible, and willing to not only adjust to but also welcome change is as key for us as business owners as it is for those resume clients we may occasionally coach through their job search process!

I hope I've inspired you . . . and I promise to provide as much support and encouragement, and as many practical ideas and recommendations as I possibly can in the chapters that follow to encourage *you* to begin your own secretarial services business!

> *All this will not be finished in the first one hundred days.*
> *Nor will it be finished in the first one thousand days. . . .*
> *But let us begin.*
>
> —John Fitzgerald Kennedy, *Inaugural Address*
> (January 20, 1961)

CHAPTER ONE

PRELIMINARIES AND ASSUMPTIONS

Congratulations on your decision to investigate starting a home-based secretarial service. The first steps are usually the most difficult. This book is designed to provide specific information to help ease your transition into successful business ownership in the months—and years—ahead.

There are probably an infinite number of reasons for wanting to start a home-based business providing secretarial and office support services; perhaps some of these points describe you:

- You possess specialized secretarial skills and a strong administrative background.

- You already own some or all of the necessary equipment.

- You would like to leave the "corporate rat race" and capitalize on your experience.

- You have young children—or plan to have them—and want to take advantage of the flexibility a home-based business affords.

- You have decided that working for someone else is not as appealing as working for yourself.

- You have informally been typing "this or that" for any number of people over the years and decided that it now makes sense to structure what you've been doing all along by calling it a business, charging for your services, and growing it into a truly viable business.

- Your children are now grown, or perhaps you opted not to have children and have decided that growing a business from your home appeals to you.

- You want to capitalize on the potential to earn more money and achieve greater job satisfaction than you've been able to in the past.

- You have an unused room and a need to earn some extra money and have decided a home-based business might be the solution—plus offer tax advantages you've often considered investigating.

- You are newly retired—or about to retire—but wish neither to give up a full-time income nor to be tied down to a full-time position working for someone else.

- You recognize that you've always had "entrepreneurial blood" running through your veins and that there's no time like the present to start to enact the dream you've always had to own your own business.

These are all good reasons to consider starting a home-based secretarial service. With in-depth investigation and planning, the appropriate level of skills, seed money, a credit card or two or a line of credit for start-up costs and equipment, and possibly more energy, motivation, hard work, and enthusiasm than you've ever channeled toward a "job" before, you will find it possible to realize the professional and financial success as well as experience the high degree of satisfaction that accompanies the achievement of a goal of this magnitude.

This book is designed to provide you with proven techniques and key information culled from my experience as well as the experiences of many other successful home-based secretarial service owners. (In addition to the detailed profiles of successful home-based secretarial service operators appearing in chapter 8, you'll find helpful tips and quotes from some of these professionals interspersed throughout the text of this book to expand on some of the suggestions and recommendations I provide.) Specific details are included that will guide you through every step of starting and running a successful business.

ASSESSING PERSONAL AND PROFESSIONAL GOALS

Let's get down to specifics . . . and reflect on the earlier reasons mentioned for wishing to start a home-based secretarial service. Keep in mind as you work your way through the questions that these are simply discussion points to consider, both personally and perhaps with family members. Remember that anyone sharing the same home from which you plan to operate a home-based business will be affected by your decisions. There are no right or wrong answers to these questions. They are essentially guidelines to understanding the reasons underlying your desire to own a business and may highlight certain areas that could present special challenges to you in the future as your business grows. Jot down on paper your thoughts in response to each of the following points—and save this information for later reference.

1. Consider the importance to you of being your own boss and reporting to no one other than yourself. Is this extremely important to you—or not that important?

2. Consider the ability to have unlimited income potential. (You may see this claim appearing in magazine advertisements, but in this business it really is possible, with certain constraints—number of hours you are willing to work; external factors, such as whether you have young children in your home; client base; and so on.) Is this extremely important to you—or not that important?

3. Consider the flexibility of your work schedule, from the standpoint of hours, days, and weeks that you choose to work. Also consider being the individual who determines those things and has the ability to change them almost at a moment's notice. In other words, you set and alter the schedule to suit your needs. For everyone from women with young children at home to retirees wishing to remain "footloose and fancy-free" as they travel periodically throughout the year, a home-based business can ideally provide the necessary flexibility. Is this extremely important to you—or not that important?

4. For many business owners there is a great deal of pride and self-esteem that accompanies being able to say, "I own my own business." Is this extremely important to you—or not that important?

These are the primary areas that most home-based business owners cite when asked why they started their own companies. They are also an individual reflection of your own personal goals and values in life. These questions create a good framework for discussions with other family members as you explore your own reasons for establishing a business.

The following comments were shared by home-based secretarial service operators from around the country—their experience ranging from just one year in business to nearly twenty years as successful business owners. These remarks represent just some of the key sources of satisfaction for operating a home-based secretarial services business.

"It's hard to choose just 'one thing' I like most about owning my own business. Fulfilling my youngest daughter's wish (to have me home when she gets home from school) is certainly one of them. I like the flexibility of my schedule—sleeping later in the mornings and working late at night if I so choose. But networking has been an equally enjoyable aspect of owning my own business. I have met some of the greatest people through networking, and my work on chamber committees and with Toastmasters International is very important to me."

—Cindy Kraft, Executive Essentials

"The sense of being my own person—the respect I get from other people (especially compared to being 'just a secretary' working for someone else. The flexibility to work any time I want to (i.e., get up late, work late in the evening, take time off in the middle of the day). Feeling proud of my accomplishments. Not having to deal with office politics. (On the other hand, I miss some of the goofing off and office socializing we used to do at work.) Being able to 'fire' a client I can't stand instead of having to put up with a tyrannical boss."

—Nina Feldman, Nina Feldman Connections

"Owning my own business gives me the opportunity to make my own decisions and set the direction the business takes. I can work with clients that I want and do the type of work that I enjoy. I love the fact that my business is what it is because of me. I love being at home and having the best of both worlds—home and work. I have some flexibility to change my schedule and do things with my daughter or husband during the day and then work in the evening if necessary. I love my commute during bad weather!"

—Kathy Mandy, Select Word Services

"The flexibility. I love what I do—I do not see it as work, I actually look at it as a hobby! I have to literally force myself to stop working, shut the lights off in my office, and walk away."

—Brenda Lorencen, Word/Pro Connection

"I find myself able to work harder, stay at it longer without a break, and enjoy my work 100 times more than at any other time in my working life."

—Joyce Moore, Moore Business Services

"What I like most about starting my own business is having control of my time and my destiny. I like being in a position to make key decisions. I like being able to help others—if someone really needs a price break, I can choose to provide one."

—Vivian Lee Adkins, Adkins Resume Services

"I like being able to make my own decisions and not have to deal with the 'red tape' of a corporate environment. When I was shopping for my first DOS computer, a secretary for one of my corporate clients was looking for the same system. I researched, shopped, and purchased the computer I wanted in just one month. The corporate secretary received a dedicated word processor eight months later. I also like the feeling of accomplishment. I'm proud of the fact that I can support myself and my son on my own, and that I've been able to grow my business to its current level of success."

—Kathy Keshemberg, Computron—A Career Advantage

"Owning my own business allows me great flexibility in my schedule which in turn allows my husband and me to work together in our commitment to raising our son 'the right way'! Although Christopher does attend day care two mornings each week, we do this primarily because we want him to have social interaction with other children. It is a great relief not to have to depend on an outside caregiver in order to have a second income!"

—René Hart, First Impressions Resume/Career Development Services

"I like the freedom that I have in being able to choose who I do business with. If the chemistry is not there, then it doesn't have to happen. I like the unlimited potential and the ability to deduct more things on my taxes."

—Beth Quick, Q & A Business Solutions

"Everything! I'm in control, I make all the decisions, I can do things my way, I don't have to worry about a boss's fragile ego, no office politics, coffee breaks when I want them, setting my own hours, learning everything I can about business. (I never thought it could be so much fun!) And, best of all, I can buy 'nifty doodads' and software all in the name of the business. Of course, explaining to

my husband why I just had to have another piece of hardware or software (or both!) requires some creative explaining sometimes, but—hey—that comes under R&D [research and development] anyway. It's funny how priorities change: I used to enjoy going to the mall . . . now it's office supply stores like Office Depot!"

—Josie Smith, An Executive Assistant

LEGAL TECHNICALITIES AND ZONING ISSUES TO CONSIDER

Before plunging into the secondary level of concerns related to starting a successful business, you must address several critical issues early on in the process. First, you must ascertain if your proposal to operate a home-based secretarial service is sanctioned within your own city or town's planning and zoning regulations. Your city or town clerk's office can serve as the best source of information in order to begin the application process. As home-based businesses have proliferated through the 1980s and 1990s, so too have the regulations and application processes developed that are designed to contain and control them within many municipalities nationwide.

Typically, most towns will require that you complete a simple, one-page application that details the type of home-based business you wish to operate. Two or three lines are all that would be required, such as "Home-based secretarial and office support services. Will meet with clients on an individual basis, occasionally in their offices and occasionally in my home office. Will provide professional word processing/typewriting/desktop publishing services."

There are generally several key areas with which most local agencies are primarily concerned:

1. That you do not plan to operate a business that will have any associated disturbing noises or smells, use or produce any type of hazardous chemicals or materials, or create any other type of potentially hazardous condition.

2. That you do not plan to operate a business that could in any way disrupt the neighborhood in which you live, create a nuisance situation, or alter the character of the community.

3. That you do not plan to operate a business in which significant traffic and associated problems would be a component.

4. That you do not plan to operate a business that will have many or, in some communities, any employees.

5. That you do not plan to install any form of signage beyond what is permitted. In some communities no outside visible signage is allowed, particularly if you reside in a town's historic district or in a condominium association or apartment complex. In other areas specific size limitations are provided for the posting of one business sign.

6. That you do not plan to operate a business that occupies more than a certain percentage of space available in your total living area. (Generally, a home-based business must occupy 25 percent or less of the total living space.) A simple hand-sketched map, depicting your proposed office space as it relates to the overall size of your dwelling (using square-footage measurements), is generally required.

7. That if you own your home, you can demonstrate appropriate parking, if requested. Using an A2 survey map, as-built plan, or plot plan that shows your house, the portion of your house proposed for your business and the proposed parking for your clientele should be depicted. The parking plan for a business of this type is quite basic: typically indicating that no more than one client will be visiting your office at a time, together with a statement that "ample parking is available in the driveway, along a street, or in a parking area."

8. That signatures of approval have been collected from adjacent neighbors attesting to their support of (or lack of objection to) your operating a home-based business.

9. That you have included the small fee accompanying the application that is generally required (usually between $20 and $50). This should be your first business expense; you don't want to expend money on expensive business cards, stationery, and a telephone line if you haven't ensured that operating a home business in your community is permitted by the zoning regulations. Until such time that you have selected your permanent business name and opened a checking account, you should use your own personal checks, carefully annotated to reflect the business costs incurred (and retaining the checks once canceled). These later become deductible expenses for your income tax return.

If you have a business plan or outline, this can become part of the zoning application package, but it is generally not required. (Chapter 3 discusses development of a business plan in detail.)

When you initially obtain the blank application form, you will be advised of the procedure for submitting the application package. You will probably be asked to attend a meeting of the planning and zoning commission for your town. You should ask to have sent to you a copy of the agenda for the meeting at which your application will be discussed; you should also plan to attend that meeting. While practices vary from city to city, you may be asked to briefly explain the nature of the application to the commission chartered to review home-based business applications. You would simply respond by reading from the description you have provided on the application.

Once you have secured approval from your town to operate your business, you should check with the secretary of state's office regarding registration of your business name. (See chapter 3 regarding selection of your business name.) Again, your city or town hall can provide valuable assistance in completing what is known as a *trade name certificate*. The information you must provide includes the type of business (secretarial/word processing service), name you have selected for the business, address of the business, and your name; the city or town clerk will notarize the certificate. There is typically a small filing fee (approximately $20).

At this time you should also investigate obtaining a sales and use tax permit registration number (if your state requires that sales tax be collected on the type of services you plan to provide; this varies). Your town or city hall can provide information, as can your accountant, if you choose to have one. I have been in business since 1983 and not utilized the services of an accountant; however, I became acquainted very early on with my town clerk and have found her to be an excellent source of information regarding the types of documents I was required to complete as a start-up business owner. Provided that you determine a sole proprietorship is the optimum form of business organization (discussed in chapter 3), your Social Security number serves as your tax identification number.

Your city or town also may require you to complete a Personal Property Declaration form. This document is to collect information so that local taxes can be assessed on your business equipment. Information that will be requested on the form includes your name and address, the business name and type of business, the type of ownership of the business (sole proprietorship, partnership, corporation, LLC, or Subchapter S; discussed in chapter 3), the date you physically occupied your dwelling, the overall square footage of the dwelling, and the purchase value of your business equipment and furnishings.

A second form accompanying the declaration, typically called Confidential Information Report—Manufacturers, Merchants, and Traders, will require you to repeat most of the same information and indicate for each piece of business furniture and electronic/computer equipment the year acquired and the purchase

SAMPLE ZONING PERMIT APPLICATION

Town of _____
ZONING PERMIT APPLICATION

Date _____   Fee _____

OWNER: _____   APPLICANT: _____
(your name)   (your name)

Address _____   Address _____

_____   _____

Phone _____   Phone _____

Affected Address _____   Block # _____ Lot # _____
(same as above)   (above information available through your city or
                                           town's land records)

APPLICATION FOR (check the block for "Home Occupation")

Approvals from (various city/town agencies . . . leave blank for their initials upon approval)

Current Use _____(residence)_____

Proposed Use It is my intention to operate a secretarial service from my residence located at (specific address). The proposed office is located on the first floor, adjacent to the living room (or wherever you've decided to place it). There is a separate entrance serving the proposed office (or the entrance is through the existing front door of the dwelling). No physical alterations to the outside of the dwelling are planned; there will not be any external evidence of the business that would change the residential character of the dwelling.

The office occupies 10% of the total dwelling living area (or whatever the percentage, usually cannot exceed 25%), approximately 400 square feet (again, the specific number should be calculated). No employees are planned at this time. A sign in accordance with the regulations is planned for the future. Ample off-street parking is available for clients; it is anticipated that there might be several clients stopping by the office in a given day to deliver work or pick up completed materials. This business will not have a deleterious effect on the neighborhood and its property values. This home business will not cause an increase in traffic-producing safety hazards. A site plan of the neighborhood (can be your own drawing) is attached; it also details the site plan of the house and parking area (again, can be drawn by hand).

The following neighbors own property adjacent to the proposed home business (list names and addresses) and (if required) have signed the attached sheet demonstrating their support/approval of this proposed home occupation.

(A clause is generally included requesting you to attest to the accuracy of all information provided.)

Your signature/date _____

Zoning Enforcement Officer/date _____

price. A depreciation schedule is provided, and you will be asked to calculate the depreciated value. For example, if you purchased a $2,000 computer in 1998, the depreciated value (as per the percentage listed on the form) might be 80 percent in 2001; therefore, the number you would list under depreciated value would be $1,600. This number is then used as the basis for your personal property tax (if your locale assesses one; most communities do).

Once again, your best resource in determining the types of information required by your town or city would be your accountant or your city or town clerk.

CHAPTER TWO

QUOTIENT FOR HOME-BASED BUSINESS SUCCESS

A t this point we've reviewed the basic information essential to knowing that it is legal and viable to operate a home-based secretarial service in your community. Now you can continue the evaluation process regarding your "quotient for home-based business success."

Again, this is not a scientific process; rather, it is an exploratory path for understanding your unique strengths (and weaknesses) and then utilizing this knowledge to best establish and position your business for success. Review your earlier notes about why you want to be in business for yourself. Then consider the following discussion areas.

CONDUCTING A SKILLS ASSESSMENT

Evaluating what skills you possess is important, from knowing your keyboarding speed to understanding your style in dealing with problem situations. Being a successful business owner involves managing many tasks simultaneously, some of which you may never before have had the opportunity to handle. Most people considering an entrepreneurial career providing secretarial services have office experience, usually as a secretary or an administrative assistant. Many take for granted their skill at the keyboard but often overlook their lack of experience in the critical business areas of planning, marketing, sales, and customer service. Your skill in handling deadlines, dealing effectively with irate clients, managing customer relations, and solving problems is nearly as important as the professional techniques you will use in properly typing and formatting your clients' work.

Owning and operating your own business means that you will be wearing many and probably all of the following hats, at least in the first few years.

- You'll be required to be the president and CEO when it comes to decision making, long-term planning, and strategizing for your company's growth and future.

- You'll be the controller and manager of the Accounts Receivable Department when it comes to decisions regarding granting credit, pursuing slow-paying accounts, and terminating service for nonpayment.

- You'll be the director of public relations, marketing, and advertising when decisions need to be made concerning those publications in which to advertise, what organizations in the community to support, which direct mail pieces to implement, and how much money to spend on Yellow Pages advertising.

- You'll be the sales manager—doing all cold calling, promoting, cultivating of potential leads (every client is first a lead or a prospect), and selling of your business services. (P.S. This never ends, even when you've been in business five, ten, or more years. There will always be the need to cultivate new business.)

- You'll be the Customer Service Department manager, handling all client issues—work orders, scheduling matters, problems, corrections—and receiving those "Project looks great!" kudos from satisfied clients.

- You'll be the computer/software technician, learning and becoming proficient in the frequently complex systems and software (including the Internet and, quite possibly, designing your own Web page) you'll need to professionally produce your clients' materials.

- You'll be the receptionist, greeting each visitor to your office and every caller by phone.

- You'll be the supply clerk, maintaining a reasonable but not overly costly supply of inventory.

- You'll be the billing clerk, handling all invoicing promptly to ensure a healthy cash flow for your business.

- You'll be the repair technician, replacing used toners, cartridges, and printer ribbons; adjusting copy quality; and the like.

- You'll be the cleaning person, emptying the trash each night, dusting the office surfaces each day, placing a fresh flower on the desk in the morning, and running the vacuum over the floors to maintain a professional office appearance in your home office.

- If you're a parent with young children or a caregiver for an elderly parent residing in your home, you'll be managing the challenges of integrating your family responsibilities with growing your business.

- *And* you'll be what you probably describe yourself as—a crackerjack typist/ word processor/desktop publisher who wants to operate a successful home-based business!

In which of the aforementioned areas do you have practical experience? Where are your talents at the expert level? Consider all of the positions you've held in your career. Don't overlook any expertise you might have acquired in a volunteer capacity that would be relevant, such as the cold calling involved in fund-raising for a nonprofit organization.

In what areas might you require some additional assistance or training? For many entrepreneurs the sales aspect of their business is the most difficult. This book later delves into marketing, promotion, and sales in great detail and will provide you with lots of easy-to-implement, creative, and time-tested techniques to help you with effectively marketing your own business. There are also many excellent publications available through the Small Business Administration (SBA) and on the shelves of your local library or bookstore to give you added inspiration; see also this book's suggestions for periodicals to consult or subscribe to (listed in the Appendix). Lastly, don't overlook the vast resources and information available through the Internet.

REVIEWING MINIMUM REQUIREMENTS AND ANALYZING YOUR STYLE

If you research start-up businesses (in any field, not just the secretarial services business), you'll quickly find that a significant percentage fail within the first year . . . and probably only 10 percent of those started will still be in business five years later. Dismal statistics! You can greatly optimize your chances for success in a number of ways, not the least of which is comparing your skill set against the minimum requirements outlined subsequently. This listing of skills is aggressive—and if your skills fall short, even in a number of areas, don't become discouraged. That does not necessarily mean that you're doomed for failure before starting. What follows is, however, a realistic appraisal of some of the "given" attributes a successful secretarial service owner should possess—or work to improve—in starting a business.

Keyboard Skills

The suggested *minimum* words per minute that you should be able to accurately type is 70. While it's possible to operate a service typing at a lower speed, recognize that your earnings will be significantly less than those of an individual who can type 90, 100, or 110 words per minute.

For example, the industry standard for producing eight pages of double-spaced text is one hour. This is based on a typist with a keyboard speed of 70 words per minute (assuming two to three errors per page, frequently corrected in automated spellchecking features typical with most computer word processing software).

If you have determined that your hourly rate, for the purposes of this illustration, is $20 (information on determining appropriate pricing appears in chapter 5), your charge to the client for this project, eight double-spaced pages, would be $20. Now, if you can type 90 words per minute, you would probably complete the project in forty-five minutes. Using industry standards, the fair charge for this project is $20, based on one hour. Therefore, by being able to finish in three-quarters of that time, you would effectively "earn" $26 per hour. *But,* if you can only type 50 words per minute, the project is likely to take you one and one-half hours. Because one hour is the standard for this work, your charge to the client should be $20, based on that being your hourly rate. Therefore, you would actually be earning only $13 an hour for your efforts. And, by the way, these are gross numbers that do not take into account your expenses.

Many other factors are taken into account when considering industry standards. Industry production standards have been developed by the Association of Business Support Services International, Inc. (ABSSI; see information in the Appendix) for use by members of this professional association for the secretarial services

---

SELF-ASSESSMENT: KEYBOARD SKILLS

On a scale of 1–10 (1 being the weakest, 10 being the strongest),
I consider my skills in this area to be _____.

Remedial action required* (if any) _____

_____

_____

_____

---

* An example here might be: Obtain an advanced typewriting program for computer with which I will practice to improve my typing speed and accuracy.

industry. The standards provide information for fairly assessing the time necessary to perform specific work within certain parameters.

Industry standards in many industries have been developed for the benefit of both the customer or client and the service provider. By using standards, superior typists avoid penalizing themselves. In looking at the example provided, if the 90-words-per-minute typist charged just for the actual time of forty-five minutes expended on that project, instead of using the industry standard of one hour, the charge to the client would be $15 (three-quarters of an hour at the $20-per-hour rate). Utilizing standards is fair to the client and to the service provider.

Skill with the English Language

While some clients may insist that you type material exactly as they have presented it, the majority will welcome your "automatic" correction of any errors—spelling, punctuation, grammar, vocabulary, syntax. Most secretarial services do not charge extra for correcting these types of errors in client work. Obviously, if significant editing is necessary (and this should always be authorized by the client first), an additional fee is appropriate. But simply spelling words properly and using correct punctuation are typically expected by a client engaging the services of a professional secretarial service.

Your strong command of the English language is an asset to your clients. If you have particular expertise in this area and perhaps are a writer as well, your skills can naturally lend themselves to an additional profit center for your business—editorial services.

SELF-ASSESSMENT:
SKILL WITH THE ENGLISH LANGUAGE

On a scale of 1–10 (1 being the weakest, 10 being the strongest),
I consider my skills in this area to be _____.

Remedial action required* (if any) _____

_____

_____

_____

---

* Examples here might be: Enroll in a college-level course in journalism, editing, or writing to further enhance editorial skills; supplement personal library of professional resources by adding relevant reference books.

A Word about Profit Centers

Profit centers are specific areas of business that can be segregated for the purpose of reporting and collecting data on your expenses and your revenues. For example, if you have a copy machine in your office and provide copies to clients, the charges for copies should be noted separately on invoices (more on this later) and tracked as an individual profit center. You should also be tracking your costs for the copier separately (lease expense or purchase cost, paper and toner expenses, and service calls or maintenance contract expense). At year's end you will know, for the "copy profit center," exactly what your expenses were to provide this service as well as your income from this service. This same formula holds true for every aspect of your business—from tracking stationery costs and fax services to producing a breakout of your hourly rates for different services. (See Recordkeeping in chapter 5.)

Proofreading Skills

Automated spellchecking features in word processing programs have removed some of the need for proofreading for the misspelling of words in documents. Most spellcheckers, however, are not sophisticated enough to notice a dropped ending on a word (you typed *possess* when the word should be *possesses*), catch homophone errors (*principal* used for *principle* or *to* in place of *too* or *two*), or distinguish a correctly spelled but misused word (*that* should be *than* or *in* should be *is* or *it*). Nor can a spellchecker alert you to dropped text (when typing a lengthy document containing repetitive terminology, you glanced away from the original page, and when you looked back, your eyes picked up the word you just typed—*neu-*

SELF-ASSESSMENT: PROOFREADING SKILLS

On a scale of 1–10 (1 being the weakest, 10 being the strongest),
I consider my skills in this area to be _____.

Remedial action required* (if any) _____

_____

_____

_____

---

* An example here might be: Enroll in a proofreading workshop through an Adult Education program or at a local community college.

ropsychological—but at a different place on the page). These examples point out the continued need for excellent proofreading ability.

Of course, there will be occasions when you are asked to prepare a draft document and use computer spellchecking only—the client is planning to edit anyway and will catch typographical errors during that review process. You should factor in time proofreading all other work, however, with particular emphasis placed on resumes and cover letter materials. The hallmark of a great secretarial service is the ability to produce work professionally, promptly, and *accurately*. While everyone is human and will make an occasional error that will slip through even the best spellchecking system and careful proofreading, the successful business owner wants to keep these to a minimum.

Visual Layout/Desktop Publishing Ability

Although this skill is somewhat intangible and difficult to define, most successful secretarial service owners recognize the need for producing work that is not only accurate and to a client's specifications but visually appealing as well. While a true graphic arts background isn't essential (although it is a plus if you have it and an ideal add-on profit center!), formatting text and layout as well as determining font size and any special design elements require an eye for detail and visual appeal. This includes such formatting features as italicizing, using boldface, using a lighter font, using a contrasting font, underscoring, and indenting. Two documents perfectly typed can look entirely different depending on the typist's ability to employ good visual layout. Over time your skill in this area will be rewarded by

---

**SELF-ASSESSMENT: VISUAL LAYOUT/
DESKTOP PUBLISHING ABILITY**

On a scale of 1–10 (1 being the weakest, 10 being the strongest),
I consider my skills in this area to be _____.

Remedial action required* (if any) _____

_____

_____

_____

---

* Examples here might be: Read books devoted to desktop publishing, subscribe to relevant periodicals, and practice-practice-practice DTP skills in designing my own brochures and flyers.

a reputation for producing work that not only is accurate but looks professional too. This emphasis is reflected in my business slogan: *"Our Business Is Making You Look Good!"* Many of my clients over the years have either their own computers or their own secretaries . . . yet still utilize my services. Why? They tell me it's because, "You work 'magic' and make me look good."

Many secretarial services today also offer desktop publishing services to their clients. These may range from basic or simple desktop publishing (sometimes known as "enhanced word processing") to high-end, professional-quality desktop publishing. The ready availability of desktop publishing software allows many word processing experts to adapt their skills (and upgrade their computers) to offer this more lucrative end of the business. Coupled with strong visual layout ability, the secretarial service operator employing desktop publishing skills can easily offer this high-end profit center. (Consult the Appendix for information about Louise Kursmark's definitive book on the topic, *How to Start a Home-based Desktop Publishing Business*, and learn how she added full-service desktop publishing to her successful secretarial service.)

Over the years, mostly because I was resistant to learning the new software, I have grudgingly worked my way into desktop publishing. Once comfortable upon learning Adobe PageMaker (surprisingly quickly), however, I found my desktop publishing skills greatly improved the appearance of many documents that I had "thought" looked fine by using the bells and whistles I'd mastered in Microsoft Word. I believe there's an old adage about using the right tool to do the job most efficiently . . . this certainly bears out with desktop publishing. And now proficient in PageMaker, I must say I love using my desktop publishing skills for not only my clients' work, but my own publishing projects as well.

Math Aptitude

This is a fundamental requirement—from the standpoint of both managing your business's financial health and working with clients. A small calculator is essential. You may periodically be required to calculate or verify statistical information in client materials. You will probably need to calculate sales tax on most if not all of your services and products sold (paper supplies, postage, etc.). You need to feel comfortable with handling at least the preliminary accounting for your business so that you can quickly spot trends, respond to projected cash-flow crunches, and so forth.

I highly endorse using a computer software program such as Quicken to handle all your business's financial records—and using it on a daily basis. Over the years, I've committed every sin with regard to recordkeeping (more details appear in chapter 5)—from being "too busy" to enter my financial data for *a whole year* to simply not tracking the *essential* information necessary for me to recognize the profitable and not-so-profitable segments of my business.

In the case of the full year in which I accumulated a nearly 6-inch stack of client invoices, it was during a mad dash in April of the following year (yes, just before the deadline for filing my tax return) that I hastily built records into Quicken in order to produce the reports necessary to complete Schedule C on my tax return. It wasn't until way too long after the fact that I was able to observe my "good" months and those months in which numbers were slightly off. Only then was I able to see the most profitable segments of my business (confirming, in most instances, where my "gut" had told me the good money was) and those profit centers that really were costing me money. Because of my sloppy bookkeeping, I wasn't able to keep track of accounts receivable in an efficient or timely manner. The biggest drawback to this "method" of bookkeeping was that I'd deprived myself—on an ongoing daily, weekly, monthly, and quarterly basis—of feeling good about how well my business was really running: I was literally flying by the seat of my pants. By the way, I'll admit that this was *only* a few years ago (for the calendar year 1995) that I, a seasoned business owner, committed this ridiculous "you-would-think-I-would-know-better" mistake, which only goes to show . . . do as I say, not as I do!

SELF-ASSESSMENT: MATH APTITUDE

On a scale of 1–10 (1 being the weakest, 10 being the strongest),
I consider my skills in this area to be _____.

Remedial action required* (if any) _____

_____

_____

_____

---

* Examples here might be: Double-check all math on quotations for client projects and invoices; invest in, install, learn, and *use* a good recordkeeping program *regularly*.

Interpersonal and Communication Skills

Probably even more important than your computer/keyboarding skill and technical know-how is your ability to deal effectively with people. Providing secretarial services will expose you to many types of people. From professionals, white-collar senior management types and college and graduate students to blue-collar laborers and gray-collar techni-professionals, you will be in contact with all of these people throughout nearly every business day, by telephone and, to some extent, in person. Your ability to "change hats" and relate with impact and empathy will largely govern your overall business success.

Why is this so important? The services you provide are a commodity—secretarial services are probably available from a number of sources in your area. Why do people choose to do business with the firms they do? *People.* You are what will make your business a true success. Your ability to make all clients comfortable, secure, and confident in your ability to handle their work—and to follow through on your promises—is what will make for repeat business and build that all-important client base. Likewise, satisfied clients will do the single thing that's most important for your business growth (besides pay for your services)—*they'll tell others.* No other advertising is as important as the referrals your happy clients will provide. (More on this later.)

The more genuinely interested you are in your clients' businesses, the more valuable they will perceive you as being. Your aspiration should be to be a team player with each of your clients. For example, with every resume client you handle— even those merely having their resume typeset exactly as they've written it—you

---

SELF-ASSESSMENT: INTERPERSONAL AND COMMUNICATION SKILLS

On a scale of 1–10 (1 being the weakest, 10 being the strongest), I consider my skills in this area to be _____.

Remedial action required* (if any) _____

_____

_____

_____

---

* An example here might be: Research library and bookstore shelves for books regarding communication skills and relationship management techniques.

want to convey your sense of involvement and caring. When a resume client contacts you several weeks after the initial resume/cover letter project to ask for your assistance in preparing additional cover letters, you should express interest in the previous correspondence the person sent seeking interviews. "How did that opportunity at the university turn out for you?" Your ability to utilize quick memory recall can be a real plus here! I have a very poor memory—but a good filing system that enables me to quickly pull out a paper file for each resume client with copies of the correspondence and resume attached. This prompts me in asking appropriate questions.

Likewise, with your business/corporate clientele, staying abreast of their industry or field is equally important. "What did the results of the survey reveal?" might follow a survey project for a business client in your next telephone contact. "How was your lecture received?" "How did that sales call at XYZ Company go?" Whatever could logically follow a project you handled recently is the perfect question to ask in a follow-up call (whether initiated by you or the client). We're all flattered when people remember what we do and those activities in which we're involved. Clients will be impressed by your interest in their business.

Professional Demeanor and Polish

Establishing a professional presence from a home office setting can be challenging for some unless you're planning to offer services strictly over the telephone and via the Internet. I am firmly of the belief that if you are *always* professional in your client dealings, produce a top-quality product, and cultivate solid working relationships with your clients, you will naturally convey a highly professional demeanor. Whether you choose to dress in a corporate suit or a jogging suit is your decision . . . and you have the flexibility, from a home office, to quickly change to appropriately meet the requirement. For example, when meeting with a first-time corporate client in my home office, I always assume a more traditional "corporate" look. I've long since disposed of my constricting matched-jacket-and-skirt business suits, but I do have a nice wardrobe of unconstructed jackets, coordinated skirts, and the like. The same is true when meeting with a resume client who is a professional. (Information exchanged in the preliminary call to my office typically reveals something of the person's background; when I know that I'm meeting with a health care professional to update her CV [curriculum vitae, as a resume is typically called in the health care, education, and psychological professions], I "dress the part".) I will also dress down ("professionally and neatly casual") when I'm meeting with a student to discuss typing a thesis or when a factory laborer is meeting with me early in the morning following his third-shift job.

* An example here might be: I'll consciously give thought to my wardrobe on days on which client appointments are scheduled, and I'll deliberately pay attention to the manner in which I speak with all clients.

Believe me, I don't spend a lot of conscious time on this aspect of business—it has evolved naturally and, occasionally, I do err. Although all appointments are scheduled and I don't offer drop-in times, clients will periodically swing by to drop off a project if they are in the area. They may not expect to see me and simply plan to use a drop-off envelope I provide at the door. But they may catch me on a "writing" day when I have only a few client appointments scheduled with professional clients who work from home offices (and dress casually, as do I, for our meetings). I may be barefoot and dressed in shorts and a T-shirt, but I accord them the same respect, friendliness, and professionalism I do when "dressed for business." Our relationship does not in any way suffer; in fact, many of the professionals with whom I work frequently sigh and tell me how much they admire the ability I have to work comfortably from my home office.

Professionalism is an attitude—how you convey it is a skill of combining words, direct eye contact, open body language, and a genuine appreciation and respect for your clientele.

Customer Satisfaction

Your commitment to delivering customer satisfaction cannot be overemphasized. When you were working for someone else, chances are good that "the buck" did not stop with you; there was always someone higher in the organizational chain to whom you could refer problems during a customer dispute. When you are the business owner, all issues, positive and negative, typically start and stop with you.

Your ability to defuse a hot situation in which a client is agitated is critical. Your ability to remain objective and not be overly sensitive *or* defensive is just as key. The bottom line in any strong business is pleasing the customer . . . the adage we've all learned: "The customer is always right." No one wants unhappy clients—and we'll do all that is within our power to make a client satisfied.

If you are facing a situation in which a client has a complaint, be open and receptive to hearing and really listening to what the client is saying. Whether or not you believe there actually is a problem is irrelevant. If a client says there is a problem, then there is a problem. Your objective should be to discover as quickly and calmly as possible how the situation can be remedied. For an obvious problem, such as a typographical error appearing on a resume, a simple correction is all that is in order (accompanied by profuse apologies; by a reminder—if applicable—that the client did have an opportunity to review and approve the proof copy prior to printing and therefore must assume the cost of the correction, if a large number of originals are involved; and by a quick repair).

In some cases it may make the most sense for you to absorb the cost of correcting a typographical error, even if you do include on your work order a statement that "final proofreading is the responsibility of the client." (More information on this in chapter 5 under Organization—Client Work Order.) Client goodwill and word of mouth are worth protecting at nearly any price. Because you are the boss, you can adjust your own rules at any time. It's well worth your quarter-hour of time to make a free correction and provide twenty newly printed laser originals of the corrected resume at no charge—graciously, courteously, smiling all the time—to a client who is highly and perhaps irrationally irate. After all, what ill will is a client likely to spread when you've bent over backward to appease and satisfy the person?

Business analysts have calculated that, in terms of money and time, it costs nearly four to eight times as much to cultivate a new client as it does to retain an existing client. If you already have a client through the door, it's much more effective to work with that client to resolve a dispute than it is to begin the sales process all over again with someone new. Of course, as in any other aspect of life, there may be the occasion when you simply don't value a particular client's work enough to make it worth the aggravation . . . and would prefer to not handle the work. In this case there may not be a personality fit between you and the client, the client may be one of those fortunately rare individuals who simply can't be pleased, and you determine it is not of mutual benefit to cultivate a relationship any longer. In that case my recommendation is to indicate professionally that continuing a business relationship appears not to be in the best interest of either party and to provide a

* Examples here might be: Develop a client satisfaction policy, including a service guarantee, and post it prominently in the office; read business books on the topic of delivering service excellence and ensuring customer satisfaction.

referral to another service. No law requires you to work with any client. If you've entered into a relationship, plans do need to be made for ceasing that particular business arrangement, including a reasonable period of time for notice; provision of work completed to date and of disk copies, if appropriate; return of client stationery; final payment of account; and so forth. In my years of being in business since 1983, I've never had this scenario play out. But I do have colleagues in this business who have done just this to eliminate such a difficulty.

Marketing and Sales Skills

Polished marketing skills, the ability to promote yourself and your business, and the capability of selling are all important attributes to developing and maintaining a successful business. While probably only a few lucky entrepreneurs naturally possess these skills and attributes, the rest of us can quickly learn and develop our techniques in this area. Just by implementing many of the ideas appearing in chapter 4, you will become more comfortable with the function of marketing for your secretarial services business. And there's truth in the phrase, "Nothing succeeds like success." As you capture new business, successfully turning callers into clients, you'll develop "recyclable" phrases and terminology that you can use again and again in speaking on the phone. Far from sounding "programmed," you'll develop a professional polish that is conveyed to the listener.

Many periodicals devote monthly columns to the topic of marketing. (Some of the best for the secretarial services industry are listed in the Appendix.) Bookstore and library shelves overflow with books proclaiming the virtues of their own techniques for enhancing your ability to promote and sell your business. The

Appendix includes the titles of just a sampling of some of the best of these books. Pore through your own favorite bookstore and public library shelves to unearth others. Keep in mind that professional periodicals to which you subscribe can become tax deductions for your business. So too can the professional seminars and programs you are encouraged to attend in your locale—they have double impact, educating you through exposure to different marketing ideas and providing you with valuable opportunities for networking with other professionals and possible clients in your community.

Check with the Business Development Office in your city (or nearest large city) for additional information. The Small Business Administration (SBA) office in your area can also provide information about upcoming seminars. Local colleges and universities frequently offer programs in conjunction with the SBA. Local telephone companies may also offer programs for developing your business that you would find beneficial. I try to attend at least two professional workshops

---

SELF-ASSESSMENT: MARKETING AND SALES SKILLS

On a scale of 1–10 (1 being the weakest, 10 being the strongest),
I consider my skills in this area to be _____.

Remedial action required* (if any) _____

_____

_____

_____

---

* Examples here might be: Read business columns in newspapers and magazines for marketing and sales techniques; attend as many seminars and workshops (including industry-specific professional conferences) as possible in which the topic of marketing is prominently featured.

or conventions per year, including one in our industry. (ABSSI sponsors an outstanding convention each year, and local chapters also host regional annual conferences; see chapter 5 and the Appendix.)

Desire to Be Successful . . . and Drive to Work Hard

This may be an understatement, for to be truly successful, you must sincerely *want* success. Success must be defined in your *own* words. For most secretarial service owners, the ultimate plan is to work a full-time schedule (or perhaps slightly less) for *greater*-than-full-time pay in relation to a comparable position in a company. For example, if as a secretary a person earned $25,000 for working a typical 8:30 to 5:00, five-day-a-week job, as the owner of a business, this person would want to have as a salary (*not* the revenues of the business, out of which must come taxes, expenses, and all other costs of doing business) at least $25,000, generally $35,000 or $40,000, and optimistically anywhere up to $50,000 or $75,000 or even $100,000! These numbers should, of course, be adjusted for your geographic area of the country and whether or not you live in or near a large metropolitan area. Essentially, the potential is limited only by you and your desire to build your business.

Many entrepreneurs have as a realistic goal working *fewer hours* than they did in what I like to call "the real world," while at the same time earning *more money*. This is a great goal and highly achievable, with hard work and planning, particularly at the outset.

It's a fair statement, and you'll hear it from every successful entrepreneur, that you will work harder building your business and for yourself than you ever have in the past. But you'll also derive infinitely greater job satisfaction and, hopefully, more income than you ever did working for someone else. There are probably no successful entrepreneurs in any field doing what they love who dread "going to work." For most of us it's a pleasure to be in our offices, working with clients, doing work we enjoy, and receiving good money for it. In fact, for many of us where a key difficulty can rear its head is in finding the all-important balance necessary to sustain a life *and* a business.

For many successful entrepreneurs the tendency to be a perfectionist is a natural characteristic. It's easy to get carried away with working too much when your business is thriving and reaching a point where you must make critical decisions

---

SELF-ASSESSMENT: DESIRE TO BE SUCCESSFUL . . . AND DRIVE TO WORK HARD

On a scale of 1–10 (1 being the weakest, 10 being the strongest), I consider my skills in this area to be _____.

Remedial action required* (if any) _____

_____

_____

_____

---

* An example here might be: Regularly monitor business growth and development relative to initial goals and objectives—always set new goals and stretch objectives for the future.

regarding its overall future as you manage its growth. We'll talk more about this later. For most budding entrepreneurs dealing with too *much* work is a problem they would love to manage in the first year!

Ambition and Inner Motivation

When you answer to only your clients and ultimately yourself, you must have within you the pride that is associated with owning your own business. No one will criticize you in your performance evaluation for taking too many sick days. (Clients may complain and, worse, go elsewhere, but there's no one to dock your pay if you decide not to show up for work one day; however, in this business if you aren't working, you aren't generating what are known as "billable hours".) This is not to say that it isn't appropriate to take well-deserved days off. They simply must be planned reasonably, far in advance if you have clients who utilize your service very regularly and on appointed days.

High energy level and good health should accompany your own motivation and drive to succeed. You'll need these characteristics as your business grows. The work of a secretarial service is generally not able to be grouped into perfect work segments. Some periods of the year will find you overwhelmed if you accept student work on top of regular client requirements, particularly during term paper or thesis season at a nearby university. You'll pull "all-nighters" characteristic of when you were back in college. Other times of the year may find you working at less than capacity. For some secretarial service owners, the weeks between Thanksgiving and Christmas are characteristically slow, as are the months of July and

---

**SELF-ASSESSMENT:
AMBITION AND INNER MOTIVATION**

On a scale of 1–10 (1 being the weakest, 10 being the strongest),
I consider my skills in this area to be _____.

Remedial action required* (if any) _____

_____

_____

_____

---

* Examples here might be: Build a list of "to-do" strategic business planning activities and marketing ideas to work on during slack periods; create a personal library of motivational books and articles, tapes, or videos (depending on the learning style you prefer).

August. Once your business has hit its stride, you'll welcome these brief respite periods. They allow for the necessary time to rejuvenate your batteries and devote resources to strategically planning your business.

Years ago I used to panic if I looked at my daily to-do list (see Other Relevant Forms—Project Status/Deadline Sheet in chapter 5) and had fewer than five or six client projects and deadlines listed. I'd worry that I would run out of work. For at least eleven years, I really haven't had the pleasure of thinking I might run out of work for a day or two and actually have time to catch up on some of my filing for the business . . . or play with a new software program . . . or experiment with a different layout for my company's newsletter. Now the only time my to-do list ever has fewer than ten or fifteen projects on it is when I'm gearing up for a vacation. Then I really have to work double time to accomplish all my projects before leaving (and work twice as hard when returning to get back on track). But I'm calling the shots—and I love it!

I always advise newcomers to this industry to relish the times when things are relatively quiet. That's not to say that if your phone isn't ringing at all, you shouldn't be taking proactive steps to build your business. But if you've got a fairly regular client base and an expectation from regular clients of ongoing work, an occasional quiet day or two can provide essential time for refocusing and exercising continual development of your business. In the first few months and years, you should plan to spend a specified amount of time each day on marketing your business. More details are provided in chapter 4 as to the types of activities that can be most beneficial to growing your business.

Outstanding Organizational Ability

Being a home-based secretarial service owner, like any business owner, requires extraordinary skill in juggling multiple priorities, tasks, and work responsibilities. For those also caring for young children or aging parents, your management skills will be tested even more. But the rewards derived from operating a successful business in your home are unmatched, and throughout this text I'll provide many suggestions and tips for getting the most out of your valuable time.

ADVANTAGES AND DRAWBACKS TO OPERATING A HOME-BASED BUSINESS

There are infinitely more advantages than disadvantages to owning a home-based secretarial service, but it's worthwhile to review both sides of the picture. First, the positive aspects of such an enterprise.

* An example here might be: Implement an effective planning/scheduling system (I love the Franklin Planner!) and utilize a computerized tickler file. (First Things First works well for me.)

Advantages

- Because you will most likely be meeting with clients on an appointment-only basis (as opposed to a storefront operation, where drop-ins are common and the hours are generally fixed), you maintain greater flexibility in your work schedule. This works particularly well in helping to balance business with your personal life. Whether it's taking an afternoon off occasionally to attend a professional meeting, go to a doctor's appointment, participate at your children's school, poke around in your garden or an antiques store, or simply do nothing, you are in charge of arranging your own schedule.

- Nothing beats the commute to a home-based business! This translates into significant savings in terms of the rent or leasing costs of an external office, commuting costs, professional wardrobe (you can get away with far fewer professional outfits when you're not appearing in the same business office five days a week), power lunches, and possibly day care. (More in chapter 6 on this aspect of operating a business when you have young children.)

- You directly control your income. Unless you were in sales, you probably had a fixed salary, had little opportunity to earn bonuses, and waited twelve to eighteen months for an increase. When you own the business, you set the prices, determine the timing and amount of increases in your rates, and have the ability to aggressively market, offer promotions, and work harder or more hours to generate greater cash flow. Overtime in "the real world" was probably mandated or available only at your employer's discretion. Here you make the decisions when you will work and how much you will work.

■ In this business you can opt to handle only the types of work you actually *like* handling. For some, transcription is a bore, difficult, or hated . . . so, your secretarial service doesn't have to provide this service. Maybe you dislike typing statistical copy—don't solicit this type of work. Perhaps your greatest enjoyment is working with lengthy manuscripts—you should actively seek this kind of work. Because you are the manager, you dictate what services your business will provide. Most brand-new secretarial service owners find they'll take any and all work in the initial months—and perhaps years—"as long as it's legal." As your business develops, however, you may find that specializing in certain areas of the business appeals to you and that doing certain work does not. You make the call!

■ While you do have clients to answer to, owning your own business provides the greatest flexibility in emergency situations. For me emergencies have ranged from simply being available to pick up a sick child at school on a moment's notice and having three preschoolers home over a period of six weeks as they all battled chicken pox (not quite simultaneously) to having a chance to get away at the last minute for a week in the sun. All that I needed to do was coordinate my calendar with my clients', work more at night, and maintain regular communications. My former employers from the corporate world might not have been as flexible over a six-week hiatus with the chicken pox! My clients had no objection to meeting me on my porch (for those who hadn't been exposed) or in the evenings.

■ There are significant tax advantages to owning your own business, particularly when it is home-based. While this book is not intended to provide specific legal or financial advice and you are encouraged to seek professional counsel in these areas, throughout the text I will share some of the benefits I've found in these areas.

■ In addition to scheduling client meetings and appointments to suit your schedule, you also have the flexibility of determining the best times of day (or night) that you'd like to work. When my twins were infants, I found I worked during assorted pockets of the day and night, whenever they were napping or sleeping. Sometimes that meant I'd be at the computer from 5:00 A.M. until the next feeding at 8:30 A.M.; in other instances I'd sit down to work after the 11:00 P.M. feeding and work until their next feeding at 3:00 A.M. before I decided to retire for the night. As the children got older, my work habits changed to reflect my true biological clock—a night owl's. When my children were all still preschool age, I could rarely meet with clients between 8:00 A.M. and supper time; consequently, most of my client appointments were evenings and weekends and I worked nearly every night until midnight or later. Now, I'm generally not at my desk until 9:00 A.M. (once all my boys are on the school bus), and I'm able to talk or meet with most of my clients during "regular" daytime business hours. I still work an evening or two a *month* (by choice—and typically to compensate for a day spent out of the office volunteering at my sons' school or going on a field trip), but I'm no longer a slave to my desk every evening until the wee hours of morning as I was during my business-building-around-babies mode. Herein lies the great flexibility of owning your own business. Whatever your particular lifestyle requirements, this business can flow right around it. Many of my colleagues are empty-nesters and keep very traditional business hours, rarely if ever working evenings or weekends. That was once a future aspiration for my business which I have now achieved!

With few exceptions, home-based secretarial service operators *love* the advantages of working from home. Here's what a few people in the business have to say:

"The thing I like most about owning my own business is that I can work on what I want, when I want, and where I want. I can choose what hours to work and be able to do some gardening, take the dog for a walk, or even take a nap after lunch."

—Shawn Teets, WordWise

"Owning my own home-based business allows me the freedom and flexibility that I need in my personal life."

—Theresa Mills, Mountain View Office Support

"What I enjoy most about working from home is being able to keep my wonderful golden retriever, Jake, company . . . being able to dress casually and comfortably . . . access to a cold pop in the refrigerator when I want one . . . able to take a two-hour shopping trip when work is slow or I know most of my regular clients are out of their offices."

—Sue Faris, Word Processing Plus

"Working in my pajamas and not having to drive in rush hour!"

—Cindy Kraft, Executive Essentials

"Being able to start dinner while working and to work late at night if I feel like it. Being able to work family and friends into my schedule when needed."

—Nina Feldman, Nina Feldman Connections

"I can work in my pajamas, if I please. Many a night I have worked well into the wee hours of the morning (doing a rush job). What other place could I work in such attire? Again, I will say: I love my job! Life is good!"

—Brenda Lorencen, Word/Pro Connection

"I like the commute. I get dressed and walk into my office. I don't have to go out and get in the car during snow, ice, thunderstorms, or fog and hope that I've allowed enough time to reach my destination without being late. I am warm, dry, and at work the moment I walk in there. My office is in a spare bedroom, next to the bathroom, and only 30 feet from the kitchen coffeepot. I can take a break when I want to, without having a supervisor or boss counting the minutes. If someone in the family needs me, I'm here. (I have a daughter with MS, and it means a lot to her to know I'm here in case she needs me.) I finally trained the rest of the family not to call during business hours or, if they do call me, to ask if I'm busy or if I can talk."

—Joyce Moore, Moore Business Services

"I like working out of my house because it's much more time-efficient. There's no time lost traveling to and from work, going out to lunch, etc. I'm able to be with my son much more than if I worked at an outside job. I'm able to much more easily mix my personal and professional lives. If I have an hour to spare between clients, I can do a quick errand or I can do a load of laundry or whatever. Working for other people, that's not usually possible. I often use the computer equipment and business inventory for the good of the church I go to and other nonprofit organizations that I'm involved in and believe strongly in."

—Vivian Lee Adkins, Adkins Resume Services

"The flexibility—being able to throw in a load of laundry and make dinner in conjunction with finishing up client letters or waiting for a FedEx pick-up is convenient. Also, the ability to schedule clients to fit around my schedule is a luxury. Doctor, dentist, and hair appointments can be scheduled during the day, and I can work during the evening to catch up on my work. Being here before and after school as well as during the summer to monitor my son is a definite advantage. The independence: not having to be 'somewhere' at a specified time, or having to rely on an employer who could go out of business or downsize. I put in more hours in my self-employed status, but it's easier to put the hours in when my office is only steps away from my home."

—Kathy Keshemberg, Computron/A Career Advantage

"Freedom! I can work when I want. I can dress however I want. When the mood hits me, I can take a break and go outside to garden or play with my son. I enjoy working by myself."

—Josie Smith, An Executive Assistant

Drawbacks/Challenges

■ Managing your personal and business time will probably be the single greatest hurdle facing you as a home-based secretarial service owner. While the flexibility such a business provides is wonderful for you, your clients may begin to think it is designed for them. In fact, when I first started my business, I still held a full-time traditional day job. I could *only* meet with my clients after hours and on the weekends. I sold this as an *advantage* to them—"I'm available to meet with you during your off-hours so that you're not losing valuable business time." In the many years since I took my business to a full-time status and gave up my external employment, however, I found clients still wanting to utilize the perceived advantage of my availability after hours. I'm flexible and structure my time to meet their needs, while at the same time being cautious not to let it spill too much into my family's time. This can be a constant struggle for some. (See Cultivating Client Relationships in chapter 5.) Many secretarial service owners describe their own experiences, some hilarious, in which they were disturbed at home on holidays, late in the evening (after going to bed), or in the early morning before they had dressed for business. About the latter I have my own funny story, which you can chuckle over in chapter 6.

■ Security for a home-based business is paramount in the minds of many. Because many secretarial services businesses are owned by women who work from their homes alone, at least during the daytime hours, it's important to give consideration to this and plan accordingly. I believe it's a fair statement that even in a traditional office setting or executive suite arrangement, it's impossible to prepare for all possible problems.

But you can take steps, as a home-based business owner, to ensure the greatest peace of mind and security for you, your home, and its assets. By not permitting drop-in appointments, you should never be surprised by an unannounced visitor. When scheduling appointments over the telephone, you will need to develop an almost "sixth sense" in discerning true callers (99 percent) from the occasional prankster. I make it a practice never to reveal my street address in any advertising (including Yellow Pages) or promotional literature; I utilize a post office box. When responding to a telephone inquiry from an unknown prospective client who has asked, "Where are you located?" I indicate that I am off the main street in my town. I quickly add that once we've discussed the person's requirements and are at the point where we are scheduling an appointment, I'll be happy to provide specific directions. A prankster is not going to engage in five minutes of telephone discussion over a nonexistent project simply to learn your address. (At least that's been my finding.) Use your own common sense and good judgment. There have been occasions when I've felt uncomfortable over the telephone, even after discussing a project. In such cases I then attempt to schedule an appointment at a time that I know either my children or, preferably, my husband will be here. I will also sometimes fictitiously state, "Yes, 3:00 will be a convenient time. My associate will be speaking with another client at that time, but the office is large and we can accommodate that." Only twice in my years of doing business have I actually asked a neighbor (retired and, incidentally, my father) to physically be present in the office during questionable appointments. I've never had a problem.

Some secretarial service owners I know have established a calling system with colleagues in their communities. Someone I know even went so far as to make a telephone connection with a neighbor by calling that person's number and leaving the telephone on her desk so that if a problem arose, she could simply scream and the telephone could transmit her plea for assistance to the neighbor listening on the other end. This is somewhat drastic, but whatever makes you most comfortable is worth doing. Many home-based businesses have installed professional security systems that include a feature whereby you can punch in a quick code in an emergency to alert a monitoring station that you're in distress. This can impart a feeling of confidence and security.

Some secretarial service owners I know keep a radio turned to a talk station on low volume in a room adjacent to their office, to provide the illusion of someone else being in the home during their appointments.

Physical location of your office comes into play here as well. Ideally, you do not want to situate your office (at least the portion of your office where you will be meeting clients) in the bedroom or living areas of your home. The perfect location would be somewhere separate from these areas—a room adjacent to your home, a renovated garage or closed-in porch, or perhaps even a basement room. (That's where I started out.) In my own case, after outgrowing my basement quarters I moved with all my equipment to what was then a spare child's room. With the exception of one client who became a family friend, I never brought a client down to this "office"; instead, I always had all the necessary supplies for an initial client meeting at my dining room table, and that's where I met clients for several years, until the point where I had a large office constructed adjacent to my home. A disadvantage to not having your computer equipment where you meet clients is during those times when a quick correction is necessary while a client waits. By this time, though, the client is in the office for at least the second time, or maybe the third, and money has already exchanged hands. In such situations I always found I could comfortably (and quickly) scoot down to my bedroom office, make a change, and return to the dining room. I always provided relevant reading material and information for my clients to peruse while I was gone—and was never away for more than five minutes. If lengthy changes were required, I scheduled a follow-up appointment.

■ Turning off your professional work self is more difficult when your work space is physically located in your home. In the early years this may not present itself as a problem, but as business grows you may find that it's hard to stay away from your desk—especially if your office is located in eyeshot of other living areas—when you have deadlines encroaching. Similar to managing client interruptions on your personal/family life, structuring time off for yourself and your family can be a challenge. Some secretarial service owners find it's useful to dedicate at least one day per week, and possibly two (frequently on the weekends), when they simply will not go into their offices, respond to messages on their answering machines, or "think" work at all. This type of discipline is not always easy to impose on yourself but should evolve quite naturally with time.

Your colleagues have been very candid in revealing their opinion of the drawbacks to operating a home-based business. They add, however, that the benefits more than outweigh and compensate for any perceived disadvantages.

"The biggest challenge of being home-based is seeming credible to other people. From the beginning, I worked hard to set limits on interruptions from others during the day. I set a schedule of hours I worked each day. When I first started and my daughter, Becky, was in preschool, I worked while she was at nursery school and while she napped. As she got older and in school full days, I worked while she was gone. Of the sixteen years I've been in business, the last ten years have been full-time. I go down to my office at 8:30 to 9:00 every morning, break for one to one and one-half hours for lunch and running errands, and finish work at 5:00 to 6:00 each day. I turn down requests from family and friends for lunch or outings during the day if my schedule doesn't permit. Even if relatives from out of state come to town, I have turned down requests to visit because of work. I think because of this, people know my boundaries and call to set things up with me in advance. Then I'm able to plan and put it on my calendar. But when I'm not really busy with work, I can sure relax and enjoy the free time. I love the flexibility of enjoying a nice, sunny day!

"The other challenge of being home-based is the lack of live interaction with people, face to face. Sometimes you can feel so isolated. The cure for me has been membership in a home-based secretarial association, the Association of Professional Office Support Services. The third Monday evening of the month is sacred at our house. Everyone knows I'll be at my APOSS meeting. It's wonderful to network with people doing the same thing and facing the same hurdles. It's also a great place to share accomplishments. Some of my very best friends are women I have met through this group. We've been together for a long time, and some women are now doing other things, but a small group of us still stays in almost daily and weekly contact with each other. We do things together socially, as well as professionally.

"During the last two years, the other thing I've done is make myself get out of my house at least three to four times a week. I do really exciting things (like go to the post office, the bank, and go to McDonald's for a Diet Coke). But this at least gets me out of the house and breaks up the day. Prior to implementing this plan, I found I was really getting homebound, only going to the mailbox each day."

—Kathy Mandy, Select Word Services

"The biggest challenge to being home-based, for me, is separating my work from the rest of my life (it's always staring me in the face when I come into the house) and allowing myself to stop and feel it's okay to leave things unfinished. I do this a lot, but I haven't gotten over feeling bad about it. Getting out of the house

enough. Realizing it is 'okay to make money.' Most women I encounter don't really believe that it is all right to earn a profit for our services. Rare is the woman I find who is willing to be more than minimally compensated for her labors without feeling guilty about it. The idea that it might be legitimate for me to make a profit (that is, more than just a 'wage' for helping people) is still a hard thing for me to believe with conviction."

—Nina Feldman, Nina Feldman Connections

"Helping people (friends . . . relatives . . . a certain spouse) understand what's involved behind a home-based business. I get really annoyed when I have work scheduled and people can't understand why I won't go mall-hopping or run errands for a spouse. ('But you're home all day! Why can't you go and get my fishing bait so I have it for the weekend?') To overcome this challenge, I've learned the fine art of just saying 'No!'"

—Josie Smith, An Executive Assistant

"My biggest challenge is not letting my home-based business take over my entire life and neglecting my family and friends. I find myself being absorbed by my work, and sometimes family and friends do take second place. I seem to not have much time for social activities with friends since my business has begun. I have to step back and reprioritize. After all, the reason I wanted my home-based business to begin with was to spend more time with my family and be available for them. I find this to be my biggest challenge. I am attempting to overcome it, however, by shutting the door to my office at the end of my work day and not entering again until the next day. This is not always possible—but it's something I'm working on. There have been many nights that we have sent out for burgers or pizza. I have always provided home-cooked meals for my family, and this area seems to be most difficult—finding time to prepare a meal when I have deadlines upon deadlines. The Crock-Pot and microwave have been a tremendous help. But this balance is definitely something that I am struggling with on a day-to-day basis."

—Brenda Lorencen, Word/Pro Connection

"The biggest challenge that I face is finding adequate time for rest. I've been blessed so far with a very successful and busy business. Sometimes it doesn't seem like there are enough hours in the day to do everything. I work hard at disciplining my time and staying focused on the work that I need to be doing at the

moment. My business has become my top priority. Service to my clients comes before everything else in my life right now. I will probably subcontract extra work out to a good friend who is computer literate, has her own computer, subscribes to the same on-line service that I do, and uses the same software that I do. When that time comes, we can upload/download files to each other."

—Vivian Lee Adkins, Adkins Resume Services

ENTREPRENEURIAL ANALYSIS: DO YOU HAVE WHAT IT TAKES TO BE SUCCESSFUL WORKING FOR YOURSELF?

Unlike tests in school, this analysis isn't graded. Rather, as you respond to each of the questions and then read the profile of a typically successful entrepreneur, assess how you "stack up." This forms a good framework for understanding your strengths . . . and your potential weaknesses.

1. How good is your health, and how much sleep do you require?

    Entrepreneurial success will depend almost entirely on your efforts—including your ability to work hard and sustain momentum once your business is running smoothly and has a fairly regular cash flow. Do you have staying power? Are you able to pull occasional all-nighters when necessary? Are you in generally good health, and do you eat properly and exercise? These factors can all play into your general ability to maintain a successful business.

2. At what age did you first begin to test the entrepreneurial waters? Did you deliver newspapers, babysit, wash pets or cars, organize tag sales, clean houses for pay, or sell juice drinks before you were old enough to hold a "real" part-time job?

    Most successful entrepreneurs can recall evidence in their childhood of their ability to promote as well as their sales skills. The thirst for being in business for oneself and making money begins early.

3. Do you have a close relative who is or was a successful entrepreneur?

    Statistics have typically shown that "entrepreneurial blood" runs in families—or perhaps you are starting the trend in your family. In my own case my grandparents were successful restaurateurs, building a popular restaurant/banquet hall/resort in a remote area of Connecticut during the Great Depression, then growing it to success, operating it for fifty years. Even before that successful enterprise, my grandfather proved his entrepreneurial worth—and honed his sales skills—selling Watkins products for many years around the state of Connecticut. My dad also worked for himself successfully for nearly thirty years with a home-based office. Being an entrepreneur seemed the natural thing for me to do: I recall seeing my name inscribed after my dad's on the hallway leading downstairs to his basement office: "Manton H. LaFountain and Janice, Inc." I was probably four or five when I first understood what this meant.

4. How competitive were you in organized school or college sports? Do you continue competitive involvement to this date?

Once again, the "true blood" of an entrepreneur tends to become established early on. This relates to organized activities as well as business pursuits.

5. What kind of a student were you?

While excelling in English positions you for success in providing secretarial and editorial services, developing a new business and managing its myriad aspects—including accounting, reporting, and planning—rely heavily on your expertise in general business administration. Any training you may have had in business, accounting, management, and organization will be very useful.

6. Are you an early riser or a night owl? Do you possess the ability to work for long stretches of time, seemingly without a break?

Entrepreneurs tend to get so caught up in their business that they never watch clocks, except to be alert to appointments, and they frequently work both ends of the clock (called "burning the candle at both ends"). This item relates to question 1 as well.

7. How good is your memory? Or, phrased another way, do you have good work habits established with regard to making lists, maintaining a to-do list, and keeping a calendar?

A successful secretarial service owner must manage many priorities, project deadlines, and appointments. Already being familiar with tracking time and making lists can be a real asset. Memory also plays a big role in learning more about your clients and their businesses. Many secretarial service owners track birthdates and other important dates in their clients' lives and send out greeting cards on a regular basis. Being able to ask a follow-up question or simply remembering at a Monday client appointment that the past weekend was the person's university's alumni weekend can put you in good stead with your client base. Become an avid user of small Post-It notes; use them everywhere as reminders!

8. How much of a risk taker are you?

    Starting any business is, of course, a risk. But beginning a secretarial service when you have assessed your skills and strengths can be an excellent venture and opportunity for you. As your business grows, will you continue to be willing to take risks? These can include the decisions to add new services and equipment as well as buying and learning new software. Being a successful entrepreneur almost goes hand in hand with being a calculated risk taker.

9. How well do you handle your personal finances? Are you organized? Do you reconcile your checkbook the minute the statement arrives? Do you pay your bills on time and avoid bouncing checks by keeping good records?

    A successful entrepreneur must have a good handle on money at all times. Managing cash flow is quite different from anticipating a weekly paycheck from an employer.

While considering your responses to this questionnaire, think about the traits cited by most successful entrepreneurs when asked to name their most important characteristic: self-confidence, high self-esteem, high energy level, ability to set and achieve long-term goals, persistence, highly driven style, motivation, ambition, ability to take initiative, ability to learn from mistakes, risk taking, resourcefulness, creativity, and innovative style. What do you think? Do many of these terms describe you? If so, then you're on your way to achieving your goal!

CHAPTER THREE

PLANNING

BUSINESS ORGANIZATION

Nearly all home-based secretarial services businesses are sole proprietorships (as compared with the other most common forms of business organization: partnership, corporation, LLC, and Subchapter S, all of which are discussed later in this chapter). I have been a sole proprietor from day one and have never had any reason to change; however, I'll briefly discuss these four types of business ownership and outline the pros and cons.

Sole Proprietorship

Being a sole proprietor means exactly that—working by yourself, for yourself. You can simply hang out a shingle, once you've obtained the necessary permits. No attorney is needed for structuring complex partnership agreements or laws of incorporation; nor is an accountant absolutely required for filing your tax return. (You fill out a one-page Schedule C [stating your profit or loss for the year] and Form 4562 [detailing your company's property and its value] and attach these to your federal income tax return.) There may be, however, a number of areas in which you believe professional advice from both accounting and legal professionals would be of value and, if so, you are encouraged to pursue this avenue. Still, your costs are significantly reduced as a result of not *requiring* these services at the onset of establishing your business. Other advantages to sole proprietorships over other forms of business organization include the following: You are the sole "boss," with ultimate authority and responsibility, and there are potentially significant income tax advantages to being a sole proprietor who is home-based. Disadvantages include some of the more obvious items, such as the following: You have full exposure and unlimited liability in the event of a legal suit (highly unlikely); if you were to become seriously ill or die, your business activities would cease; and a home-based business structured as a sole proprietorship is limited, in terms of expansion and growth, by your ability to work.

Partnership

Most partnership arrangements have the benefit of a legal agreement between parties. (Although this can be an oral agreement, that method is not recommended.) Agreements are necessary to provide for disposition of assets in the event that one or both parties wish to disconnect from the business at some future point. There are greater costs in entering a partnership as compared with a sole proprietorship, from both an accounting and a legal standpoint. Advantages to this method of business organization include having a partner with whom to consult and pool resources and ideas (financial and creative) and having someone with whom to share the problems. Disadvantages beyond added costs include difficulty in determining a compatible partner with whom you can establish clear working guidelines and a division of workload and managerial responsibility, blurring of managerial control over the business, difficulty encountered if the partnership doesn't work out, potential loss of friendship if the partner is a friend (worse if the partner is a family member), and lifespan of the business in the event of the partner's death.

LLC and Subchapter S

Before jumping all the way to the traditional structure of "corporation," there are two intermediary steps that you may wish to discuss with an accounting professional to determine their applicability to your personal situation—Limited Liability Company (LLC) and Subchapter S Corporation. Both have several advantages over formally incorporating, but their relevance to you and your specific financial situation would need to be carefully investigated and assessed.

Corporation

This is the most expensive and complex way to begin a business, although it does limit your liability. Establishing a corporation will require legal and accounting fees, but this method of business organization generally allows for greater ease in raising capital for your business and provides for continuity in the event of your death. Disadvantages include higher taxes, restricted ability to "act like an entrepreneur" (depending on the covenants and restrictions of your charter and the board of directors), and perhaps a false sense of security.

While your own advisers should guide you, I highly recommend beginning as a sole proprietor. For nearly every home-based business in this field, a sole proprietorship is the most popular form of business organization. It's the least expensive way to run a business, requires the simplest and easiest-to-keep set of books and records, and is practical. Keep in mind that even as a sole proprietor, you do have the ability to have subcontracted freelance people handle work for you and even to have employees. (More on this in chapter 7.)

The next two aspects of planning—assessment of your competition and selection of your business name—should occur before spending the considerable time necessary in developing a business plan.

RESEARCHING AND ASSESSING THE COMPETITION

At this point it makes good business sense to find out who the competition is. It's unlikely that you're the first person to consider offering these types of services in your area. Find out who're out there, what they're doing, and how long they've been in business. Find out what they charge and if they're home-based. Try to determine their clientele profile and the niche they service. See where you can fit in—be more competitive pricewise starting out, perhaps, or offer a better-quality product, or offer a version of a service not currently available.

How do you do this? Obviously, the library does not provide copies of your competitors' business plans and sales records. Nor is this information likely to come easily by simple telephone inquiry. To gain information about your competition requires a little creativity and some solid market research. Start with your town's telephone directory, consulting all Yellow Pages listings under such categories as Copying, Desktop Publishing, Editing, Facsimile Transmission Service, Notary Public, Office Services, Photocopying, Proofreading, Resumes, Secretarial Service, Transcription, Typesetting, Typing Service, Word Processing Service, and any other category where services you're interested in providing might be listed.

Next, through either the library or an office of the local telephone company, obtain directories for all neighboring communities and repeat the process. You might also try to pull up businesses in your county through searches on the Internet. Finally, check with your chamber of commerce for a membership listing (also a good networking source for prospective clients).

With these data in hand, use the following Assessment of the Competition Worksheet (two samples are included: one filled in as an example and one blank) to develop your data analysis of the competition. Develop a separate set of worksheets for each business area in which you are interested (i.e., group all information gleaned about those businesses providing typing services together, group separately those companies providing resume services, etc.).

Once you've collected these data for each directory and in each category, use the following Advertised Categories Worksheet (again, two samples included) to tabulate your findings. This will form the backbone of your research into the competition. Keep in mind, too, that if older telephone directories and listings are available, you should compare these data with those of the previous year or years. Doing so will help illustrate who is new to the industry (at least from the standpoint of advertising), who has dropped out from a prior year, and who has been around for a while. This last category—businesses that have been in existence for longer than just a few years—represents the prime target area about which you really want to obtain information about pricing and services offered. You should also repeat this exercise at the time of year each telephone directory is published for your area. This will keep you up to date on who your competition continues to be and will allow you to spot trends quickly (e.g., if in your area there is a trend toward using the color red in ads or if everyone in the business is going from an in-column to a display ad, you may want to follow suit; more information on this topic is available under Yellow Pages Advertising in chapter 4).

Now, armed with the results of your excellent research, it's time to begin the real analysis. One common way to obtain information about your competitors is to contact them directly. Disable Caller ID and place telephone calls to competitors to inquire about getting a resume typed (if that's a service you are thinking of offering). You might wish to say you are calling for information for your spouse or friend if you'd rather not state your name. Call another day and inquire about having a term paper typed (again, if this is an area that interests you). Be sure to have your question checklist ready: What equipment is used? a laser printer? Do you charge per page? per hour? What about corrections? How many copies are included? What type of paper is used? What is the charge per sheet? Enlist a friend or spouse to assist with placing the calls if you feel uncomfortable making them. Ask about the experience of the individual you talk with, that is, how long the operation has been in business. If you think you may be speaking with a home-based secretarial service owner, ask if you are calling a home office. Record on your worksheets all information obtained—and retain this information. It will be useful when you "test the market" each year to determine where the competition is heading in terms of the services provided and the costs charged.

Another valuable way to conduct research and gain extensive knowledge is to contact businesses outside of your market area, perhaps in another area of your state where you represent no threat. Ask to speak with the owner and identify yourself, indicating that you are beginning your own word processing service (or whatever you've decided to offer). Immediately mention that you deliberately selected this company to call because it's not in the area and, therefore, you are not a competitive threat whatsoever. Ask if the owner would be willing to spend a few minutes (hopefully, more) with you on the telephone to answer a few questions—if not then, perhaps at another scheduled time. Ideally, the person you'll be talking

ASSESSMENT OF THE COMPETITION WORKSHEET

Directory for City/Town of _____ Mapleville _____

Category _____ Typing Service _____

Total Number of Companies Listed under this Category _____ 6 _____

Company Name	Town	✓*	Telephone	Services Provided	Size Ad **
A Good Word	Mapleville	✓	555-0001	laser documents, corresp., theses	2" in-column
Business Pros	Mapleton		555-0002	not itemized	Bold listing
Data Documents	Mapleville		555-0003	"	Single line
Debbie's Sec. Svs.	"	✓	555-0004	FAX, typesetting, laser, business svc.	1.5" in-column
Typing Techs	"		555-0005	Word Processing	Bold listing
Word Wizards	Maple City		555-0006	Copies - FAX complete sec. svs.	3" in-column

* Check if you know or suspect the business is home-based; a good "giveaway" is if no address is published (or only a P.O. box is provided).

** For in-column ads this would be the depth of the ad in inches. For display ads size is computed using width and height so that a 2 x 4 ad is two columns wide by 4 inches deep. Also note if there is no ad but simply a single line listing, a boldface/caps listing, or a reference to see an ad elsewhere in the book.

ASSESSMENT OF THE COMPETITION WORKSHEET

Directory for City/Town of _____

Category _____

Total Number of Companies Listed under this Category _____

Company Name	Town	✓ *	Telephone	Services Provided	Size Ad **

* Check if you know or suspect the business is home-based; a good "giveaway" is if no address is published (or only a P.O. box is provided).

** For in-column ads this would be the depth of the ad in inches. For display ads size is computed using width and height so that a 2 x 4 ad is two columns wide by 4 inches deep. Also note if there is no ad but simply a single line listing, a boldface/caps listing, or a reference to see an ad elsewhere in the book.

ADVERTISED CATEGORIES WORKSHEET

City/Town Directory for ___Mapleville___

Substitute headings from your area's directories; these are just examples. Using the data collected in the previous exercise, enter each company's name under all of the categories under which they advertise. You should begin to see some patterns develop and be able to recognize the "heavy hitters" in your geographic area, that is, the companies that are the most heavily advertised. In all likelihood, they are the businesses that are the most successful.

Desktop Publishing	Resumes	Secretarial Service	Typing Service	Word Processing Service	Multiple Listers
ABC Press	ABC Press				2
Business Pros			Business Pros		2
Fran's DTP					
Typing Techs		Typing Techs	Typing Techs		3
Word Wizards	Word Wizards	Word Wizards	Word Wizards	Word Wizards	5
	Business Res.				
	Career Dev. Pros.				
		Sec'y Svs. Plus			
		Typing Svs., Inc.		Typing Svs., Inc.	2
		Yolanda's Svs.			
			A Good Word		
		Data Docum.		Data Docum.	2
			Debbie's Sec. Bus.		
				Alladin's Bus. Svs.	
				Imaginings Words	
TOTALS					
5	4	5	6	5	6

ADVERTISED CATEGORIES WORKSHEET

City/Town Directory for _____

Substitute headings from your area's directories; these are just examples. Using the data collected in the previous exercise, enter each company's name under all of the categories under which they advertise. You should begin to see some patterns develop and be able to recognize the "heavy hitters" in your geographic area, that is, the companies that are the most heavily advertised. In all likelihood, they are the businesses that are the most successful.

Desktop Publishing	Resumes	Secretarial Service	Typing Service	Word Processing Service	Multiple Listers
TOTALS					

with once started his or her own company (perhaps initially home-based, or still home-based) and knows what you're going through. With that type of empathy, you could obtain very useful information. The person might even be willing to meet with you in his or her office for an hour or two. If so, take advantage of it, and if you hit "pay dirt" and acquire some great information, remember to acknowledge it professionally and promptly with a thank-you note.

You might try calling your local competition and asking them "how to get started." But as nice as people are, that generally is ineffective. Just jumping out of your local telephone dialing area should be adequate and well worth the toll charges on your telephone bill.

SELECTION OF YOUR BUSINESS NAME

Now you're ready for the *fun* part—selecting a name for your firm. This is also very serious business because once you've selected your name and gone to the expense of creating all your business materials using that name (and then developing name recognition among your clients and in your geographic area), you won't casually want to change it. So give this exercise a great deal of thought. If you're like many would-be entrepreneurs, you probably have some ideas in mind and may already have designed some preliminary logos and even slogans for your stationery. If so, take a close look at the suggestions provided to see if most of these criteria have been incorporated in your selection process. If you haven't given extensive thought to determining your company's name, here are some recommendations to get you started.

Many business owners, secretarial services included, opt to use their own name and call themselves something like "Jane Brown Associates." Depending on how your telephone directory lists names, this could be fine, because many will show the listing as "Brown, Jane," followed by "Jane Brown Associates" in the actual ad copy. This is good—because strategic placement within the alphabet *is* key! Unfortunately, most of the business words you might readily think of tend to start with letters that are not located near the beginning of the alphabet—*professional, secretarial, typing, service, word processing*—as do many of the clever catch phrases used in our industry: Letter Perfect, Wordsmith, Ways with Words, Typing Pros. Don't let that stop you from becoming creative. If your name doesn't lend itself to good placement alphabetically, begin experimenting.

I recommend staying away from the obvious AAA Services or Aardvark Systems, employed solely for alphabetical placement. If you're not using your own name or initials, attempt to select a name that will describe some element of the business services you intend to provide, yet be as expansive as possible. I know of people in this business choosing to name their service something like Quick Typing Service ten years ago, then updating it to Quick Word Processing Service five years later, when word processing nearly replaced typing from a technological standpoint. Now a change to Quick Desktop Publishing Services is being considered. Who knows where technological advancements will take this field in the next five to ten years? For that reason a less focused approach might be better with regard to name selection.

Getting back to alphabetical placement, why is this so all important? Because how you are listed in the Yellow Pages of the telephone directory (or directories) in which you will appear is *critical* and can't be stressed enough. Even clients who know you and your company name will frequently use the Yellow Pages to look you up in order to call . . . and prospective clients who need a service and don't know whom to call will start at the top of the heading they're looking under (say, Secretarial Service) and work their way down.

Once you've selected a name, experiment with it. Try out various styles and fonts. See how it looks on drafts of a letterhead or business card, or a mock-up of a Yellow Pages ad. Ask opinions of others. Then wait a few days. If you still love it when you go back to it a week later, go with it. Finally, refer to the section on Legal Technicalities and Zoning Issues to Consider in chapter 1 for information about properly recording your name with local and state agencies.

DEVELOPING A COMPLETE BUSINESS PLAN

Don't let this scare you. Development of a business plan for your secretarial service can be as simple and uncomplicated (or as complex) as you choose. This section presents a description of the basic components of a business plan which you will need to consider. (An edited version of my actual business plan, with "fabricated" financials, appears in the Appendix.) A business plan is really nothing more than a road map of how you intend to start, develop, and operate your business, with an eye toward the future. A business plan is essential if you are seeking funds from a lending institution. But it's a good idea to have a business plan even if you are not obtaining any loans, because developing the plan will help you focus on all the necessary aspects of properly planning your business for success. Once developed, a good business plan will allow you to evaluate your business periodically as well as monitor sales growth and profitability.

The following sections should be components of your business plan. (Some categories require only a few lines or a paragraph.)

Executive Summary

Although placed at the front of the business plan, this is generally written last, after you've pulled together all the other pieces of your plan. This should stress the most important sections of your business plan clearly and succinctly. Information

* An example here might be (in addition to company name, location, rationale for starting business, and financing): My office support services company will focus on providing professional and timely services through concierges located in the 20+ high-end hotels located in my geographic area.

typically included would be your name, the business name, the location of the business, the services you intend to provide, the market niches you intend to serve, the rationale for starting your business (i.e., why you are able to offer a "better mousetrap" than the competition), and—if you are seeking financing from a lending institution—the amount you are requesting and your plans for disbursement. (See above.)

General Description of Business

Here you repeat the information from the executive summary and also mention your form of business organization (usually sole proprietorship). If you've already started your business, indicate the actual date commenced. Describe in detail the types of services you will provide and the intended clients. For example, you might indicate that because you are located within 10 miles of four colleges and universities, you intend to develop a strong market niche providing services to students (term papers, theses, doctoral dissertations, and resumes/cover letters upon graduation).

Also included in this section would be information about the planned financial status of the business. If you haven't actually started the business, you would provide projections based on your anticipated charges. (See Establishing a Price Structure in chapter 5.) Using the example of providing services to students, you might indicate that your hourly rate will be $24, that you anticipate fifteen billable hours per week (on average) in your first year of business, and that you plan on working fifty weeks in the first year and therefore project revenues of $18,000.

* An example here might be (in addition to other information detailed in this section of the text): I am currently cultivating potential subcontracting relationships with two other secretarial service providers in my immediate area; these competitors are also members of the same professional network to which I belong.

A final segment in this section includes your short- and long-term goals for the business. In continuing our example, you might present as your short-term goal fully developing the niche servicing students in your first year. In year 2 your goal might be to average twenty-five billable hours per week, with an increase in your rates to $26 per hour and three weeks' vacation (thereby working forty-nine weeks). This would project annual revenues at nearly $32,000. For a longer-term goal you might project expanding your services to include professional word processing and transcription services for the business community that supports the neighboring universities. For year 5 you might project implementing a two-tiered price schedule, having thirty billable hours per week at a rate of $35 and five billable hours per week at a rate of $45 (editorial/transcription). You might also project four weeks' vacation (working 48 weeks). This yields $61,200 per year in gross annual revenues. Included in your long-term planning might also be speculation of hiring part- or full-time assistants, either as freelance, subcontracted typing help or perhaps as a part-time, in-office person to cover telephones, handle filing and copying, and so forth. (Note: These numbers are purely hypothetical and not necessarily representative of the norm in your geographic area.)

Products and Services

This component of a business plan is where you would describe your physical setting. (Outline the basic furniture and room in your home that will be devoted to the business.) Mention procurement of local permits for the business. Examples of

---

WORKSHEET IDEAS: PRODUCTS AND SERVICES*

_____

_____

_____

_____

_____

---

* An example here might be (in addition to other details explained in this section of the text): Because of my bilingual ability (English and Spanish) and the increasing need for this attribute throughout the city in which I reside, I plan to specialize in and offer translation services to the business community.

your work could be included (e.g., a formatted resume or a brochure or newsletter). A complete listing of the services your business will provide should be included, accompanied by typical charges. For example, if you plan to handle resumes, you will probably want to establish different pricing for different levels of service—simply typing a client's handwritten, one-page resume might have a flat charge of $25, whereas meeting with a client, conducting a consultation, then writing "from scratch" a one-page resume would naturally cost more, perhaps $75 or $100 or even more, depending upon your geographic area. If you plan to handle document preparation, such as theses or reports, you might show what your hourly rate is and then give an estimated per page rate. (For instance, if your hourly rate is $20 and you follow the industry standard of producing approximately eight double-spaced pages per hour, you would quote a price of about $2.50 per page.)

This section regarding products and services should also discuss the advantages of doing business with you. What unique attributes do you offer? You might mention your professional experience before beginning your own company or discuss your educational background, either in learning the various skills required of an excellent secretary or in earning a business degree. You would also mention specialized services you can provide. Are you bilingual? Do you offer translation services as well? Can you take shorthand in addition to providing transcription? Will you provide pickup and delivery services? Do you plan to offer rush, overnight, or even same-day service (for an increased charge)? These are all business attributes to mention.

Market and Industry Data

This is where your hard work collecting competitive research information comes in handy. Merely compile the statistics you collected about your competition and their service offerings and pricing and rank them against your planned services and fees. It will probably be impossible for you to know or calculate market share by your competitors (as might be done by a cosmetics giant in launching a new line of skin care products), but you may be able to compare your geographic proximity to the intended clientele with that of your competitors and cite again the unique attributes you will offer.

WORKSHEET IDEAS: MARKET AND INDUSTRY DATA*

_____

_____

_____

_____

_____

---

* An example here might be: Include copies of the information gleaned and developed in researching competitors through the Yellow Pages and via the Internet.

Marketing Strategy

There is substantial information on this topic in chapter 4. You'll want to review it, certainly, before including information in your business plan. Basically, you should outline how you plan to acquire clients. Using our student example, this could include placing flyers under the windshield wipers of cars in student parking lots; posting flyers throughout campus buildings and classrooms; advertising in university newsletters, university telephone directories, and regular telephone company Yellow Pages; using direct mail (to department heads); and perhaps providing discount or repeat client offers or coupons toward future services. You might structure a student discount price for cash in advance. All these items would be mentioned.

WORKSHEET IDEAS: MARKETING STRATEGY*

_____

_____

_____

_____

_____

* An example here might be: I will plan to directly market (with a series of direct-mail pieces) my bilingual abilities and professional translation and secretarial services to the outsourcing or vendor relations managers of all companies within a 50-mile radius that have more than 100 employees.

Operational Plan

This section describes the equipment you will use in your secretarial services business. There is an outline to which you can refer later in this chapter. If you haven't purchased equipment yet, you would include in the operational plan the anticipated cost of equipment, software, and supplies. Include anticipated vendors you will be using. (Consult the Appendix for recommended supply vendors, in addition to your own local sources.) If you are starting out your business as the only employee (the most common way to begin), you will be handling all the work. Describe your skills briefly.

WORKSHEET IDEAS: OPERATIONAL PLAN*

_____

_____

_____

_____

_____

* An example here might be: Prepare a fully inclusive listing of all hardware and software as well as a skills summary; also include secretarial service operator's own resume.

Management "Team" and Organization

Once again, if you are starting out as the only employee, you'll be wearing all those hats described in chapter 2. Include in this section a brief summation of those various responsibilities.

WORKSHEET IDEAS: MANAGEMENT "TEAM" AND ORGANIZATION*

_____

_____

_____

_____

_____

---

* An example here might be: In referencing your background as a former administrative secretary with excellent bookkeeping skills, also note prospective arrangements for subcontracting and networking.

Financial Plan

This, for many, represents the most difficult part in developing a business plan. Forms are provided in this chapter for you to use in compiling and calculating the appropriate information.

Appendix

In addition to attaching your business card, brochure, and/or newsletter (if you have developed any of these pieces) to your business plan, you should also attach your resume and any letters of reference. (These could include letters from past employers as well as clients.) If you have received any publicity in local newspapers (you will; more on this in chapter 4), include copies with your business plan.

Expense Worksheet

You will probably find that you do not have as expenses some of the items listed on the Expense Worksheet Form for your business, particularly in the start-up phase. This worksheet should be completed after the close of each month to maintain an accurate picture of the financial health of your business.

Balance Sheet

From an accounting standpoint, a balance sheet is simply a "snapshot" in time at any given point of the overall financial health of your company. It represents a summary of your assets, liabilities, and net worth. The numbers on a balance sheet must "tie"; that is, your assets minus your liabilities equal capital or net worth. A brief definition of each of the categories on a balance sheet follows.

Current assets—whatever your business has of value that can be converted to cash within a short period of time (under a year). This includes cash in your business checking and savings accounts and in your petty cash fund, as well as equipment, office supplies, and accounts receivable.

Fixed assets—your equipment investments and office furniture, minus depreciation.

Liabilities—the unpaid expenses of the business for which you are responsible. These include your business telephone bill, any maintenance contract costs, office supply bills, and so on. Also included would be any debts you incurred to start your business, such as bank or personal loans.

Capital (also known as equity or net worth)—the number resulting when you subtract your liabilities from your assets.

Profit-and-Loss Statement

This is also referred to as an income statement and should ideally be prepared monthly or quarterly, but some companies prepare them just once per year. This is another important document that can be used to assess the economic health of your business.

Cash-Flow Projections

The final form included in your business plan represents a month-to-month comparison between estimated and actual income and expenses (and should be updated on a monthly basis). In any start-up business you will naturally have more cash "outgo" than income. This reinforces the reason for having a solid savings base on which to draw for at least the first six months of your business. Many start-up secretarial service owners pay themselves no salary for the first few months or even year in business. Instead, they constantly reinvest any profits in the beginning to further develop their business, adding to their promotional and marketing efforts and the like.

See chapter 5's recommendations under Recordkeeping for techniques in establishing your business records as well as creating sales analysis documents by client and by profit center to truly help you manage your business growth. All of these

EXPENSE WORKSHEET FORM

Month/Year _____

Salary	$ _____
Payment on note/business loan	$ _____
Equipment lease costs	$ _____
Telephone	$ _____
E-mail account	$ _____
Yellow Pages advertising (usually itemized separately on telephone bill)	$ _____
Other advertising	$ _____
Fax telephone charges	$ _____
Office supplies	$ _____
Printing costs (business stationery)	$ _____
Stationery and supplies	$ _____
Postage	$ _____
Bank service charges	$ _____
Federal Express/other delivery charges	$ _____
Professional dues	$ _____
Professional subscriptions	$ _____
Taxes and licenses	$ _____
Insurance	$ _____
Travel and entertainment	$ _____
Medical insurance	$ _____
Mileage and parking expenses	$ _____
Maintenance contract costs (computer, copier, fax, etc.)	$ _____
Repairs and maintenance expense	$ _____
"Rent"/contribution to utilities	$ _____
Security system/monitoring expense	$ _____
Office cleaning expense	$ _____
Freelance subcontractors	$ _____
Courier service	$ _____
Miscellaneous	$ _____

BALANCE SHEET FORM

FOR _(name of your company)_

AS OF _(specific date)_

ASSETS

Current Assets/Cash:

Cash in bank	$_____
Petty cash	$_____
Accounts receivable	$_____
Supply inventories	$_____
Total Current Assets	$_____

Fixed Assets:

Office furnishings	$_____
Office equipment	$_____
Less allowance for depreciation	$_____
Total Fixed Assets	$_____
TOTAL ASSETS	$_____

LIABILITIES AND CAPITAL

Current Liabilities:

Accounts payable	$_____
Notes payable, due within 1 year	$_____
Sales taxes	$_____
Quarterly taxes	$_____
Total Current Liabilities	$_____

Long-term Liabilities:

Notes payable, due after 1 year	$_____
TOTAL LIABILITIES	$_____

Capital:

Proprietor's capital, beginning of period	$_____
Net profit for the period	$_____
Less proprietor's draw (salary)	$_____
Increase in capital	$_____
Capital, end of period	$_____
TOTAL LIABILITIES AND CAPITAL	$_____

PROFIT-AND-LOSS STATEMENT FORM

FOR _____ (name of your company) _____

FOR THE MONTH (OR YEAR)_____

GROSS SALES $ _____

COST OF SALES:

Opening inventory/supplies on hand $ _____

Purchases _____

Total _____

Ending inventory _____

TOTAL COST OF SALES _____

GROSS PROFIT

OPERATING EXPENSES:

"Rent"/contribution to utilities _____

Loan payments _____

Depreciation _____

Mileage/parking costs _____

Telephone , e-mail account, and advertising _____

Office supplies/printing costs _____

Postage _____

Fax expenses _____

Bank service charges _____

Dues/subscriptions _____

Delivery and courier expenses _____

Maintenance contract costs/repairs _____

Office cleaning expense _____

Security system _____

Travel and entertainment _____

Medical/office insurance _____

Taxes and licenses _____

Freelance subcontractors _____

Miscellaneous _____

TOTAL _____

NET PROFIT [before your salary] $ _____

CASH-FLOW PROJECTIONS FORM

FOR _____(name of your company)_____

FOR THE MONTH _____

	Estimate	Actual
1. Cash on hand (at start of month)		
2. a. Cash receipts		
b. Loan receipts/injection of $ into business		
3. TOTAL CASH AVAILABLE (1+2a.+2b.)		
4. Cash paid out		
a. Salary		
b. Taxes/licenses		
c. Office supplies/printing/postage		
d. Delivery services/courier		
e. Office/medical insurance		
f. Telephone/fax/Yellow Pages ad/e-mail account		
g. Other advertising		
h. "Rent"/contribution to utilities		
i. Mileage/parking		
j. Professional dues/subscriptions		
k. Legal and professional fees		
l. Maintenance service contracts/repairs		
m. Loan payments/interest		
n. Bank service charges		
o. Travel and entertainment		
p. Office cleaning/security system		
q. Freelance subcontractors		
r. Equipment purchases/leases		
s. Miscellaneous		
t. SUBTOTAL (4a. through 4s.)		
u. Any of your withdrawals		
5. TOTAL CASH PAID OUT (4t.+4u.)		
6. End-of-month cash position (3–5)		
· Non-cash-flow operating information for the month		
· Sales volume in dollars		
· Accounts receivable at month's end		
· Dollar value of inventory/supplies at month's end		
· Accounts payable at month's end		
· Depreciation		

documents can be easily prepared in either a word processing program on your computer or in a spreadsheet program, such as Excel or Lotus. There are numerous software accounting packages available as well; my personal favorite is Quicken.

CAPITAL EQUIPMENT ACQUISITION

While some individuals operate a "typing" business with just a typewriter, most clients will expect at least basic word processing capability; many will want and gladly pay for additional services, including desktop publishing, laser printing, and photocopying, as well as fax and notary public services.

A significant advantage to starting this type of business is that you can begin small and build as your client base and revenues grow. Plus, there are generally significant tax advantages and legitimate write-offs the first few years of beginning and operating a business.

The following lists detail suggested basic equipment as well as recommended add-on equipment to enhance your services. Expanding your service offerings with the additional equipment will increase your earnings potential as your client base broadens. The timeframe in which to add equipment can be determined by you as funds are available, as your earnings increase, and so on. Some services never offer all of the enhanced services; others start out offering "everything" from day one. Most home-based businesses find they successfully and reasonably add to their service offerings on a gradual basis, stretching out their acquisitions over several years' time. That's the flexibility you have as a business owner.

Estimates vary substantially based on geographic area, brands, and so forth. Also, don't overlook "gently used" equipment. (See Highly Recommended Tip later in this section.)

Basic Start-up Equipment

- Computer system (ideally, with a full-page monitor) $1,000–$3,500

- Word processing software/spreadsheet software (see subsequent information regarding recommended minimum features) $300–$700 ea.

- Laser printer (necessary for resume work or handling corporate clients' material) or ink jet/letter-quality printer (if laser printer cost is prohibitive) $750–$1,800

- Electric or electronic typewriter (you'll need this for completing school, grant, and employment applications)

  $100–$250

- Business telephone and line (separate from residence telephone line; a phone set that includes both your residence line and your business line is ideal, in particular, if you have the "hold" button feature—perfect when children interrupt you when you're speaking with a client; you can place your caller "on hold" like a "real" office). Explore the availability of home-office business telephone service in your area. This is typically less expensive than traditional business service, though a little more costly than residential telephone service. It does, however, allow you to obtain Yellow Pages advertising.

  $25–$150+ (*phone set*)

  $20–$40 (*monthly base*)

- Answering machine for business telephone and/or voice mail service through the telephone company or an individual service provider.

  $45 and/or
  $8–$10 monthly fee

- E-mail account; highly recommend America Online because of access to support, networking, numerous resources, and forums (see details in the Appendix).

  varies, from free to
  $20 per month

Highly Recommended Tip: Telephones

A telephone set with a *portable phone* is a wonderful aid in being able to handle myriad responsibilities—from filing "silently" while on a lengthy call with a client who likes to chat and throwing dinner (quietly) into the oven to tossing laundry into the dryer or checking on a napping baby, all while conducting business over the phone. It's well worth the $150 or so. It also will enable you to work outdoors and not miss business calls, if you so choose (especially nice when weather allows and you have a lengthy proofreading project).

Recommended Basic Features for Word Processing Software Program

Over the years, Microsoft Word has become pretty much the standard for word processing with widespread acceptance in both the IBM (and compatibles) and

Macintosh communities. If this is your first foray into word processing and you're uncertain of what capabilities a program should have, look for these minimum (or basic) features in any package you may be assessing.

- Ability to open more than one document at a time
- Ability to search and replace text within a document using one command or simply search for specific text
- Ability to bold, underline, italicize, expand, condense, outline, shadow, type all caps, type small caps, undo all caps
- Ability to key information into header and footer menus, including separate menus for "first header" and/or "first footer"
- Well-designed margin feature that provides for automatic tabbing as well as a number of margin settings, including left and right (flush left and flush right), justified, centered, decimal tabbing, word wrapping
- Ability to scale font sizes easily in 1-point increments
- Features for indexing and footnoting functions
- Ability to set and reset page numbers at will
- Ability to set text leading and key single, single plus a half, or double spacing
- Ability to set superscript and subscript in 1-point increments
- Ability to conduct automatic hyphenation and word counting
- Ability to set page layout to portrait or landscape
- Ability to select word, paragraph, and document segments easily
- Ability to set margins to exact sizes (all four sides of page)
- Ability to set "smart quotes"
- Ability to spellcheck and create unique dictionaries
- Ability to consult thesaurus
- Ability to create a data document, then set up a mail merge easily
- Ability to apply borders and shading to sections of text
- Multiple column capability

Furniture

- Solid work space/desk with an area of the proper height for your monitor and keyboard — $75+

- Good quality, ergonomically designed chair (the best you can afford—you'll be "living" in this chair!) — $125–$300+

- Small file cabinet for client records and files (temporary cardboard files that stack are a satisfactory alternative) — $25–$75

- Area devoted to storage supplies (free from humidity and the curious fingers of young children; a shelf or two in your probably already crowded linen closet is fine—but not in the bathroom: too much humidity, which is not good for paper supplies); keep in mind that if you have young children, you don't want them to be able to access such supplies as correction fluid, markers, and toner cartridges, which contain chemicals and could pose health problems if ingested. Safety is paramount! — $0

Other Start-up Costs

- Professionally prepared business cards (see details under Business Cards in chapter 4). — $25–$100+

- Business checking account (a d/b/a account— "Susan Smith doing business as Wordsmith Associates") and first order of checks; a d/b/a account is the most common way to establish a business account as a sole proprietor. I'd recommend talking first with your hometown banker (where you have your present checking and savings accounts and, perhaps, mortgage). More and more, banks and credit unions are becoming increasingly small business friendly and offer a wide array of attractive services. Shop before you open accounts, but recognize some possible advantages to doing all your business with one — $30+

institution. There are three key things I suggest you seek in establishing your business checking account:

1) free or minimal monthly fee (typically available through relationship banking links if you have other funds on deposit totaling a certain amount).

2) overdraft protection (as you might already have available on a personal checking account); with business accounts, this is sometimes called a line of credit. The key point is to have immediate "float" coverage for times when either a client check bounces after you've written your own checks against those funds or cash flow in a given week or two is very light and you have bills that must be paid.

3) ATM card on the business checking account.

From the start, it is important to build a good relationship with your banker and, for this reason, doing business in your own community can be a big advantage. In my case, I've banked at the same building in my town from day one. I say "building" because my bank has changed ownership/names five times since I began my company in 1983 . . . compared with the two times I've changed my business name!

- Basic stationery/office supplies (see Proposed $75–$300
  Start-up Office Supply Inventory later in this
  chapter); your best buys will undoubtedly be
  through bulk supply warehouses and discount
  mail firms (see the Appendix for suggested mail-
  order vendors); however, it's strongly suggested
  that you establish and cultivate a good relationship
  with a local printer and an office supply store—
  they consistently stock the same brands, unlike
  the warehouse; are convenient for last-minute,
  rush merchandise (usually offering delivery); and
  are an excellent source of new client referrals.

■ Maintenance service contracts on equipment during postwarranty years. This is one of those expense items that some folks opt to gamble with. They take a chance that there won't be an equipment failure or, if there is one, that the per call service to repair the problem will still cost less than repeated annual service contract payments. I think the bigger consideration is what the "cost" will be to your business if your computer system is down and you don't have a backup in the office, particularly if you live in a more rural area without access to Kinko's and such where you could easily take your files and continue working (albeit at a cost). As my children have gotten older, I no longer immediately sell a "retired" system when upgrading to a new one. Hence, I have four Macs varying in age from one to nine throughout my home office (and home). As a result, and because they are all perfectly compatible, I have allowed service contracts to lapse. Just a few months ago, I did have to place a service call for one of the CPUs; a fan needed replacing. The total cost (labor plus parts) was less than $200, less than one year of service contract fees on one system alone and the first money I've had to allocate to computer repairs in probably five years. If, however, your computer system is your one and only, as it's likely to be at the start-up of your business, it is definitely a good idea to have a contract that provides you with service on-site within twenty-four hours.

varies $100/yr.+

■ Business insurance policy that not only protects you from liability in the event of personal injury but also offers protection for theft, fire, and damage to your office furnishings, equipment, etc. This is an important expense frequently overlooked by start-up secretarial service owners.

varies significantly from a $6.00 annual rider on your regular homeowner's or renter's policy to $250–$350 for a business policy. Shop around!

- Discreet, professional, attractive business sign for your driveway/home (be sure it's in compliance with local zoning regulations) $75–$300
- Advertising (see chapter 4) *varies*

Highly Recommended Tip: Furniture

Purchase high-quality *used* office furniture. Save your investment dollars for early advertising and expensive computer equipment and software. Scout out quality used office furniture and equipment stores in your area, often in the nearest large town. You might also check with large companies in your locale that might be moving and be interested in selling their used equipment. Look for top-quality brands (such as Steelcase) and excellent serviceability; don't worry about appearance—yet. You should be able to find a good used desk for under $100, a used vertical four-drawer file cabinet for under $50, and a good used chair for under $75. (Prices vary depending on your geographic area; check around and you'll become an expert on what to pay for used office furniture.) Foreclosure and auction sales can also yield great buys.

If you've managed to piece together used equipment from various sources—used furniture stores, tag sales, basements, and so on—give consideration to having a professional office furniture refinishing company electrostatically repaint all of the metal portions of your furniture and equipment to match. If you've saved hundreds of dollars through carefully selecting quality used merchandise, you might feel comfortable justifying the cost of this repainting (especially if the furniture is otherwise in good condition—just scratched, marred, and unmatching, e.g., a black desk, a brown file cabinet, and a putty tan typing stand). The cost of such repainting is usually under $500.

I assisted with organizing a sale of used office furniture for my full-time employer back when I began my own company. As was the case with all of my colleagues helping out, we were able to have "first pick" of the used goods at great prices. I purchased a 6-foot mahogany-look conference table, a single pedestal desk with a return (for my computer), three upholstered chairs on wheels, a large credenza, two bookcases, and a four-drawer file cabinet—all for under $100. I had every color in the business furniture rainbow represented, however—black, tan, beige, putty, and gray! But the quality was excellent, and there was virtually no damage or wear. The following spring I had all of the colored surfaces electrostatically refinished in a gorgeous burgundy color that beautifully picks up a color in the wallpaper of my office. I coordinated the deep forest green background of the wallpaper with a thick pile carpet of the same shade bearing maroon flecks—so I'm completely "decorated," all on a shoestring! Best of all, even the refinishing of my furniture was a bargain: In my state's annual public television auction, I was the successful bidder on a refinishing package. The item was auctioned at 12:30 A.M. and, because I'm a night owl, I was practically the only bidder as well as the successful one. I got the $500 package for a mere $220! And the company handled all of the painting right in my office. No one would ever guess that my furniture didn't start out as a coordinated set. Considering that the aforementioned furniture was purchased *used* back in 1983 for under $100, I think it probably represents my best investment ever! Just this past spring I finally retired the three Steelcase office chairs to my children's playroom. There's still plenty of serviceability but, at nearly 20 years of age, the upholstery was beginning to finally look a little tired. I also replaced the desk a few years ago with a nicer oak one; I sold the desk and return for $50 at my own tag sale. The bookcase, filing drawers, conference table, typing stand, and credenza *all* work perfectly still—a great ROI (return on investment)!

Highly Recommended Tip: Computers

Purchase your computer system and/or peripherals from a student at a local university. Stretch your investment dollars to cover a system maintenance contract (strongly advised) and additional software. If you live anywhere near a large university or college, chances are good that there are students eager to trade up their computer equipment and seeking to do so through an outside sale in the community. This is a great way to get good value for your money (I'm talking under $500 or $600!). Watch local newspapers for classified advertising under Computers. To most effectively take advantage of the bargains to be found in this market, you should ideally possess a good working knowledge of computers, have identified the type of system you want to own, and know something about the various operating systems, model numbers, and so forth. Also, computer magazines usually publish second hand pricing to give you a negotiating point (e.g., *MacWorld* provides pricing for used Macs each month). Most students are more than willing to share their knowledge about their computer systems; many sell their equipment "as is"—thus giving you the added benefit of hundreds, even thousands of dollars of "free" software (already installed on the system), albeit usually without documentation. For documentation you'll be able to purchase guides from a large bookstore (a campus bookstore is ideal) that will help you with much of what might be included. Over time you'll eventually want to buy your own software, with upgrade privileges, complete documentation, registration, support resources, and the like. But this is a great way to start small and build up.

When I converted to the Macintosh at year 5 in my business cycle, I purchased my first and second Mac SEs exactly in this fashion from students at a nearby university. (I watched for their newspaper ads.) I successfully negotiated excellent

SAMPLE LANGUAGE FOR PURCHASING USED COMPUTER EQUIPMENT

(Present to the individual selling you a used computer for signature.)

I hereby guarantee that the _____ (brand

name and model of computer) as well as all included peripherals are in excellent

working condition and warrant to _____ (your

name), d/b/a _____ (business name),

_____ (town, state) for a reason-

able period of time in which to provide for a premaintenance service contract

inspection by _____ (name of your

selected service provider), _____ (town, state),

not to exceed 72 hours. If the system is not found to be in excellent working condi-

tion and, therefore, cannot be placed under a computer maintenance service

agreement, I will refund the purchase price of $ _____ upon return of

all above-mentioned equipment plus _____

_____ (any peripherals, supplies)

provided as part of the sales agreement of _____ (date)

between _____ (your name

and your business name), and myself.

_____   _____   _____

signature   date   time of signing

purchase prices and never regretted getting into the "Mac world" in this way. As I've expanded my business, I've outgrown the need for my smaller Macs and sold them through my own newspaper ads in the same way.

Again, regardless of the manner in which you acquire your computer equipment, it is highly recommended that you place all of it under a maintenance contract or agreement. If you successfully negotiate a sale with a private party, be certain that your conditions of sale include a clause that provides you with a reasonable period of time in which to ensure that the system is inspected by a qualified computer maintenance organization and suitable for placement under a service agreement. If prearranged with a service company (and it should be), a twenty-four to forty-eight-hour period of time should be adequate, and most students are reasonable and will accept this as a condition of final sale.

Always be sure to have a copy of the bill of sale for your tax records. And be certain to obtain the telephone number and address of the party from whom you buy your system—a good source of free troubleshooting support for as long as school is in session that year.

Other good sources of equipment include the large variety of publications specifically aimed at certain brands. (There are magazines for the PC world, i.e., IBM and IBM-compatible, and for the Macintosh, the two most prevalent small business system types in the country.) If you're not already "into" computers and decide to make this your point of entry, you'll probably find yourself aligned with either the Mac or the IBM (or one of its many clones). Depending on whom you talk with, you'll be heavily steered toward one or the other. The general finding is that graphics people, writers, and creative sorts tend to prefer the intuitive Mac, whereas true business types like IBM. My background with computers was with Digital—the other "biggie" out there—and I converted to, and love, the Macintosh. I've also used IBM systems successfully, but I keep returning to my Macs. With ongoing technological advances and good file exchange utilities, you can generally convert documents from one system type to another relatively easily. My present system configuration (primary computers: an Apple Power Macintosh 6500/250 and an Apple Power Macintosh 7100/66 PowerPC) accepts IBM disks and allows me to easily save documents to an IBM format for those clients requesting such; my secondary and laptop computers, a Macintosh IIvx and Apple PowerBook 100, both allow transfer of documents via file transfer to IBM formats.

Enhanced Equipment and Furnishings

- Desktop publishing software program $300–$700

- Modem (many new computer systems are $75+
  sold with a built-in modem; however, if purchased
  separately, buy the fastest available)

- Domain name on the Internet; if you plan on $70 annual fee
  doing business "over the Internet," you might   to register and
  wish to have your own domain name (so that   retain exclusive
  clients and prospects key in directly with   use of your url
  whatever you've registered; in my case, my   (web address
  url [address for the Internet] is   on the Internet)
  www.yourabsoluteadvantage.com

- ISP (Internet Service Provider); if you're spending $15–$30 per
  much time at all "surfing the net" and using e-mail   month
  to correspond with clients and/or family and friends,
  having an ISP provide your Internet access is much
   more economical than simply accessing the Internet
  through an e-mail provider (such as AOL). If you do
  have an ISP, you can still have an AOL account (to
  benefit from not only e-mail, which would also be
  available through an ISP, but also to retain access to
  all the user forums and great support boards), paying
  a reduced AOL fee of $9.95 per month in addition
  to your ISP's monthly fee.

- Caller ID; I have found this service from my telephone $5-$9 per
  company to be one of the best business helpers ever   month
  for a busy home-based office. Many people who know
  me know that I rarely answer my business line. (I'm
  simply too busy working and know that all my regular
  clients will happily leave a message.) But, to avoid playing
  endless phone tag with a client I've been trying to track
  down, having Caller ID lets me know that it is Bob Edwards
  returning my call—and I can selectively pick up if I choose.
  I also opt to pay for this service on my personal phone line
  for the same reason—I know when it's important to put
  a client on hold to take a family member's call. And, not

so incidentally, I'm able to avoid most of the annoying telemarketing calls on *both* lines with this service!

- Pitney Bowes Personal Postage Meter; I found this to be one of those expenses that I held off on incurring for years, only to do it and then say, "How did I ever live without it?" In my case, securing a large credit union as a secretarial service client was the justification I needed. I process a mailing to its new members every other day on a year-round basis, typically 50-60 pieces per day. It is *much* more convenient and professional to meter the first-class postage. In addition, for mailing completed projects to clients as well as my own client newsletters, it is simply far more convenient to meter everything here at home and then drop it off at the post office. This compares with waiting in line to buy postage and write a check, returning home to affix it to a large mailing, and then going back to the post office at another time, only to wait in line once again to mail everything. *after a complimentary 90-day period, the monthly fee is about $35 to rent the metering scale; postage is "refilled" into the meter through a modem link and billed automatically to a credit card*

- Additional filing, cabinet, and storage space — *varies*

- Bookcase — $50+

- Fax machine—this is frequently considered a start-up necessity. It's a fairly good profit center *and* brings in additional word processing business. Keep in mind that you don't need to lay out additional monies for a separate line for the fax—most home-based businesses use their personal house telephone line for their fax. (However, a dedicated fax line is a luxurious plus, one that I installed, finally, after ten years in business.) While you can't deduct the base monthly charge of the personal telephone line on your tax return when it is used for the fax, you can keep track of the toll charges incurred when transmitting faxes and deduct these as legitimate business expenses. Be sure to check for the most current guidelines with regard to the ability to deduct any business expense. — $200

- Good quality photocopier*—almost a necessity, but this can be deferred at start-up if you can't swing the financing. (Remember, though, that producing copies of text, reports, resumes, etc. represents an excellent profit generator.) Check also into refurbished copiers. $1,200–$2,500

* For the photocopier, most companies offer lease packages, many with an option to purchase the equipment at the end of the lease. Although you end up paying more for the machine, you can own it at the end of the term and finance it in smaller increments as you grow your business. For some this is an excellent option. Check, too, with your accountant regarding the potential tax benefits to leasing versus buying your equipment.

PROJECTED START-UP COSTS WORKSHEET

Fixtures and equipment (information earlier in chapter 3) $ _____

Remodeling, renovation, and decorating expense $ _____

Installation of equipment $ _____

Deposit to telephone company $ _____

Cost of business telephone line $ _____

Legal and professional fees $ _____

Licenses and permits $ _____

Business insurance for a home-based business $ _____

Starting inventory of office supplies/stationery $ _____

Initial advertising/promotion costs $ _____

Operating cash $ _____

Miscellaneous $ _____

TOTAL $ _____

20-pound paper suitable for both laser printer and copier (cheaper by the case and you will use it; buy 24 pound for final originals if you can afford it) . . . . 1 case (10 reams)

manila file folders . . . . box of 100

8½ x 11 writing tablets . . . . package of 12

oversize white envelopes (9 x 12) . . . . box of 100

#10 business envelopes (white) . . . . box of 500

small pads for telephone messages 6

Post-It notes (2-inch-square size) . . . . small package

paper clips . . . . 1 box

stapler with staples . . . . 1 box staples

pica stick and ruler . . . . 1 each

scissors . . . . 1 pair

rubber cement and Elmer's glue . . . . 1 each

cellophane tape with dispenser . . . . 2 rolls

self-inking stamp: "First Class" 1

first-class postage stamps . . . . roll of 100

extra incremental ounce postage stamps . . . . sheet of 100

small postage scale 1

small desktop calculator (portable is ideal) 1

disks appropriately sized for your computer . . . . 3 boxes (10 per box)

pens (blue or black ink) . . . . box of 10

pencils . . . . box of 10

fine-point black ink pens 2

highlighting markers . . . . 4 different colors, 1 each

labels suitable for use in laser printer or copier . . . . box of 100 sheets

If you opt not to have preprinted letterhead and envelopes, be certain to have an appropriate quantity of your preferred stock and matching envelopes in storage for printing your own as you need them. Invoice forms are typically printed individually as you generate billing on your computer and, therefore, do not require preprinted forms.

Optional (depending on if you will be offering resume services; this would be the minimum start-up inventory for this service)

24-pound ivory parchment . . . . 3 boxes (100 sheets each)

matching envelopes . . . . 4 boxes (25 to a box)

24-pound ice blue or stone gray parchment . . . . 3 boxes (100 sheets each)

matching envelopes . . . . 4 boxes (25 to a box)

24-pound pure white parchment . . . . 2 boxes (100 sheets each)

matching envelopes . . . . 3 boxes (25 to a box)

CHAPTER FOUR

ADVERTISING AND PROMOTION

As the owner of a secretarial services business, you are your own best public relations person. As a goodwill ambassador for your company, you have the opportunity to promote yourself and your services every time you speak with someone—friend, neighbor, local businessperson, and so on. Some of this speaking might be directly promotion-oriented; the majority will be subtle.

What types of clients do you wish to attract? (Keep in mind that you are providing a service to your *clients*; never make the mistake of calling them customers.) What niche are you hoping to fill? Gear your marketing, promotional, and advertising efforts accordingly.

BUSINESS CARDS

Business cards will no doubt be your first business expense after arranging for installation of a business telephone line. Be certain *not* to order your cards until the telephone line is actually installed. In some infrequent instances the number does change from the one the telephone company may have originally promised you. You don't want to go through the expense of having your business cards reprinted simply because of an incorrect telephone number.

Basic information you'll want to include on your business card includes your business name (see Selection of Your Business Name in chapter 3), *your* name, and the business telephone number. You should also select and use a title for yourself. In my years of doing business, I've observed that, as a rule, female entrepreneurs frequently choose not to use a title—or they might say "owner," "operator," or "proprietor." On the other hand, most male entrepreneurs use titles and nearly always call themselves "president." While perhaps awkward to some at first, this *is* your company, and, male or female, you are certainly entitled to call yourself president, even if your business is not incorporated. Place your title right after your name on your business cards and on all other written materials where your name appears (e.g., letterhead).

If, like most home-based business owners, you do not wish to have drop-in clientele and prefer to schedule by appointment, I recommend omitting your physical street address and instead obtaining a post office box number—use that, plus your town, state, and zip code, on your business card. A quick summary of your key services should be included also, in particular if your business name doesn't describe what you do (e.g., "Allen Associates" is great for placement at the top of the alphabet but doesn't indicate what the company does). You should also include a "subhead" or a slogan beneath the company name that says something such as "Professional Word Processing and Typing Services." (See detailed information on slogan creation later in this chapter.)

If you offer multiple services, you might briefly itemize half a dozen or so in small, legible type. Try not to crowd too much onto one little card, but do be somewhat descriptive. Perhaps consider a two-sided business card or one with an overflap. (Both cost more, however.) Play with the layout and text over and over again until you're satisfied with the look. I recommend typesetting the copy for your business cards using your own laser printer (if you have one) so that you can exactly match your letterhead and other business documents you will later be preparing on your equipment. Then let it "cool" for two days' time. Go back to it with fresh eyes and take another look. This is a step that's suggested every time you write copy for promotional and advertising purposes. Once it's finalized, you're ready to take it to a printer.

I used a standard-size business card for my first eight years in business but found that I was frequently asked at business meetings and conventions to jot down on the back of the card some of the specific services I provided. This began to become a nuisance, so I converted at that time to a double-size card with a folding flap. The card is distinctive and attracts positive attention, plus it enables me to detail some of the more specific services my company provides. I have found the cards to be well worth the cost (about $120 for 1,000 as compared with around $40 or $50 for standard-size cards of the same quantity).

Obtaining printing services for your business cards is a great opportunity to affiliate yourself with a professional printer in your area. Not only will you want to refer some business to that firm, but the printer also will be pleased to know of your existence, and once you've proven yourself as a professional with "staying

power," the printer will refer business to you that he or she doesn't handle (e.g., typesetting a resume). Call different vendors to obtain quotes for your business cards. The recommended start-up quantity is the minimum, usually 500. That way, as you expand services and equipment, your cards can be updated in a shorter amount of time with minimal waste of the outdated cards.

Go for the highest grade stock (paper) you can obtain. Crisp black ink on white linen vellum is tough to beat, in particular, because you can obtain a nice white stationery and reasonably priced envelopes instead of going with a much more costly colored stock that's difficult to obtain. You'll want a consistent, cohesive look to all of your printed materials—same type font, same stock (or similar stock but same color), and so on. Keep this in mind before deciding on "wild strawberry" as the color for your business cards! Choosing a pure white card stock costs less and, for businesses in the start-up phase, allows you to order inexpensive but professional-quality return labels, mailing labels, business-size envelopes with your return address, and so forth from such supply catalogs as Walter Drake and Spencer. If you pick an ivory or gray for your letterhead or business cards, for example, you won't be able to coordinate these other supplies as economically as when using white paper.

In addition, the availability of unique business stationery and forms for customized use in your laser printer (see the list of sources in the Appendix) allows for quick personalization of professional-looking brochures you write, design, and print yourself in quantities of one or more as needed.

If you've developed a logo, use it on your card as well as all other printed materials. I highly recommend that a slogan be created and used in all print marketing materials as well as in Yellow Pages advertising. A short slogan that's catchy and memorable creates a professional image and impression of your business. Make sure your slogan reflects you. The following slogans have been shared by your colleagues:

- "Providing *Comprehensive Secretarial Services* For ALL Your Business Needs"
  —Cindy Kraft, Executive Essentials

- "We can help you with any project that uses the computer"
  —Nina Feldman, Nina Feldman Connections

- "The Wise Choice for Word Processing Solutions"
  —Shawn Teets, WordWise

- "Office Services with the Personal Touch"
  —Kathy Mandy, Select Word Services

- "Making Your Job Our Top Priority!"
  —Brenda Lorencen, Word/Pro Connection

- "Helping You Get *More* from *Your* Business"
  —Joyce Moore, Moore Business Services

- "Our Product Is Your Success!"
  —Vivian Lee Adkins, Adkins Resume Services

- "Providing Desktop Publishing, Secretarial, Editorial, and Resume
  Services for Businesses and Individuals in the Fox Valley Since 1983"
  —Kathy Keshemberg, Computron/A Career Advantage

- "Committed to Excellence and Client Satisfaction"
  —René Hart, First Impressions Resume and Career Development Services

- "We Are in Business to Help You in Business"
  —Beth Quick, Q & A Business Solutions

- "Secretarial Support and Transcription Services for Businesses and
  Professionals"
  —Sue Faris, Word Processing Plus

- "Presenting you at your best!"
  —Lisa Freeman, Advanced Office & Resume Services

- "Behind every busy office is An Executive Assistant, taking care of the paperwork so you can take care of business"
  —Josie Smith, An Executive Assistant

I use two slogans in my business: "Our Business Is Making *You* Look Good!" and "Whatever Your Requirements Are, Absolute Advantage Will Make *You* Look Good!" In addition, with my change of business name in 1996, I added a twist to my slogan in my Yellow Pages advertising to ensure a smooth transition and continued name recognition/identity: "Absolute Advantage . . . division/ Comprehensive Services Plus—Our name has changed . . . our commitment to quality and you has not." I continue to mention the name change and link back to Comprehensive Services Plus in my ongoing Yellow Pages advertising because of the large number of repeat clients who still know me as CSP but refer to the Yellow Pages to find my telephone number. In my resume service Yellow Pages ad only, I also add the following subslogan: "When quality absolutely cannot be compromised, call us. We'll help give you the competitive edge!"

BROCHURES

If you plan to be in the business of providing enhanced word processing or desk-top publishing services, then you'll undoubtedly want to pursue the market for preparing brochures. The best way to capture this business? Develop your own eye-catching and professional brochure that showcases your talent and creativity! With the wide range of specialty papers available through such companies as Paper Direct (see the Appendix), you can stylize a unique, customized brochure and print only the quantity you need for a given promotional mailing. You'll be able to cus-tomize your message while at the same time tailoring services to the anticipated needs of certain client groups.

Also discuss with the printer you selected to handle your business cards the options and specialty papers available for large runs. While I always recommend against printing too many, particularly in the beginning, you may find it is more cost-effective to have 500 brochures produced on a distinctive paper carried by your printer.

What should a brochure include? Beyond the obvious information (name, address, telephone number, and, if you have one, fax number and/or web address), you should detail *benefits* to your clients as well as services available. I am firmly of the opinion that you don't want to simply provide only a "laundry list" of your services. Some clients may be unable to interpret from this listing how you can help them with their requirements. Include prose that connects directly to the client. For example, if you plan to provide resume services, don't just list "resume services and cover letters." Be certain to include text regarding your experience in this area (I include a line in my brochure that says I've produced more than 8,000 resumes in my sixteen years in business) as well as how you can help the job-seek-ing client—for instance, "Distinctive and eye-catching cover letters help to profile your unique background and accomplishments and will assist in getting the door open to the all-important interview. Let us work with you to effectively highlight your achievements and the salient points of your career experiences." Promo-tional copy for all aspects of the services you provide will convey the right message for your business. Take advantage of this vehicle for showcasing *your* abilities in the public relations field!

Included in this text is an actual (reduced) copy of my current brochure for Absolute Advantage. I created this using Paper Direct brochure stationery. Over the years, there has been a subtle change in the focus of my business toward an emphasis on the business consulting/partnering my company now provides. In addition, I've strengthened the copy in my brochure as it relates to the resume/career services side of my business. Both of these changes reflect the higher end (and more lucrative) side of the business. I still handle a significant amount of

Absolute Advantage

division / COMPREHENSIVE SERVICES PLUS

Providing the Professional Consulting, Business, and Strategic Planning Services Your Business Needs!

Jan Melnik, CPRW
President
Member, PARW, ABSSI,
NRWA, NAJST
Middlesex County
Chamber of Commerce

Absolute Advantage

division / COMPREHENSIVE SERVICES PLUS

Absolute Advantage

division / COMPREHENSIVE SERVICES PLUS

Job Search Coach, Professional Resume and Career Services

Business Consulting, Promotional and Strategic Planning

Desktop Publishing, Editorial, and Office Support Services

Since 1983

P.O. Box 718 – Durham, CT 06422

Phone (860) 349-0256
Fax (860) 349-1343
E-mail CompSPJan@aol.com

Established in 1983, **Absolute Advantage** provides professional consulting and creative services to clients throughout the United States. We're experts at helping your business develop and implement programs and collateral materials that are action-oriented and capture the bottom-line results you're seeking.

■ ■ ■

We work closely with your staff to understand your strategic objectives and to implement effective, successful programs and materials — all while keeping a close watch on your budgetary constraints.

■ ■ ■

In short, whatever your particular requirements, you can rely on **Absolute Advantage** to deliver the professional assistance you need to succeed and prosper in this challenging business climate. We help turn opportunities into realities!

■ ■ ■

Our Business Is Making You Look Good!

traditional word processing for a number of my corporate accounts, but my brochure copy doesn't specifically focus on this service offering. (There's only a very short paragraph.)

YELLOW PAGES ADVERTISING

In nearly every location throughout the United States, this will be your single biggest—and best—advertising mechanism for bringing new business through the door. This is so important that I'll say it again: Your ability to get into the Yellow Pages will do more to determine the likelihood of more immediate success for your business than any other marketing step you take.

At the time you arrange for your business telephone service, be certain to obtain the advertising schedule for the directory in which you'll be listed. Contact the Yellow Pages advertising department immediately to determine the possibility of making it into the next edition. Depending on timing, this could be up to sixteen months away. Therefore, it's especially important to make these contacts the minute you've determined that you are going to establish a business and have arranged for a business telephone line. By the way, you can advertise in the Yellow Pages only if you use a business or home-office business telephone number—you can't use your home number. This timing is so critical that as you are conducting your evaluation of whether or not beginning a secretarial services business is right for you, you may want to establish your timetable around this very important deadline.

Highly Recommended Tip: Yellow Pages Categories

Be listed under as many categories as you can afford. Once you've determined the services you plan to offer, advertise under as many of the appropriate categories as possible—even if the listing is only a one-line company name listing with your telephone number. Suggested categories to consider (based on the services you plan to offer) are as follows:

- Copying
- Editing
- Notary Public
- Photocopying
- Resumes
- Transcription
- Typing Service

- Desktop Publishing
- Facsimile Transmission Service
- Office Services
- Proofreading
- Secretarial Service
- Typesetting
- Word Processing Service

Your own Yellow Pages may have slightly different versions of these headings or additional headings to consider—the key is to be as expansive and visible as possible. Interestingly, research has shown that while technology continues to improve the methods of keyboarding (from typing to word processing to desktop publishing), the majority of consumers and potential clients still think of "typing" when they need a document professionally prepared. And, of course, some clients actually do want something "typed" (e.g., completion of a preprinted application form on a typewriter). Therefore, it's highly recommended that you place your biggest ad under the Yellow Pages category of Typing Service (or the equivalent version in your directory), even if your competitors aren't doing this. Other than my resume service and Yellow Pages ad for that category in two different directories, my Typing Service ads have always pulled in the most new business for my company—and this has been true since I started out in 1983.

Another important factor to keep in mind is analysis of your competition. (Refer back to your earlier notes from Researching and Assessing the Competition, in chapter 3.) Examine closely the current telephone directory: Who are your competitors? Look under all applicable categories and make a list. Where are they advertising? How large are their ads? Where are the most or biggest ads run? If your competitors have been around for any length of time, you can bet they've determined (if they're smart business managers) the categories under which it makes the most sense to advertise heavily. Take their cue and align your advertising accordingly. While you might not match competitors' advertising in the first few years, you could certainly choose to run your bigger ads in those categories where the competition does.

Another interesting thing about Yellow Pages advertising for this field is that small, in-column informational ads seem to draw better than large, out-of-column display ads. Exceptions to this are usually but not always found in large metropolitan areas—New York City, for example. The single biggest factor in determining which way to go is, again, to look at what your competition is doing. If all of your competitors are running large display ads, that may be what pulls in your area. It's more likely, however, that the in-column informational ad—somewhere between a half inch (most economical) and approximately 2 or 2 ½ inches— is the best way to proceed for this industry.

To discourage drop-in clientele (important for most home-based businesses), you can specifically request that the telephone company not include your street address in your advertisements and in your White Pages listing. You can have your post office box address included; however, there is probably little value to doing this other than soliciting junk mail. Instead, simply list your town and the telephone number, the latter in large type.

Over the past few years, I've experimented successfully with adding my own name to my Yellow Pages copy (followed by one of my credentials—Jan Melnik, CPRW [for Certified Professional Resume Writer]). I've found this has the advantage of letting first-time callers feel as though they already "know" me . . . and increases prospective clients' comfort level with leaving a message with my voice mail service. Because I'm usually meeting with clients during most of the available business hours, it's rare that a caller actually gets through to me directly; instead, I rely heavily on voice mail for nearly all client communications. Again, although I advise against including a street address, I do think there is a significant advantage to including your own name in your advertising.

If you opt to also advertise in the telephone directories of adjacent towns (e.g., you might be located near a major route that commuters use to travel to adjacent towns), consider including a line like "conveniently located in [your town]" as a means by which to encourage traffic. I advertise in a directory that covers three towns, two of which border my town but are currently in a different dialing area. Because I want to stress my location as adjacent to these two communities, I include a line in my ad stating that I'm "conveniently located in Durham." This has attracted numerous callers from these towns who are already commuting right by my street on their way north to the next largest cities. If I didn't state that, they might think I was located half an hour farther from their homes than I am and not bother to call.

In addition to specific product offerings and new services, always advertise special features that you offer:

- Competitive rates
- Business hours, evenings, and weekends
- Notary Public services
- Photocopying
- Telephone dictation
- Number of years in business (once it's significant; I always include "Serving Clients Since 1983")

- Convenient appointments
- Pick-up and delivery (if it's free, add that as well)
- Fax service
- Rush service
- Same-day turnaround
- Discount for referrals

Try to include something "free" in your advertising, whether it's "free resume guidelines upon request," "free review of your existing resume," "free photocopies (ask for details)," or "free pick-up and delivery"; these items catch the reader's eye and usually don't cost you that much. Obviously, something like free pick-up and delivery is practical only within a certain geographic area and may make sense only for larger "corporate" clients.

Be certain to request proofs of your ads from the sales representative; push hard if this request is met with resistance. One year (early on, when I didn't request proofs), my ad was omitted from one category altogether. I received the ad free of charge for the next entire year. Another year the Yellow Pages representative showed me a sample of my ad prepared with red ink in a quarter-page size. This was to encourage me to sign up for larger ads. But the proof spelled *transcription* incorrectly and was not designed as I had envisioned it. I frequently see the word laser misspelled as *lazer* in a number of related Yellow Pages ads. And one of my competitors has had a misspelled word, *develoment*, in its ad for six years. While the initial error wasn't the competitor's—unless a proof was approved—I'm surprised a correction hasn't been requested in the subsequent years.

Above are copies of actual ads I run for my company in the Yellow Pages of two directories.

COMMUNITY TELEPHONE DIRECTORY

Some communities have their own small telephone directories, usually published by local civic organizations (Exchange Club, Rotary, etc.). Advertising in these directories is a good way to get established, a nice way to support local causes, and a viable way to begin bringing in business. A half-page ad in a small directory generally costs under $200 per year and is very visible. Design an ad yourself or use the organization's graphic design services—perhaps "blow up" your business card if you're very satisfied with what it says and how it visually attracts the eye. Consider laying out your ad in reverse (the appearance of white lettering on a black background).

PUBLICITY AND PROMOTIONAL ADVERTISING

Generating news and obtaining free publicity are two of the easiest and best ways to get exposure at little or no cost, particularly when you are starting out. Simply starting a new business is news, and you should be certain to get the word out to all newspapers (daily and weekly) that cover your geographic area and the market you intend to serve.

Keep in mind that, as your business grows, you'll want to establish relationships with all media contacts in your vicinity to garner future publicity. New equipment, new service offerings, and unique promotional discounts are all potentially newsworthy items, as are celebrations of your company's anniversary. Develop a media contact list in your computer database and keep it up to date.

A few years back, I experienced great success with obtaining some outstanding newspaper publicity—all the result of a telephone call I initiated to the business editor of my state's largest daily. I've provided an edited version of the letter here, annotated to reflect the rationale behind each key point so that you can focus on what would be applicable to you and your situation. I've also shared some of what happened as a result of the article that was published on the cover of the business section of the newspaper—just three short weeks after I phoned the business editor with my "pitch" (and then followed up with this letter).

(date / inside address information)

RE: "Building a Home-based Business While Raising Kids . . .
    The Trend for the 90s . . . *and* the next century!"

The angle (or hook) that I decided to present to the newspaper was one that captured the essence of my business and its relevance to these times: It's home-based, can be done while raising little kids, and is clearly a trend for our times.

Dear Business Editor *(personalize your letter)*:

Thank you for speaking with me recently regarding my story idea for an "Inside Business" feature. I believe three factors strongly support the relevancy of an article spotlighting my business.

> *This is the benefits statement that attempts to introduce the reasons (beyond personal, egotistical, or in order to obtain "free publicity") that I developed to give the story idea real "news appeal." If writing this today, I would reflect the continuing trend projected well into the next millennium for starting home-based businesses.*

1. Home offices are growing at an accelerated rate in the '90s. A trend first started in earnest during the early '80s by corporate telecommuters, many entrepreneurs have since jumped on the bandwagon. In part fueled by the recession and continued corporate "right-sizing," these talented people with diversified skills and experience are drawn to the myriad appeals of a home-based business (unlimited income potential, creative license, decision-making authority, business autonomy, sometimes significant tax advantages, etc.). Nearly every home office in the United States today (more than 20 million) requires (or will require in the near future) either ad hoc or regular assistance from a professional word processing/secretarial service to handle work ranging from basic copying and fax services to preparation, formatting, and editing of complex documents, development of databases, and handling of mass mailings.

> *This paragraph includes statistics (newspapers love to run stats), buzzwords for the times ("right-sizing," "fueled by the recession," "telecommuters," etc.), and touches on the industry of which home-based office support services are a component. It also provides a significant angle—the fact that interest in this type of business is extremely broad-based (and, therefore, should have substantial reader appeal; again, important information for the newspaper publishing field).*

2. Project managers, administrative assistants, writers, secretaries, paralegals, and middle managers have not been exempt from the corporate cuts that have occurred. It's a fair bet that many already possess a number of the skills needed to successfully launch a home-based business. *And* a good percentage of these workers have skills that would allow for success in my business—there's hardly a person today who hasn't used a PC or learned to "keyboard" (type).

Who could potentially get into this business (and succeed)? I rhetorically point out that nearly anyone could begin a home-based business providing office support and ancillary services. Once again, this provides "reader appeal."

3. Celebrating my tenth anniversary in business this year, I've shown it can be done successfully and profitably. And with my background as a speaker to members of the Association of Business Support Services International, Inc. at their annual conventions, my positions of contributing editor for several key industry publications (*Keyboard Connection, Bootstrappin' Entrepreneur* and *Homeworking Mothers*), and my status as an author of a book on starting a home-based business providing word processing and secretarial services, as well as publisher/editor of an industry periodical, *The Word Advantage*, I'm an expert in the field.

    An unabashed plug for my business, a bit about my credentials so as to position me as "someone in this field" who knows what she's talking about, and another story hook—a tenth anniversary celebration.

By way of giving you a thumbnail sketch of my company's background, I began providing freelance word processing and secretarial services on a part-time basis in 1983 from a home office. My intent from the start was to convert to full-time status as soon as a regular client base was established. Concurrent with building my business, I maintained a full-time career with Digital Equipment Corporation from 1981 through 1988 and was even promoted into management (in 1985, from an administrative assistant's position). In 1986, I was offered another promotion with DEC, this time accompanied by a relocation offer to Boston; I accepted, and once again found myself "starting my business from scratch." After my identical twins were born on Thanksgiving Day in 1987, I used my maternity leave and accumulated vacation time to put plans in motion for operating my business full time. When my husband (also a "DEC-ie") was relocated by Digital *back* to Connecticut in 1988, Comprehensive Services Plus was officially launched as a full-time home-based business.

As briefly as possible, I provide the preliminary history of the business. I mention Digital and DEC because it's a company that gets a lot of press in the Northeast and thus carries name-recognition power among readers. I always include mention of my twins and their Thanksgiving birthday—this has captured attention before and led to publication of stories in other papers. People seem to be fascinated with twins. Plus, it points to a possibly interesting "photo opportunity" to accompany the story! The actual photo that was shot certainly depicts the "life in a circus" lifestyle of man-

aging a business with young kids! The photographer really enjoyed herself the morning we spent together.

One hears a lot these days about home offices, home-made money, and making a living while working at home. I believe my sales records reflect the success I've experienced in the office support and editorial services niche. While I'm not comfortable sharing my actual numbers, each year in business has shown steady growth and 1993 will be CSP's best year ever. My first-year revenues from the part-time venture were $74 (it was only for a six-week "year," mid-November to the end of December) and with each relocation (Boston in 1986 and Connecticut in 1988) the numbers went back to zero. In less than 18 months of operating CSP in Connecticut on a full-time basis, my earnings had exceeded the $36K salary I'd left behind at DEC. And with annual growth of between 20 and 35 percent each year since 1989, my decision to take a risk and leave the security of the corporate rat race (as well as a solid earnings potential there) has been reaffirmed more than once.

> *The all-important numbers are mentioned in this paragraph. Using numbers and percentages, I convey the information the editor was seeking. I also reference a critical decision-point factor—leaving the corporate rat race and quickly exceeding my previous earnings. Business articles love to include stuff like this.*

My business has grown beautifully over the years and includes an interesting and highly diversified client base. Areas into which *I've* diversified include writing and publishing. Always a freelance writer of articles and reviews, the only books I had written until a year ago were children's stories. In 1992, I decided to put together a guide in order to address the increasing number of telephone calls I was receiving from friends and strangers alike asking, "How do I start a business like yours?"

> *Where the business is today and more plugs for the work I do are included in the foregoing paragraph. I also try to build a little credibility about my background as a writer. Who knows? Maybe the paper might be interested in having me do some freelance stories for them.*

I determined that the focus of this guide should be on developing a home-based desktop publishing and typing service *while raising young children* and, to date, I market the guide exclusively through a national network for home-based mothers to which I belong. Sales have been strong and it was word of this guide that led to my receiving an inquiry (and ultimately a contract) from The Globe Pequot

Press in Guilford, Connecticut, to write a 300-page book that would become an integral part of their home-based business series (by the way, this book does not focus on raising kids, although indirect references are, of course, included). My publisher, too, recognizes the tremendous market potential for such a book, given the country's current economic climate, the skill set of so many Americans today, and the anticipated trend of home-based businesses into the next millennium. I believe I mentioned when we spoke that the manuscript was submitted to my editor just last week; the book will hit shelves nationwide (chains and independents) in the spring of 1994.

> *I obviously wanted to promote my upcoming book while, at the same time, mentioning that my first guide is already selling well. Again, this reinforces my image as an "expert in the field." I include mention of the fact that the book does not focus on starting a business with kids because I don't want childless readers to think that it's not a serious business book. By referring to my publisher's impressions about the market potential, I believe I provide a somewhat objective "professional" opinion that underlines the significance of the story to readers of the newspaper.*

Beyond financial success, I believe it's equally important to note the personal satisfaction achieved with operating a successful home-based business. After my twins were born, I had another baby in 1990, hardly skipping a beat in terms of my business (even with a C-section, I was back at my desk the day I got home from the hospital with Stephen nursing in my arms!).

Maintaining a home-based business has afforded me the luxury of caring for my children in my home while I work and provides immeasurable benefits personally. Plus, there's nothing that beats kicking off in the middle of the morning to go for a walk or pull weeds in my flower garden . . . helps to compensate for those many nights of working that go well into the early predawn hours! I love being an entrepreneur and especially enjoy sharing my experiences with others, (both the success stories and the mistakes that have enabled me to grow), helping them in their business pursuits.

> *I try to show that raising a business and a family can be done successfully and afford benefits beyond strictly financial gains. I also attempt to convey a lot of the enthusiasm and energy I have for this business and talking about this business. (I'm hoping to show I'm an "interesting" subject for an interview, so try not to be too dry or overly, unapproachably professional—in other words, I'm a "real person.")*

I believe I've rambled on enough here . . . and sincerely hope I've provided you with the framework of information you will need to make a decision on whether or not such a story idea has merit. I'll look forward to talking with you after you've had a chance to review this. Thanks for your time and interest.

This is probably the only area where I take a more humble, modest, and reserved approach . . . again, I'm trying to keep things "warm and friendly" and clearly place the decision in the editor's lap as to whether or not these ideas are deserving of a story.

Sincerely,
Jan Melnik

Enclosures
(I included my business card, business brochure, and resume)

The following are just some of the things that happened after the article appeared in the newspaper:

- I received seven checks (and numerous other queries) for the guidebook I wrote on starting a home-based desktop publishing and office support services business. All of these calls were from women wanting to do the same thing.

- *Five* of these callers asked to consult with me. (At the time, I charged $50 an hour and freely provided copies of anything they wanted that was not confidential or proprietary; this included copies of my Yellow Pages ads, the many promotional and marketing letters I'd written to prospective clients, to clients seeking information, and thanking clients for their first-time business, copies of all my newsletters to clients, etc.) The consultations held were each two hours in duration, and I made a promise of providing telephone support, complimentary, after the consultation, if desired, for a reasonable amount of time at my convenience.

- I booked two complete resume consultations from the article, both from towns that were nearly an hour from me. Interestingly, the clients did not respond to the article's claim about how quickly I'd turn their stuff around. Rather, they both indicated they liked how the story depicted me and hoped I'd enable them to enjoy success. (One client was a CPA, the other an attorney.)

- A woman living in an adjacent town noticed the article and contacted me, asking if I typed term papers. Of course, I did (although I still prefer "adult" students and don't actively solicit this market; usually, it's ancillary to working with a client for other reasons: When they return to school for a master's or a doctorate, *then* I type their papers). Well, this woman carried the good news to her entire class at nursing school. Nearly all of the students were women balancing full-time positions, families, *and* nursing school! They all hired me to type their papers and, sure, this first project of the semester was just a two-page abstract each ($20.35, including tax, per student), but I got nearly the whole class (eleven or so students) *and* a commitment to type the rest of their papers for the semester (ten-page and twenty-page papers *each*), plus requests for resumes once they graduated! Not bad . . .

- An interesting call came from a vanity company in Tampa, Florida, with an offer "without obligation" to professionally mount the news article and forward it for my inspection. I actually opted to "allow" them to do this. I was pleased with the results, as they figured I would be (they know the egos of their market niche, no doubt!), and paid the $119 fee. I've had this company mount all of the newspaper articles about my business appearing since this time.

- A professor from my alma mater wrote, enclosing a clipping of the article, and inviting me to address the college's Phi Beta Lambda group.

- The director of my town's Adult Education program (and a part-time journalist for the daily newspaper in the city adjacent to my town) noticed the article and readily accepted my offer to teach in the Adult Ed program beginning that October. I instructed a two-class course on resume development and creation of a distinctive cover letter. For the spring semester, I taught a course in the art of self-promoting a business!

- A woman offered me a complimentary facial massage and makeover from Mary Kay—I declined, as I already had a "Mary Kay lady"—however, I thought this a rather clever and creative approach to marketing *her* business and may consider doing calls of this sort to people *I* read about in the paper who have been recently promoted, offering to give them the first half hour of a consultation free in updating their resume to reflect their new position.

- Several calls and letters came from former resume clients (now successfully employed), a mother of one of my son's friends, the town clerk in my town, the Airborne delivery person (I don't even *know* him and typically receive most of my software, paper goods, etc., via UPS or Federal Express!), lots of folks in town, my printer up in the next city, and a president of a company here in Durham who sits on the Planning and Zoning Commission with me—all nice recognition.

- Assorted calls came in from insurance people (one specializing in health coverage for the self-employed; I'm covered by my husband's policy and, therefore, wasn't interested).

Business Services Plus

Main Street · Anytown · USA

(343) 343–3333 · E-mail: Bizplus@aol.com

MEDIA CONTACT: Jessica Turner, 343–3333

DATE: 3/6/00

FOR IMMEDIATE RELEASE

Jessica Turner of Anytown, USA, is pleased to announce the recent opening of her new secretarial service, Business Services Plus. A former executive secretary with JKL Manufacturing Corporation for six years, she has more than ten years' experience providing professional word processing and secretarial services. A graduate of Smith Business School, Your City, USA, she holds a degree in business administration.

Business Services Plus will furnish professional services to executives, sales personnel, individuals, and students in the tri-county area. From an office fully equipped with state-of-the-art computer technology, laser printing, and fax services, Turner promises to "be a partner in each client's business success." Office hours will be scheduled to suit client convenience on an appointment-only basis. During the month of April, she is offering a 20 percent-off-first-invoice discount to each new client.

Turner states, "Today's challenging economic climate demands cost-efficiencies and high productivity—I can offer exactly that to each and every client." Call today to find out how Business Services Plus can service *your* requirements.

- A salesperson for an independent telephone company offered to save me "lots of money" on my phone bill. (The article in the paper mentioned I spend about $400 a month . . . however, most of this is advertising expense for the Yellow Pages and I really wouldn't dream of switching carriers.)
- My twins started school a few days before the article appeared in the paper; their teachers each posted the article in their respective classrooms, and the boys were quite proud.

So, dollar-wise, what was the initial yield? It was more than $1,500. And over the years, there's been significant repeat/referral business from clients initially seen as a result of this article. Resume clients are always repeat clients, for additional cover letters, updates, etc. And just the general publicity alone was good for business.

Getting publicity is the best way of achieving free advertising. The added credibility gained by having a story appear in a respected newspaper is priceless. I highly encourage all business owners to find *their* angle and then contact the media to "get the word out." You'll love the results—I guarantee it!

YEARBOOKS, FUND-RAISING MATERIALS, AND THE LIKE

Once you're "in business," you'll quickly become the target of many telemarketing efforts—from large, national companies wanting to sell you insurance to the local Little League organization and Police Officers' Benevolent Association seeking donations. The latter groups generally want you to support their cause through purchase of an ad in a directory they are producing or in a program for a special event. It's always good to support local causes, but a word of caution: You'll probably receive more requests than you can afford, especially when you're first starting out.

Therefore, select carefully, perhaps rotating from year to year the organizations that you support. Never hesitate to say that you're a small company (one employee) just starting out, without a large advertising budget. Usually, the smallest, business-card-size ad runs anywhere from $25 in a high school yearbook to $100 in a civic program. That cost times a half-dozen different organizations can quickly add up. Ads in these types of publications do help to establish your presence and goodwill over time but generally don't directly increase your traffic or profits, at least not when you're first setting up operations. Pick and choose carefully, but save the bulk of your advertising budget for the Yellow Pages and highly select direct mail marketing. The type of direct mail marketing I've found most useful is mailing carefully developed materials in response to a prospective client's telephone inquiry about services provided.

DEVELOPING A NEWSLETTER

As with a brochure, a newsletter is a perfect way to showcase your talents. It's also the ideal tool for communicating on a regular basis with your clients and those prospective clients with whom you'd like to do business. A recommended schedule for producing your own company's newsletter is quarterly. This is affordable yet frequent enough to maintain your image before clients. Most business operators find that once their businesses are started, attempting to publish monthly or even bimonthly is simply too aggressive a schedule to follow. Whatever schedule you adopt, it's important to be consistent and stay with it.

A beginning format that is easy to maintain is a simple 8½-by-11-inch sheet folded into thirds. Check with your local postal authorities regarding sealing of the newsletter. Some newsletters are held together with a small circular seal. Others, such as my quarterly, are not sealed at all (per the request of my post office). Staples are almost always frowned upon.

You can have lots of fun designing your newsletter, from selecting a creative and eye-catching name for the nameplate (top of the newsletter where you state the name and issue number/date) to picking out a paper for producing it. Some secretarial services use the same paper for every issue—to build on a "look" that's uniquely and consistently theirs. My method is to select a different color of the same weight and type of stock for each issue; I prefer using a recycled stock with a heavy look and feel (and include the recycled emblem on the newsletter). It almost resembles a granite finish.

You may be wondering, "What can I possibly say in my newsletter?" The key to a successful newsletter, according to experts, is providing valuable information for your readers. This can be sharing any ideas you've gleaned in the time you've been doing business for better managing time, organizing files, producing promotional copy, and the like. Also equally valuable to your clients would be articles about new services you are providing, new equipment you've obtained to make *their* life easier (or their projects look even better), new paper choices that are available—whatever. Consider including a promotional offer in some or all of your newsletters, redeemable during that quarter only (if you settle on a quarterly format). Something along the lines of a percentage off the next invoice for providing a referral, a certain number of free photocopies, or a generous discount off the consultation period for a project developing a client brochure or newsletter are good ways to "give something back" to your clients.

Never hesitate to thank your clients for *being* your clients. The quarterly schedule I've developed for my newsletter calls for mailing it during March, June, September, and December. I use the December issue for my holiday message as well as an expression of appreciation for my clients' choosing to do business with me. I

Quips & Clips

a publication of Absolute Advantage
P.O. Box 718, Durham, CT 06422 • 860.349.0256 • CompSPJan@aol.com

Winter '99

Vol. 7, No. 4

S leigh Bells Ring ... Are You Listening?

Some of my favorite sounds of the season are echoing early in the halls of the school that my twin sons attend. Comprising just grades 5 and 6, the school attracts most of the 300+ students to the structured music-band program (fifth grade being the first opportunity these kids get to "be" in the school band) and they've been practicing since October. The strains of "Sleigh Bells Ring" reverberated through the halls a few weeks ago as I worked the annual book fair in the library-media center a few doors away from the band room. At home, we're making more noise than ever as, in addition to our piano, guitar, and dulcimer, we now have a budding trumpeter and an ambitious saxophonist joining the fray. Already the youngest (two years away from fifth grade) is promising to play the drums—we'll have our own ensemble!

As you prepare for the holidays, let me just share a few thoughts, reminiscent of my college motto: *carpe diem* (seize the day). Make the most of your opportunities, count your blessings, and share your feelings with those you love. And, in your work life, make maximum use of your talents, work for an organization whose philosophy you support, and strike a balance between work and personal life. If I can help you to seize new opportunities, be sure to give me a call.

— *Jan Melnik*

Ingredients for Success

A recent study of top CEOs revealed the following qualities important for success: 1) enthusiasm, 2) sincerity, 3) positive mental attitude, 4) skills, and 5) knowledge.

As you can see, your personality and outlook on life may play a larger role in your ultimate success than acquired abilities. Before checking into classes to enhance your skill base, consider taking a look at your attitude; perhaps a self-improvement or motivational tape series may be beneficial. And, during a job search, keep in mind that number-one quality of *enthusiasm* and try to convey it sincerely during interviews.

Networking — Make It Work *For* You!

Networking is widely reputed to be the best way of finding your next career opportunity. For natural networkers, this is good news. For others, the thought of networking inspires feelings of dread, nervousness, and confusion. If you are among the latter, it may be helpful to shed some light on the myths and realities of networking so that you can put this powerful tool to good use in your job search.

What is networking and how is it used in a job search?

A network can be compared to a spider web—with interconnecting strands and ever-widening circles from a central core. Job-search networking is nothing more than talking to people, gathering and following up on leads, suggestions, and referrals, and staying connected for the duration of your search.

Most of us network extensively in many areas of our lives. When we need a good plumber ... want to arrange a carpool for a child's sports practice ... are looking for an obscure gift for a special birthday ... and in many other circumstances, we talk to friends and neighbors and often find our circle of contacts growing ever wider as we pursue our quest. The process is the same when using networking in a job search.

Need Help? We can write an effective COVER LETTER to introduce you to your networking sources or as a follow-up to referrals. And don't forget: we offer one-on-one INTERVIEW COACHING—to help you communicate effectively and gain maximum benefit from those golden networking contacts!

Before you begin asking contacts for time and information, be sure you understand just what kind of help you're looking for. Are you in an exploratory phase, seeking insight into specific career possibilities? Or do you know exactly what you want to do and where you want to do it, but don't know anyone personally at the companies you're targeting? Once you've defined your goals (which may change during different stages of your search), draw up a list of people you might call to discuss your search. Networking sources can be drawn from any type of personal or professional relationship—close or not-so-close.

In his book *The Overnight Job Change Strategy*, Don Asher identifies ten categories of networking contacts and suggests that you compile a list of at least 100 possible contacts from these groups:

continued on reverse ...

Effective Networking ... *(continued)*

- Family Members
- Employers/Coworkers
- Club Members

- Friends
- Clients/Customers
- Church Members

- Acquaintances
- School Contacts

- Neighbors
- Vendors

(This book provides a great overview of the job search process and includes in-depth information on organizing and implementing a networking campaign.)

When contacting networking sources, give them every opportunity and make it easy for them to help you. Never ask for a job; instead, ask for their advice, suggestions, leads, and referrals. If they have nothing to suggest right away, ask them to keep you in mind and indicate you'll check back in a few days. When your sources give you a referral, be certain to follow up, and continue to keep your original source informed about your progress. Since one referral typically leads to more—expanding your contacts exponentially—effective networking creates a whole army of people helping you with your job search. So enjoy the process and learn firsthand how tremendously the simple process of talking to people can benefit your career.

desktop publishing, and office support since 1983

professional resume/career services, business consulting,

P.O. Box 718, Durham, CT 06422 • 860.349.0256 • CompSJan@aol.com • Fax 860.349.1343

Absolute Advantage

Quips and Clips from

<u>*Absolute Advantage*</u>

P.O. Box 718 • Durham, CT 06422

Wishing you and yours the blessings and joys of the holiday season!

devote probably a quarter of the editorial space available in each newsletter to "sit on the fencepost" and deliver my own editorial. Topics I've used for this personalized message over the years include the birth of my last baby, my twins' tenth birthday, and my company's "Sweet Sixteenth" anniversary. I also tuck in a line about upcoming vacations and professional conferences, when relevant, providing advance notice to my clients of when I'll be away so that they can plan their needs accordingly.

As for the general information articles included in the newsletters, I typically write about good suggestions I've implemented for managing workload, time, and projects. Occasionally, I subtly promote various services at the same time, as when I ran an article about the benefits of developing a brochure. Here I included a time-limited offer for a free half-hour consultation; four clients redeemed this, resulting in significant billings for the development of four brochures. Two clients remarked that they were "unaware" I provided this service. You'll find, as time goes on in this business, that although you may interact with your regular clients frequently, they still may not be fully informed as to all the services you can provide to benefit their businesses. Using a well-written newsletter is a fun and timely way of staying in touch with your clients—to the benefit of you both!

FLYERS / ADS

Flyers can be developed for many purposes. From posting them at local universities and supermarkets to mailing them out as informal direct-mail pieces, they can be highly effective. Once again, developing your own flyers gives you the perfect forum for showcasing your creative abilities. A simple flyer that's easy to develop is an enlargement of your business card copy or one of your Yellow Pages ads, provided that it is strongly written and has an eye-catching layout. Add a creative border or frame, use font features sparingly to create a clean look, and you're all set for printing and distribution!

NEW AND REPEAT CLIENTELE ACKNOWLEDGMENTS

The easiest source of additional business is through repeat and referral business. Your current (or soon-to-be current) clients will provide the best form of advertising for your company—and it's free! Be sure to cultivate it by encouraging present clients on a somewhat regular basis to "feel free to take a few extra business cards to give to contacts" they might have. Always insert two business cards with each completed project. You don't want to be too pushy, but if you have established clientele satisfied with the services your company provides, these individuals will frequently refer you to other, potential clients.

Creative Business Services

P.O. Box 333 · Your City · USA 55555

"When Your Image Counts, Call the Professionals"

We can help with all your business requirements:

- Professionally Prepared Brochures, Newsletters, and Flyers
- Well-written Promotional Copy
- Distinctive Resumes and Customized Cover Letters
- Mass-mail Campaigns
- Transcription Services
- Editorial and Composition Services
- Fax and Photocopying Services
- Custom-designed Business Cards and Letterhead

Creative Business Services can provide whatever you need in professional office support, typing, and secretarial services!

Call 666–2020 Today!

Words that Sizzle.

Simply Magic.

Jan Melnik   **349.0256**
Absolute Advantage

It's pure magic when your communications are dazzling. And it's like having the Alladin of Words at your fingertips when you call CSP!

Jan Melnik   349.0256

It's pure magic when your
communications are dazzling.
And it's like waving a wand
when you call CSP!

Jan Melnik   349.0256

Unmask the
Magic
in Your
Communications …

call Absolute Advantage,
the Word Professionals!

Jan Melnik   349.0256

Be certain to follow up each project for a new client with a handwritten thank-you note. Obtain stationery for your business expressly for this purpose. I use notepaper with my business name on the 7 ½-by-5 ¾-inch notes (which fold in half) and my business address on the envelopes. The cost for a box of one hundred notes and matching envelopes was under $30 and well worth it for the professional look they impart. A typical message of thanks might be as follows:

It was a pleasure working with you on your grant proposal. I'll be very interested in knowing the outcome. Thanks for giving Absolute Advantage the opportunity to handle this project. I look forward to working with you in the years ahead. Sincerely,

Over the years I've had numerous clients comment on how much they appreciate receiving a handwritten note of thanks, simply for opting to do business with me. I've also noticed that my taking the time to write to my clients in turn fosters in them a desire to write back. The acknowledgment notes I've received from my clients have built an extensive "testimonial" file and bulletin board in my office.

Don't neglect your regular clients. It's just as important to acknowledge their ongoing relationship with your business. Because referrals represent a significant number of new clients for my business, I want to constantly cultivate goodwill with my established client base. For those clients referring someone to me for a resume consultation, I jot a quick, personalized note of appreciation and enclose a coupon redeemable toward future services (for the *referring* client). When I consider what I spend each month with the telephone company for my Yellow Pages advertising, this is a tiny investment yielding big dividends.

Here are examples of clients for whom I've used acknowledgments:

- A landscaper, who, using the forms I created, successfully bid on a $100,000 contract. (He received a thank-you note followed by a dinner out, including spouses.)

- A sales manager at a major cosmetics company, who got a coveted promotion—in her case, we'd been working together for several years, and she had given me samples of products her company manufactures each Christmas, a wonderful bag of goodies. (She received flowers with a balloon and, at Christmas, a gift certificate for dinner at a French restaurant.)

- An insurance broker, beginning a new business and making his first sale. (He received a note of congratulations.)

These small courtesies cost little, yet they reap tremendous rewards in terms of continuing to maintain your image as a professional dedicated to the individual successes of each of your clients. Don't overlook, either, the opportunity to communicate with your clients when you read of news of their personal or professional accomplishments in the local papers. I always clip the article and photo and send it along with a quick little note—let's face it, when you're featured in the papers, you can never have enough copies of the article for sharing with friends and family!

While your business will ultimately gain a foothold and experience true growth through repeat clientele, you'll always need to generate a continual flow of new traffic to your office. This is essential to cultivate in order to replace accounts that "disappear" (companies that go out of business, firms that contract with you seasonally for work, companies that use your services extensively for many months but then decide to hire a permanent employee to do the same thing . . . there are many valid reasons why you will "lose" a client that have nothing to do with the quality or price of your work).

Attempt to designate a regular time each week when you work on promotional materials and advertising (including direct mail). Whether it's responding to a want ad for a part-time transcriptionist (in an attempt to sell your service as an alternative) or preparing a mailing to a group of specifically identified businesses, you'll want to devote regular, ongoing time to cultivating new business. Doing so also keeps your outlook fresh and guarantees that you'll keep "selling" those services. And always remember to update current clients on new products you are now offering. This is where your newsletter can be used effectively. Periodically (say, every six months), evaluate your client list and creatively consider ways in which your current clients might utilize some of your other services. Try to introduce clients to these other services through discount offers.

SOURCE TRACKING/NEW CLIENT INQUIRY LOG

This can't be emphasized enough—especially in the first few years of business. It's extremely important to know the source of each and every new client: It's the only way you'll know which advertising dollars are pulling for you—and to what degree. It takes at least six months to gain solid numbers that you can analyze to determine what advertising methods are paying off for you. Always track this information from the very first point of contact, when you pick up your telephone and say, "Hello, Accu-Type Unlimited, may I help you?"

Don't get off the phone—even if it's a caller who's clearly shopping around for prices—without asking, "How did you learn about Accu-Type Unlimited?" If the caller indicates the Yellow Pages, be sure to ask, "Under which heading?" (if you have advertised in more than one location, because it may not necessarily be obvious) and "Which directory?" (if you're listed in more than one book). Record this information on a New Client Inquiry Log (a sample follows) and transfer the information to a Client Work Order (see next section) as soon as you schedule the prospective caller's appointment. If business is through a referral, find out who referred this call; consider keeping track of referrals and perhaps rewarding those referring clients with an occasional thank-you—a professional thank-you note, a $5 certificate toward future services, a 10 percent-off-next-service coupon, and so on.

If you determine after six months' time that you are pulling 75 percent of your new business from one specific heading in the Yellow Pages—and it's not your biggest ad—that will give you the message to possibly enhance that ad, or at least maintain its current size, in the next year's edition. Likewise, if you get only one or two small jobs from one of the headings, you might scale back on that particular ad—perhaps running only your company name and telephone number and maybe adding the line "Please see our ad under Secretarial Services."

As time goes on and you develop experience with analyzing your advertising results, you might determine that running print media ads on a regular basis is not cost-effective—and thus reserve the newspaper ads for special giveaways, 10 percent-off coupons, and so on. You'll be the judge because *you're* in charge!

Getting back to using the New Client Inquiry Log, I try to take as many notes as possible regarding the project description and what I've quoted on the phone, because quite frequently clients will be "shopping" far in advance of when they actually need a service.

If they don't call back to schedule an appointment until a few months later, I appear very professional, with an excellent memory (which I don't have), when I pull the sheet out and reread my notes. These records should be maintained in chronological order. Over the past few years, I've taken to recording this new client inquiry data into a basic document formatted with columns in Microsoft Word directly on the computer. If you are most comfortable using pen-and-paper, by all means continue to record the information that way. The point is that you truly must capture this information if you're to make informed decisions with regard to your advertising investment. By the way, I suggest that you always *ask* a prospective client for an appointment.

Many first-time callers will ask my location. (As I've stated previously, because I'm home-based, I never print my address in my ads or on my business cards and other literature.) At this point I still don't reveal the specific address, indicating only that I'm off a major route in my town. Obviously, once the appointment is scheduled, clear directions are provided. For those clients who ask why the address isn't published, I tell them that all appointments are scheduled in advance and that there are no drop-ins, so as to protect the confidentiality of my clients.

This is probably all the prospective client research you can do at this point. Once you have booked a new client, however, don't overlook taking time at the conclusion of your initial appointment to state, "You mentioned you located me

(your company name)

Name _____   Date _____

Town _____   Telephone _____

Project _____

Deadline _____   Drop-off Date/Time _____

$ Quote _____

Why call? _____   Price shop? _____   Ck. Location? _____

Comments _____

_____   Source _____

Business Booked?   Yes / No

Name _____   Date _____

Town _____   Telephone _____

Project _____

Deadline _____   Drop-off Date/Time _____

$ Quote _____

Why call? _____   Price shop? _____   Ck. Location? _____

Comments _____

_____   Source _____

Business Booked?   Yes / No

Name _____   Date _____

Town _____   Telephone _____

Project _____

Deadline _____   Drop-off Date/Time _____

$ Quote _____

Why call? _____   Price shop? _____   Ck. Location? _____

Comments _____

_____   Source _____

Business Booked?   Yes / No

under Resumes in the Yellow Pages [or wherever the client saw your ad]—what made you select [your company name]?" The response will provide you with valuable information about what works in your ad, and maybe what doesn't. It might also provide information about other companies in your area, but that's not the key objective. You want to ascertain the critical decision point information in your ad that prompted this person to pick up the telephone and contact you. Moreover, you might obtain a lead about other services you advertise that piqued the person's curiosity—and will lead to your selling additional services.

It's also especially rewarding to hear from a new client something like, "Your ad looked great, and when I spoke with you, I could tell you knew what you were talking about and were very professional, so I didn't call anyone else." I always go back to the New Client Inquiry Log I maintain to add any additional information gleaned during an appointment and "close out the form" by checking whether or not the business actually was booked. This log serves as the one place where I can assess on a regular basis what types of advertising are working best for me, what distinguished my company in my clients' eyes, and the types of projects I obtain from various sources. It also reinforces that I'm doing a good job in promoting my services to new clients via the sales techniques I use on the telephone and reminds me to "continue to smile" when speaking with these prospects on the phone.

CLIENT WORK ORDER/SERVICE WAIVER/ DEPOSIT RECEIPT

I recommend using a multipurpose form when meeting with all first-time clients as well as with regular clients at the beginning of each major project. This is to accurately record the project description and requirements, detail directions, note the deadline, and so on, as well as to confirm client billing information, provide a cost estimate, obtain the client's signature for your records, and (with a photocopy for the client) serve as a receipt for deposits.

There is an important statement in the text portion of the Client Work Order: "Final proofreading is the responsibility of the client." This is important to you, as a secretarial service owner, because it limits your liability in the event of an error discovered after the client has accepted your work.

PROPOSALS

As a secretarial service becomes established and, especially, as it branches into higher-end services (such as desktop publishing, graphic/logo design, and business consulting), the need for developing proposals for specific projects grows. It is very important to spend ample time in writing your proposal for a client

COMPREHENSIVE SERVICES PLUS

P.O. Box 718, Durham, CT 06422
(860) 349-0256 — Fax (860) 349-1343

■ ■ ■

Professional Desktop Publishing, Promotional,
Editorial, Resume, and Office Support Services Since 1983

June 1, 1997

Ms. Mary Edwards
Project Manager
Corporate Communication Cues
123 Main Street
Your City, USA 66666

Re: Project Component Quotation

Dear Mary:

It was a pleasure speaking with you. I'm pleased to provide the following quotation for your project. As we discussed, I have broken out my services by component.

1. Fortune Cookie Mailer

    Design and create "fortune" cookie insert and cookie box enclosure piece
    • creation, design, layout, prep of camera-ready mechanical: 2.5 hrs. @ $75/hour
    • includes preliminary client discussion
    • includes one set of revisions
    • additional or final revisions billed on time-expended basis at quoted hourly rate

    As you are aware, the printing of the fortune itself is arranged by the "cookie baker." Printing of the enclosure piece will be quoted once we have a firm quantity and determination of stock. I believe you were interested in the idea of matching a bright (perhaps neon?) color to the color selected for a Post-it™ Pad.

I spoke with representatives of ABC Corporation, the supplier I had mentioned which creates a very sturdy box that would be ideal for mailing the cookie (in a variety of potentially appropriate sizes). They are unable to provide a single-unit sample, but recommended that as we near "readiness," we order the minimum quantity (100) of what we believe to be the best size. *If* it is not the right size, it can be returned/exchanged for a more appropriate size (no charge). I'd be happy to handle this phase of the project at the appropriate time if you wish.

2. Post-it™ Pad

    Design and create Post-it™ Pad notes to accompany cookie and enclosure piece
    • creation, design, layout, prep of camera-ready mechanical: 1 hr. @ $75/hour

    I can obtain quotes for printing of the Post-it™ Pad notes; I believe you indicated you also had a source. We can shop for best price, quality, and delivery.

Our Business Is Making <u>You</u> Look Good!

■ ■ ■

3.   Front-End Postcard Mailer

Design and create a compelling, front-end piece designed to precede mailing of cookie by approximately one week. Objective is to build interest cost-effectively and double impact of cookie mailer, thus enhancing the likelihood of creating an impression and driving call to action.
• creation, design, layout, prep of camera-ready mechanical: 2 hrs. @ $75/hour

Again, I can obtain quotes for printing of the card from my printers; I'd recommend an oversized jumbo card (8.5 x 5.5), matching the color selected for the enclosure note and Post-it™ Pads.

4.   Evaluation of "Knowing How to Learn for Life" General Workshop Information Piece

• editorial review "with fresh eyes" to assess message, impact on audience, provide recommendations, etc.: .5 hr. @ $75/hour

5.   Project Coordination Service ... 1 hr. @ $75/hour for discussions/faxes in moving project forward and to completion

Thanks again for the opportunity to provide this proposal. Once you have had an opportunity to review the project and budget, please contact me and we can discuss the go-ahead and a timeline.

Sincerely,

Jan Melnik
President

ABSOLUTE ADVANTAGE
division / Comprehensive Services Plus

P.O. Box 718, Durham, CT 06422 – e-mail: CompSPJan@aol.com
(860) 349-0256 – Fax (860) 349-1343

■ ■ ■

Professional Desktop Publishing, Business Consulting,
Resume/Career Services, and Office Support Since 1983

June 1, 1997

Jonathan Green / David Taylor
Green & Taylor, LLC
P.O. Box 123
Cityville, USA 77777

Dear Jonathan and David:

I enjoyed the opportunity to meet with you both yesterday. I look forward to working with you on the projects we discussed as well as networking in the years ahead to the benefit of us all!

I am pleased to provide the following quotation for your brochure and related corporate i.d. materials (letterhead, business card, envelope). Other ancillary materials can be developed at your request on an as-needed basis once the design and editorial elements are in place (for instance, a partial client listing, as we discussed; mailing labels; oversized mailer envelopes; leave-behind pieces; card-stock inserts to professional invoices; newsletter/client communication device; etc.).

1. Brochure Design

Using information gleaned in client consultation and mock-up draft brochure provided, design and create brochure specifically targeting those professionals from whom referrals are sought; brochure is to serve as primary identity document for the business. Components of project include:

- creation, design, layout, prep of brochure to be delivered NLT July 8, 1997 (duplicate packages)
- creation and design of slogan and logo
- preliminary ideas for paper selection and ink/color as well as estimated printing bids

Based upon my creative/idea-generating process, I will present several options for clients' consideration.

Quotation for above services: $350

- final revisions to create camera-ready mechanical billed at $75/hour on a time-expended basis

Our Business Is Making You Look Good!

■ ■ ■

2. Business Card / Letterhead / #10 Envelopes

Once the brochure design/slogan/logo elements are approved and confirmed, these ancillary corporate i.d. pieces will be developed. Components of project include:

- creation, design, layout, prep of camera-ready mechanicals
- presentation of paper/color ideas (in all likelihood, to complement brochure) as well as estimated printing bids
- project delivery to be mutually agreed-upon (based upon final scheduling of brochure project)

Quotation for above services: $125

I will look forward to hearing from you once you have both had an opportunity to review this proposal. Please feel free to leave a message for me if I can respond to any questions or concerns. Thanks again.

Sincerely,

Jan Melnik

BEST BUSINESS SERVICES
Celebrating 17 Years! · 1983–2000

P.O. Box 123
Anywhere, USA 88888
(333) 333-4444 · Fax (333) 333-4466

Date/Time _____

CLIENT WORK ORDER · SERVICE WAIVER · DEPOSIT RECEIPT

Client Name _____

Company _____

Address _____

Office Telephone _____ Home Telephone _____

Project _____

Source _____

Font Selection _____ Stock Selection _____

\# Copies _____ Stapled? _____ # Originals _____ Min/Max # Pages _____

Cover Page _____

Special Instructions _____

_____

_____

Deadline/Pickup Date _____

Estimated Cost:	$
Tax	$
Total	$
Less Deposit	–
Approximate Balance Due	$

The above estimate is provided to the best of our ability following initial review/consultation. Final invoice is based on actual project requirements. Significant differences between estimated total and actual requirements will be discussed with the client prior to completion of the work. For resume projects, the total quoted above is a firm number except as noted in the following paragraph.*

A minimum nonrefundable cash or credit card deposit of $50 is required for all word processing/desktop publishing services; a 50% deposit is required for all resume consultations. *For resume consultations, the above-quoted total *includes* a return or telephone review appointment of up to 30 minutes in length; review discussion exceeding 30 minutes will be billed at an hourly rate of $95 for the actual time spent. Other project deposits would be as agreed upon.

All written materials and consultation services must be paid for in full upon receipt of completed product; completed work will not be released until full payment is made, unless alternative billing arrangements have been made in advance. Unpaid accounts over 30 days are subject to a $5.00 monthly late charge. **Final proofreading is the responsibility of the client.**

The client hereby agrees that any inaccurate, incorrect, or misleading information in the resume or other materials provided to the client by *Best Business Services* is not our responsibility and that the client had an opportunity to review the materials and approve its entire content prior to delivery and/or reproduction. This includes the responsibility of students to insure that all components of a paper, thesis, dissertation, etc. comply with the guidelines provided by their school. The client's signature below certifies understanding and agreement with all of the statements of this document.

Signature _____ Date _____

Professional Desktop Publishing, Promotional, Editorial, and Office Support Services

because, in all likelihood, project go-ahead and ultimate payment to you will be based upon mutual agreement on this document.

The two sample (basic) proposal letters on pages 111–14 detail the way in which I follow up a preliminary client project discussion meeting with my quotation. You can see the change in my letterhead/font that corresponded with my business name change.

SIGNAGE

Depending on the provisions and regulations in your own community, a small, well-designed, and generally somewhat expensive (can easily be several hundred dollars) business sign is appropriate and frequently necessary to assist in directing clients to your location. Every circumstance is unique—and whether you live in a condominium complex, apartment building, or single-family dwelling will largely govern the use of this advertising and promotion mechanism. A single-family dwelling is generally most in need of this device—either to help separate you from rows of other homes in a subdivision or to direct clients if you live in a particularly isolated or remote area of your town. Coupled with a visible and attractively placed house number, it's an ideal directional tool.

When designing your business sign (having first learned the maximum dimensions, if a sign is allowed), think "simplistically." You're not in the market for drop-in clientele (at least not while your business is starting out in a home-based setting); therefore, the sign does not need to "tell what you do." After you have selected your company's name (refer to chapter 3), you'll want to design a sign that highlights it to the best advantage. If your business name is Advantage Office Services, you might use the initials AOS on a business sign.

OTHER METHODS OF ADVERTISING

Each community is different, but you are probably aware if there's a well-read weekly "throwaway" newspaper or "shopper" in your town that gets good distribution. If you are not immediately successful in getting into your telephone directory's Yellow Pages, you might want to consider running a small ad every week in this type of local weekly paper to begin to build visibility and name recognition. Usually, these papers are distributed free of charge, supported by paid advertisers (you). Depending on the layout of the paper, you might choose display advertising—an attractively boxed ad of business card size—or classified advertising—ten to twenty words in an in-column classified ad under the heading of your choice. In the latter case, the heading of Typing is likely to pull the most business for a word processing/secretarial services company. A strategy many have found to be especially successful with weekly newspaper advertising is the inclusion of the following line every week in their ads: "Clip and save this ad for easy reference . . . we won't be in the Yellow Pages until next (*fill in the month publication will occur*)!"

If you have a local daily newspaper, check into its advertising rates; a standby program is probably the most cost-effective way to advertise regularly. This program typically guarantees to run a specific ad once per week—the newspaper's choice of which day, and it varies from week to week—for a certain amount of time. (The usual minimum insertion is four times.) You usually save about 50 percent over the cost of inserting the same ad on four specific days of your choosing.

Generally, advertising in a daily newspaper does not bring the results that advertising in a weekly does, because the daily paper doesn't stay around that long. And you don't build up the image of "being in the paper every issue" (which you can usually more easily afford to do with a weekly). Also, dailies cost more to advertise in, albeit they have larger circulations. Typically, once your business advertising gets into the Yellow Pages, you can eliminate almost all newspaper advertising except for occasional special promotions and offers.

There are many ways to spend limited advertising dollars. Methods that are probably not as effective (or affordable) for this type of business as would be the aforementioned ideas are radio and television advertising, advertising on placemats and telephone book covers, and advertising in television guides. Low-cost advertising options you may wish to consider, especially for promoting your new business or a special offer, include inserting flyers under windshield wipers in a neighboring shopping mall (possibly employing one or two teenagers to run around placing the flyers, if this is permitted in your community) and placing notices on campus, grocery store, and community bulletin boards. You might also think about contributing a gift certificate to a community auction or fund-raising event in your town. If you do donate your services, I recommend establishing a flat dollar value for the services (e.g., "$50 toward secretarial services of one's choosing") and placing in small type at the bottom of the actual certificate form as well as noting in the auction description: "This certificate is restricted to use by new clients only." From the standpoint of your business-building efforts, you ideally want to attract new clients to your company. I found that before I added this restriction line, my gift certificates were frequently being bid on by existing clients.

Several years ago, I ordered my state's relatively new vanity license plate, depicting a colorful background of Long Island Sound, for my vehicle. I had two objectives in mind: (1) to support an environmental cause to improve the cleanliness of Long Island Sound, and (2) to carry some kind of message promoting my business while I'm traveling the roads. Doing this can be a challenge (in six characters or less), but I settled on JAN•CSP (figuring it will be recognized first for my name and then for the initials of my business name, Comprehensive Services Plus). What response! I'm stopped on errands nearly every day and asked, "What's CSP?" Talk about a great opportunity for promoting the business. (I never did check to determine if half of the cost of the vanity plate—for the CSP—was a tax-deductible expense!) Even though I've changed my business name to Absolute Advantage, I call it "a division of Comprehensive Services Plus" and continue to use the initials CSP on my license plate.

NETWORKING AND COMMUNITY INVOLVEMENT

The 1990s have been, without a doubt, the "networking decade." If you haven't already been "bitten by the networking bug" and discovered the benefits of inter-mingling professionally with those who could benefit by your services, put this as an action item near the top of your list. Strongly consider joining your area's chamber of commerce. The chamber typically provides many opportunities for professional networking and gaining visibility within your community (or next largest city). As with membership in any professional association or organization, you must be willing to share your time and expertise with others in order to reap some of the advantages of belonging to such a group. Annual fees can range from $75 to a more typical $200 or even $300, but if you attend meetings regularly and consistently, it can be well worth it. Most chambers publish an annual member-ship directory, giving you added visibility among the very business community you wish to serve.

For women, investigate local chapters of various businesswomen's entrepre-neurial groups. (Local universities and, once again, the chamber of commerce can be good sources for checking out the existence of these chapters.) If no targeted group exists in your community, consider starting an informal organization your-self. It's a great way to gain publicity and build worthwhile professional contacts at the same time.

Leads clubs can also be useful. Membership is typically restricted to just one representative of each profession (so you won't be "competing" with your com-petitors for every potential client). Most organizations allow you to attend at least one meeting without obligation or cost to determine if there's a fit for you. Exchange clubs and other public service organizations also allow for good oppor-tunities to get to know people in your business community.

Use every opportunity in which you are already involved from a civic stand-point to promote yourself and your business. Use the slogan you have developed to succinctly introduce yourself and pique the interest of those around you. Develop good skills in asking others what they do . . . and really use those "listen-ing" ears to discern areas for potential future prospecting.

Seminars and programs offered by the Small Business Administration, local colleges, and businesses such as the telephone company provide excellent opportunities to enhance your knowledge in specifically targeted areas as well as meet with other professionals. Check into and take advantage of low-cost, daylong conferences offered in your region. The SBA frequently collaborates with other businesses to produce top-notch programs where you can further hone marketing skills and meet others in similar businesses. Don't overlook programs made available by your chamber of commerce and chapters of professional organizations.

Attend trade shows and business expos in your area. (Traveling to a city up to an hour or even an hour and a half away can still be very beneficial.) Even if they don't seem to apply to your particular situation, you may unearth opportunities for promoting your business and services. Specifically search for potential clients who might use your services. A good icebreaker to use is the question, "How might a client of mine use the services you offer?" The typical response is a question of *you* regarding the sort of business you have, thus allowing you to expand on the types of services you provide and benefits you deliver.

Kathy Keshemberg, president of Computron/A Career Advantage in Appleton, Wisconsin, and author of *Resources!* (see Appendix), has put networking to good use in her city. She states, "Networking is a wonderful source of new business; however, the key is to become active. I joined a business and professional women's group and immediately offered to handle typesetting of their name tags. This position landed me a spot on the board of directors, which led to my writing a member profile for the monthly newsletter. In addition, it yielded several new clients." Since becoming active in this professional organization, Kathy has delivered talks on topics relating to all aspects of the services she provides, including her professional resume-writing business. While she doesn't blatantly advertise or ask for business, by sharing information and examples drawn from her business, the message is clearly conveyed to dozens of professionals—many of whom have since used her secretarial services.

Kathy Mandy, president of Select Word Services in Chanhassen, Minnesota, is a strong advocate of networking, both within our industry and within the community. "A few years ago, a colleague (Heather Lee) and I started MN-ABSSI (the Minnesota chapter of the Association of Business Support Services International, Inc.). I became the president of the group. This has been a great experience, meeting new people and networking with service owners, both home-based and office-based. There's the daily and weekly interaction with many of these members, which is so vital to the growth of business. You can tend to stagnate without fresh input from a variety of people.

"I also joined Toastmasters in 1996. It's a very fun, enjoyable group. I want to work on polishing my speaking skills and get over my fear of selling myself and my business. I think this will also be an opportunity to get some business from other members. Some of the talks I've heard have been about people's businesses, and they get other members talking to them about it after the meeting. The group really made me feel so welcome when I came to visit."

Cindy Kraft, president of Executive Essentials of Valrico, Florida, shared her honest experience with networking. "The biggest challenge I face (past and currently) is marketing myself. The first time I walked into a group of strangers at a chamber function, I really thought I would pass out. My stomach was in knots, my palms were sweating, and I was feeling faint. I think for the first three months, I was terror-stricken walking into every event, but I forced myself to continue to go. Now I love attending all the events and have even joined some new ones. I still have a problem marketing myself, though. I can get up and talk at great length about the chamber and Toastmasters, but when the focus shifts to 'me' and 'my' services, I get tongue-tied. I suppose overcoming my lack of self-confidence was and is my greatest challenge. I always knew it was a problem, but being employed as a 'secretary for someone else didn't force me to do anything about it. Being a business owner has made me deal with my inadequacies—and it is a slow process. *But*, I have come a very long way in the past few years."

As you'll note in reading Cindy's "top five" recommendations to new secretarial service business owners (see chapter 8), her very first recommendation is to "network, network, network!"

Beth Quick, president of Q & A Business Solutions in St. Louis, Missouri, says this about networking: "My preferred methods of advertising are networking in local chambers of commerce and professional associations and following up with those 'warm' faces I meet using a monthly postcard. It has been marvelous. This has been the best combination for me."

Josie Smith, president of An Executive Assistant in Chico, California, offers this interesting "twist" on networking: "An area on which I'm concentrating and which I hope will reap benefits in the future is my membership in the local chamber of commerce. Because I kept nagging them about programs for home-based businesses, they offered to create a task force to investigate ways of becoming a strong resource for home-based businesses in the area—*but only if I agreed to chair it* (which I did—talk about putting your money where your mouth is!). I feel this will really propel me into the business world, and I welcome the chance to be part of this groundbreaking task force."

With every contact you make through professional organization memberships, volunteerism, civic involvement, and networking at conferences, trade shows, business-after-hours events, and the like, *always* add "suspect" names and addresses to your mailing list. These contacts should receive your quarterly newsletter, postcard mailings, and other communications on a regular basis for at least twenty-four to thirty-six months. In many cases, that's how long it took for a "cool suspect" to turn into a "hot prospect" and ultimately become a client for my business—with no additional effort or marketing activity expended!

EXPLORING THE INTERNET

Marketing via the Internet for the secretarial services industry is, as yet, a mostly untapped area. I've been an on-line user since 1992 and have only just begun to dabble on the Internet, though my e-mail (electronic mail) usage and participation in on-line forums has easily quadrupled since I started and I use it extensively to quote resume projects to prospects and to transfer completed resumes to clients. I have yet to acquire a client through any efforts or activities on-line; however, I communicate regularly (and conveniently) with several clients through e-mail. In addition, I use my e-mail account to send and receive documents, information, and materials among colleagues. Nearly all writers for my newsletter, *The Word Advantage* (see Appendix), utilize e-mail to submit their stories. In addition, nearly every respondent to my questionnaire gathering research for this updated book edition responded via e-mail. And, the secretarial service operators mentioned thoughout this book report increased use of the Internet in their own businesses. (For more details, see the professional profiles in chapter 8.)

If you have not yet "gotten on-line," you'll first need to have a modem for your computer as well as communication software. Next, you'll need to have access through an account. The most commonly recognized on-line service is America Online (AOL—and my personal favorite). Internet access and the necessary software is part of its installation package. The typical cost of an on-line account is under $20 per month, which provides unlimited usage. Unless you live in an extremely remote part of the country, you should be able to key in a local telephone number for accessing your on-line service by modem, thus *not* incurring any long-distance telephone charges. Once you have an on-line account, you'll be able to immediately send and receive e-mail messages, access a wide variety of forums and information areas, and gain access to the Internet.

It is also possible to use an Internet provider—which typically costs less for sometimes unlimited access to the Internet; while you still have the ability to have an e-mail account through this Internet provider's service, you won't be able to access the myriad interesting (and applicable, for our industry) forums that you can through an on-line service such as AOL.

Let me share below those areas in which I *believe* secretarial services can have the best possible results in using the Internet.

- Through forum participation, you can increase awareness and visibility of yourself (first and foremost) as well as the business services you provide (in a more subtle way). Blatant advertising and solicitation of business is frowned upon (except through classified ads, Web sites, and pages specifically developed for the purpose of promoting your business). When you participate in business forums, however, just as when you network at professional meetings in person, you have the opportunity to work into your discussions who you really are and what you do. If you are active on a regular basis, this *can* lead to opportunities to bid on jobs.

By having an on-line account, you, of course, have an e-mail address; including this address on your business card, notepads, brochure, and letterhead gives you a high-tech look with your clientele and shows that you are progressive and technologically up to date. As more and more clients become familiar with the Internet, the World Wide Web, and simply utilizing e-mail accounts, this is an area of use that will undoubtedly grow. In addition, if you are especially adept in using the Internet, the web, and your e-mail account, you may wish to develop customized training for your clients (where you would charge your highest hourly rate for consulting).

- At the time this manuscript was going into production, I *still* had not finalized arrangements for launch of my Web site . . . though I did have the foresight a year ago to register my own domain name: www.yourabsoluteadvantage.com. (If you access it before my site is up, your query is deflected to my Internet Service Provider.) Because my ongoing business volume is so heavy, I haven't been personally motivated by need for business-building to really pursue this avenue for promoting Absolute Advantage. Those who seem to get the best results from their Web site tend to be in an ancillary field to ours: professional resume-writing and job search-coaching services. As a future invitation to those of you out there in the secretarial services field who *do* experiment successfully with a Web site exclusively for office support services, I'd love to hear from you and report on your results in a subsequent edition of this book! You can e-mail me at CompSPJan@aol.com.

- I've benefited individually through my on-line account by staying in touch with colleagues and friends via regular e-mails as well as participating in on-line discussions (both as a speaker and as an attendee). In addition, I have found the folders on America Online specifically focusing on the secretarial services/word processing field to be especially useful in terms of an open exchange of information among colleagues (those brand-new to our field as well as some very seasoned and experienced veterans). Finally, the Association of Business Support Services International, Inc. (additional information appears in the Appendix) sponsors an open forum periodically to allow for discussion among many members on all sorts of business issues.

As with all technological advancements, I'm quite confident that the Internet and the World Wide Web hold great promise for businesses in the years ahead.

YOUR COLLEAGUES SUGGEST . . .

Culled from the questionnaire responses of a number of your colleagues are their best ideas for attracting new clients. (It was nearly unanimous that everyone selected the Yellow Pages and word-of-mouth referrals as their top two client producers; additional details and ideas follow.)

"At this point, I pay for advertising in the following places, in decreasing order of importance: Yellow Pages, which brings in the greatest percentage of new business (successful categories: resumes, typing, word processing; unsuccessful categories: DTP, transcription; haven't tried: secretarial services); individual town phone books in smaller local towns (some folks automatically look in the local book before moving on to the larger Yellow Pages, and these ads always more than pay for themselves, although they don't yield as much business as the Yellow Pages); and in one trade publication (which runs my classified ad for a small cost and more than pays for itself).

"The other major source of new business is word-of-mouth referrals, which is probably second after Yellow Pages in percentage of new business, ahead of the local telephone books. I include in the word-of-mouth category referrals that come from local printers. As far as the source of the work that fills most of my time each day, definitely repeat clientele (at least 75 percent).

"The only direct mail I've done is to existing clients. Each November, in keeping with the spirit of Thanksgiving, I send my special clients a pocket calendar/organizer along with a note to say 'thank you' for their business. The note also highlights a new service or feature or piece of equipment or something they may want to take advantage of and serves to drum up repeat business. That is always successful. My regular clients eagerly await their calendars and have been known to call to find out when I'm going to be sending them, because they need to start scheduling appointments, etc., for the coming year. New clients that I hope to see again are always delighted that I thought of them. This generates lots of goodwill, and it also generates repeat business, without fail. And, not incidentally, I always hear from several people during the year that when they needed my telephone number, they found it quickly on the calendar.

"I also pay for a few 'business card listing' ads, not so much expecting to generate business (and these ads have never done so) but because there are several groups that I want to support; e.g., local police, firefighters, etc. I figure it adds to my company's visibility, which, in the long run, pays off.

"In the past few years, I've run a classified ad in the local newspaper, which brought in new business, but very erratically. Then the paper increased its rates several times over a few years and changed its format to one based on alphabetical listing rather than seniority, so that my ad was no longer in the first position. I held my breath and dropped the ad, not sure if my business was going to suffer. It hasn't.

"I've done a few display ads from time to time but have gotten no business from them. I've also tried coupons (once, many years ago, in those coupon packs that are mailed to ten thousand households, as well as a coupon in the Yellow Pages two consecutive years that came free with a new ad I placed) with no success. The only person who ever used the telephone book coupon was someone who was already a client!

"I've never done cold calling or in-person visits. I don't belong to the chamber of commerce. Membership in professional organizations (the Massachusetts chapter of the Association of Business Support Services International, Inc.) has definitely resulted in some referral work and some subcontracting, although, again, not nearly as much as word-of-mouth referrals from satisfied clients."

—Wendy Gelberg, Advantage Resume Services

"The best method for attracting new clients is attending chamber or women's business groups and actively meeting people; also, referring work to other word processors who then refer work back."

—Nina Feldman, Nina Feldman Connections (Author's note: Please see Appendix for information about a referral resource package that Nina Feldman markets to secretarial services.)

"I ask clients for referrals to get me into a company I want to work with. Then I make a phone call introducing myself and follow up with a letter or in-person visit if possible. This is my favorite method, since it's not really a cold call with a person's name for referral. Another tactic is when people call me from the Yellow Pages or another source and ask how much I charge, I engage them in conversation, asking them questions about their project and selling them on my attention to detail, personal service, length of time in business (eighteen years), and quality of work."

—Kathy Mandy, Select Word Services

"My best method for attracting new clients is my ability to sell my expertise and experience over the telephone to first-time callers. If they've seen my Yellow Pages ad, then they already know a lot—my name, my CPRW (Certified Professional Resume Writer) designation, the length of time I've been in business. Once the caller decides to dial my number, it's up to me to convince them that I'm the best person to assist them. I price my materials very simply, offer lots of extras, and work flexibly with my clients to customize my services to their particular needs."

—René Hart, First Impressions Resume and Career Development Services

"I derive 50 percent of my business from direct mail (personalized cover letter, resume, and business card), 25 percent from my Yellow Pages advertising, 15 percent from word-of-mouth referrals, 10 percent from cold calling, and literally nothing from in-person visits. The best method? Definitely direct mail and following up with a phone call requesting an appointment to explain the benefits of my service."

—Brenda Lorencen, Word/Pro Connection

"My preferred methods of advertising are posting flyers at local universities and sending direct mail packages to businesses advertising for writers, editors, and secretarial assistance. I spend approximately $13 a month on this activity. In tracking the results, 35 percent of my business comes from flyers, 25 percent from direct mail, 10 percent from professional organizations, and 30 percent in repeat clientele."

—Shawn Teets, WordWise

"I think the best method for attracting new clients is through networking. Although there is rarely instant gratification from doing so (is there with most things?), it does promote name recognition, and people would rather do business with people they know or from whom they got a referral."

—Cindy Kraft, Executive Essentials

You'll find many more pinpointed suggestions for promoting and advertising your business in chapter 5 as the ideas specifically relate to building individual profit centers.

BOOKING BUSINESS

Converting an Inquiry to a Sale

I call this form of booking business "conversion marketing," and it applies both to cultivating new business opportunities within your existing clientele base, selling add-on or enhanced services, and to taking a first-time caller who is clearly shopping around and booking an appointment. It essentially means converting a prospect into a client. I'm sure you've heard, and it's true, that it's infinitely easier and by far more cost- and time-effective to increase sales within your current client base than it is to develop brand-new business. That's because you've already established a reputation with your current clients—they know the quality of your work, your responsiveness, and the ease with which they can do business with you.

So, what's a new secretarial service owner to do who has yet to build a client base? Use the strategies outlined here for closing the business with as many first-time callers as you possibly can. How is this accomplished? Let's consider the field of resume services as an example. In my own business this accounts for nearly 40 percent of my overall revenue, and it is the profit center that has experienced the most growth over the past ten years. In talking with owners of other services, I've found it to be their experience, too, that resumes and ancillary services account for that portion of the business with the highest margins—that is, the greatest profits.

The following scripts will take you step by step through the process of responding to a caller's initial queries about your resume services. I'll profile several distinct types of callers, representative of the market.

Resume Script A. To respond to individuals who don't *think* they need any service other than the basic typing of their resume.

You	ABC Office Services, hello.
Resume caller	Hi. I'd like some information about having a resume typed.
You	Great! I'd be happy to help you. All resumes are typeset in Microsoft Word on the computer, with laser-printed originals and a disk provided. Do you have your resume already written and are now looking to have it professionally typeset—or do you require editorial assistance in developing the content of the resume to better illustrate your accomplishments and the salient points of your career background?

Resume caller	I've written the resume completely and know exactly how I want it to appear.
You	That's fine. By the way, my name is Jane Doe—with whom am I speaking?
Resume caller	[Name].
You	Hi, [Name]. Our flat fee for a one-page resume is $XX; for a two-page format, it is $XX. You will receive a disk and one camera-ready original, as well as XX laser-printed originals on your choice of stationery.

I will just mention that ABC has been developing complete resumes and cover letters for clients for ten years, and we are specialists in presenting your background in a very professional manner. Many clients decide to avail themselves of what we call a miniconsultation, during which we would briefly review the material you've written. If you desire, we would meet for generally between fifteen minutes and half an hour, during which time I would review your resume, ask you a number of questions, and perhaps propose revisions to the actual content.

Obviously, if I believe that you've conveyed the information in a very positive light and the resume content itself looks professional and well-polished, I won't suggest any revisions just for the sake of making changes. But with my background in this field, I generally find that there are areas where I can help you strengthen your presentation to create a stronger impact and ultimately help open the door to the interviews that get the job offers.

If you decide to take advantage of our expertise, the charge for editorial/consultation services is billed at a rate of $XX per hour, so that if we meet for fifteen minutes, the fee would be $XX. Is this a service that you think you could benefit from?

(depending on response)

Now, what is your availability for the consultation appointment? We offer appointments during regular business hours as well as evenings and weekends, both in our office and via phone. |
| Resume caller | (checks schedule, discusses date/time, etc.) |

You	(give directions, confirm and reiterate date and time, and obtain caller's phone number)
	Great. Do you have any additional questions?
	(reply depending on caller's response)
	I do require a $XX deposit at the time of the consultation. We accept cash, a personal check, or a major credit card. The balance is not paid until everything has been completed to your satisfaction at the final appointment. I do want to mention that the resume is retained in our computer system completely free of charge indefinitely—there are no annual carrying fees. Most of our clients find that they are able to update their resumes for under $XX, the minimum charge. Even if you relocate out of this area, for the price of your long-distance telephone call and a small handling charge to cover packaging of your resumes so that they travel securely, you'll find that you've made an investment and you'll never again have to have your resume "done" from scratch.
	Thank you, [Name]. I'll look forward to meeting you. One final question: How did you learn about ABC?

OPTION A (referral)

Resume caller	[Name] referred me.
You	Thank you for telling me; I'll be sure to acknowledge my appreciation with a courtesy coupon for that person, redeemable toward future services.

OPTION B (ad)

Resume caller	In the Yellow Pages.
You	In the [town] directory?
Resume caller	(yes-or-no/clarification)
You	Do you recall which category?
Resume caller	Resume Services [or wherever the person found you].
You	May I ask why you selected ABC?

Resume caller	(caller's response)
You	Well, thank you. And again, I look forward to meeting you on [date]. Good-bye.

There—that gives you an idea of how to handle callers who don't believe they need anything besides the basic typing of their resume and convert the transaction into a more lucrative sale. What does this do to the bottom line? Instead of an initial sale of between $20 and $45 (depending on the flat fee you charge for a resume), billing is as much as $75 to $100 or more. Over the years I've been in business and carefully tracked each and every caller, my records demonstrate that I "convert" more than 95 percent of all resume callers into some form of consultation and/or editorial services—enhanced service for them and greater profitability for my company.

Resume Script B. To respond to individuals who have never had a professional resume prepared and don't really know the questions to ask.

You	ABC Office Services, hello.
Resume caller	Hi. I'd like some information about getting a resume done.
You	Great! I'd be happy to help you. Let me ask just a few questions. Do you have your resume already written and are now looking to have it professionally typeset—or do you require editorial assistance in developing the content of the resume to better illustrate your accomplishments and the salient points of your career background?
Resume caller	Well . . . uh . . . actually, I don't have a resume.
You	That's no problem—we're specialists in developing resumes "from scratch" for our clients through a face-to-face consultation. Let me tell you a little about the services we provide. By the way, my name is Jane Doe—with whom am I speaking?
Resume caller	[Name].

You	Hi, [Name]. ABC has been developing complete resumes and cover letters for clients for ten years, and we are specialists in working with clients who don't have resumes. We can present your background in a very professional manner that creates a strong impact and ultimately helps open the door to the interviews that get the job offers. We would schedule an appointment to meet face to face, usually between an hour and an hour and a half. For that meeting you would bring any materials that you might have available; however, this is not essential. If you do have an opportunity before our meeting, it's helpful to jot down dates—month and year—and places of employment. Other than that, I will essentially extract from you all other information.
	After we have concluded the consultation, we'll schedule a follow-up visit. Be sure to bring along your appointment book. You would be returning to the office to review and approve the final resume—and, of course, we would make any desired revisions at that time. Upon your approval—at the same appointment—we will then laser print XX originals of your resume on your choice of stationery. You'll also receive a disk and a camera-ready original of your resume, suitable for photocopying, if you desire.
	The fee for this complete package is $XX. If you would like to have us develop a pro forma cover letter for you, the flat fee is $XX. Now, what is your availability for the consultation appointment? We offer appointments during regular business hours as well as evenings and weekends, both in our office and via phone.
Resume caller	(checks schedule, discusses date/time, etc.—pick up from Script A)

Resume Script C. To respond to individuals who have an outdated resume but don't really know what they need.

You	ABC Office Services, hello.
Resume caller	Hi. I'd like some information about getting a resume done.

You	Great! I'd be happy to help you. Let me ask just a few questions. Do you have your resume already written and are now looking to have it professionally typeset—or do you require editorial assistance in developing the content of the resume to better illustrate your accomplishments and the salient points of your career background?
Resume caller	Well . . . I have pretty much written down everything, but maybe it could use some going over by a professional.
You	Wonderful! It sounds as though you'd be an ideal candidate for what we call a miniconsultation. By the way, my name is Jane Doe—with whom am I speaking?
Resume caller	[Name].
You	Hi, [Name]. As I was mentioning, a miniconsultation is typically where we work with clients who either have an out-of-date resume and need some assistance writing about their most recent position or have written the resume but would like a professional review. We generally meet for between fifteen minutes and half an hour, during which time I will review your resume, ask you a number of questions, and perhaps propose revisions to the actual content.

Obviously, if I believe that you've conveyed the information in a very positive light and the resume content itself looks professional and well-polished, I won't suggest any revisions just for the sake of making changes. But with my background in this field, and I've been working with clients for ten years, I generally find that there are areas where I can help you strengthen your presentation to create a stronger impact and ultimately help open the door to the interviews that get the job offers. You might also opt to include a few extra minutes in our consultation to discuss tailored cover letters and the most effective way to use them.

Once we've met, I will create a resume for your approval— usually, a day or two later. You will have an opportunity to approve, revise, or edit the resume—at no additional charge. Then we go into final laser printing of XX originals on your choice of stationery, plus a disk and one camera-ready original suitable for photocopying, if you choose.

The fee for this service is a flat $XX for the typesetting of a one-page resume ($XX if it is a two-page format), plus $XX per hour for the consultation time. You are billed only for the actual time we speak, so it might be as low as $XX for ten or fifteen minutes. If you determine that any modifications I suggest would be valuable and additional editorial time is required, that is billed at a rate of $XX per hour for the actual time spent writing. As a general guideline editorial time, if necessary, is typically half of the consultation time. So if we were to meet face to face for a half-hour, the editorial time might be fifteen minutes.

Now, what is your availability for an appointment? We offer appointments . . . [etc., picking up from Script A].

By now this is getting to be routine. But it works! Try doing a little role-playing, perhaps with a spouse or friend, to practice your skill in delivering a message that *you* feel comfortable with. The beauty of the English language is that there are infinite ways of saying nearly the same thing. If the text I use sounds stilted or uncomfortable to you, then substitute words you feel will roll out more smoothly. I've observed that callers want to be reassured that you are confident, self-assured, knowledgeable, and able to provide the right service for their requirements. How successfully you convey this subtle message will be key to your business growth.

As you will see in the next example, when you can successfully market cover letters, you automatically create repeat business that, particularly in a depressed job market, can easily bring a client's billing to over the $500 mark for the typical six-month job search. Let's take a look at the script I use in my office once I've completed a resume consultation.

Cover Letter Script. To deliver to individuals for whom a resume consultation has just been completed.

You	Now that we've completed the information I need to professionally prepare your resume, may I ask how you plan to structure your job search? (Note: This information is frequently conveyed in the course of the consultation, so you may just launch into "Now, let's talk about cover letters.")

Resume client	Besides talking to people I know, I will be sending out my resume.
You	Have you developed a professional cover letter?

OPTION A (yes)

Resume client	Yes. I think I'm all set with it.
You	Great! Well, I'll just mention that if you decide that you'd like my editorial expertise in reviewing your letter, I'd be happy to do so. I write a great many successful cover letters for my clients. The fee is based strictly on my time, at the consultation rate of $XX per hour. Usually twenty minutes is sufficient. And if you decide you'd like my assistance in typing the actual cover letters so that you're creating a cohesive resume/letter package where everything is done in the same type, printing, and stationery, I provide that service at the lower word processing rate of $XX per hour. Typically, I can produce eight to ten individualized cover letters and matching envelopes per hour.

OPTION A (no)

Resume client	Uh . . . a cover letter?
You	Yes. While your resume is a professional, objective statement of your accomplishments, background, and qualifications, a cover letter is essentially a marketing piece whereby you can personalize and tailor your background to the requirements of a particular reader. If you are looking primarily in one field, a well-written cover letter should ideally be applicable to most purposes—in other words, the core paragraphs could remain essentially the same on most of your letters, but the opening and closing paragraphs would be specifically tailored to each company.
	I write a great many successful cover letters for my clients. The flat fee for writing a pro forma cover letter is $XX. And if you decide you'd like my assistance in typing the actual cover letters so that you're creating a cohesive resume/letter package

where everything is done in the same type, printing, and stationery, I provide that service at the lower word processing rate of $XX per hour. Typically, I can produce eight to ten individualized cover letters and matching envelopes per hour.

OPTION C (no—for budget-minded clients who are clearly not interested in personalized letters)

Resume client   No, I'm not planning on sending out any cover letters.

You   (if the client is open to suggestions) That's fine. Essentially, a cover letter can be considered a marketing piece. While your resume is a professional, objective statement of your accomplishments, background, and qualifications, a cover letter can be personalized with your background tailored to the requirements of a particular reader. If you are looking primarily in one field, a well-written cover letter should ideally be applicable to most purposes—in other words, the core paragraphs could remain essentially the same on most of your letters, but the opening and closing paragraphs would be specifically tailored to each company.

I write a great many successful cover letters for my clients. The flat fee for writing a pro forma cover letter is $XX. And if you decide you'd like my assistance in typing the actual cover letters so that you're creating a cohesive resume/letter package where everything is done in the same type, printing, and stationery, I provide that service at the lower word processing rate of $XX per hour. Typically, I can produce eight to ten individualized cover letters and matching envelopes per hour.

Another option is to prepare a well-written cover letter but to leave it generic enough for all purposes. You would address it 'To Whom It May Concern' and not have a date or inside address. It would, however, be prepared on stationery matching your resume and is still far more effective than merely using only the "Objective" line on your resume to define your career aspiration; in recent years, a Qualifications Summary has replaced use of the more-dated Objective on a resume, meaning that a cover letter is the only tool that is selling you.

Here again, the important point to remember is constantly trying to professionally promote the services you can provide—and always with the focal point of *helping your clients*. As any successful entrepreneur will also advise, you need to blow your own horn and not be too shy or reserved in talking about what you know you do well!

Moving off the resume niche example, let's consider one of the most common reasons a caller will contact a secretarial service: the need for word processing services. You will quickly become familiar with the opening question, "Do you do just typing?" Obviously, if the client has an SF–171 government application form or a law school application or an application for a sales tax form, he or she really does need "typing services." But you should always use that initial contact to let callers know that in addition to professional typewriting services, you can, if they desire, provide a full range of support services: a cover letter to accompany the application, a professionally developed resume, and so on. And—this is important—if the caller is someone other than a student or job-seeker, try to quickly ascertain the nature of the person's business.

Here is a sample script.

Typing Script. To respond to individuals who call with a need for typing services.

You	ABC Office Services, hello.
Caller	Hi. I'd like some information about getting some typing done.
You	Fine! I'd be happy to help you. What kind of project do you have in mind?
Caller	Well, I've written a four-page letter that details a proposal to prospective educators about a consulting service I offer, and I need to have the letters professionally done.
You	That's exactly the kind of work we specialize in. We would be handling this in Microsoft Word on a computer with laser printing, and we offer disk storage. Storage is provided indefinitely—at no charge to you. The cost is based on an hourly rate of $XX; a project of the size you describe would typically require XX amount of time.
Caller	That sounds reasonable. I'd like to set up an appointment to meet with you.

You	Great! I have just a few questions. By the way, I'm Jane Doe; with whom am I speaking?
Caller	[Name].
You	Thanks, [Name]. Will this letter be individualized to the recipients?
Caller	Yes.
You	We can create a mail-merge database for your use—either one-time use for this project or maintained for subsequent mailings you might wish to have us handle. If you are interested, I'd be happy to discuss the types of information you might want to have created in the database and give you an estimate for handling this project.

Another point I'd like to mention is that I'm a writer and editor and would be pleased to lend my editorial expertise in reviewing your material if that's a service you'd like to avail yourself of. My hourly rate is $XX.

Finally, I do want to tell you that I provide full editorial and office support services to professionals with businesses like yours. If you decide in the future to expand your business or would require assistance in developing other promotional materials, including a brochure, newsletter, marketing piece, or flyer, we can certainly help you with these projects.

Now, looking at the calendar, would you prefer a daytime or evening appointment? [etc., picking up from Resume Script A].

Prior to the arrival of a "business" client, prepare a file folder labeled with the client's name, and enclose your business card and brochure as well as the most recent issue of your company newsletter (if you have one). Wendy Gelberg, president of Advantage Resume Services in Needham, Massachusetts, uses a customized label she prepares on her laser printer to affix to a standard file folder for each client. It provides her business name, address, and (most importantly) telephone number; in addition, a full range of services are listed. She has found that clients retain these folders and frequently return to her office a year (or more) later with the original folder in hand. If you know in advance that you will be meeting with a client who is, for example, a business consultant or a professional trainer and you have worked with similar clients in the past, have rough notes available to consult regarding your experience in this field. If I'm meeting with a client to develop a newsletter, besides my own newsletter I will have my sample file available to demonstrate possible layout ideas and styles. Following a consultation of this type, I will provide about five minutes of "free discussion," sharing any marketing or promotional tips I can spontaneously think of that may be applicable to the client's business.

The work of a professional office support services business brings us in contact with diverse professions and occupations. The knowledge we possess can become an encyclopedia to our clients, and general information (not trade secrets or confidential material, obviously) is a service we can provide as an add-on in building goodwill. Most of my current corporate clients began with initial calls—usually, rush service in nature—to get a document word-processed. By opening the door to the full menu of services my business provides, I create a wonderful path into these companies, and they make up the foundation of my regular, ongoing clientele. You will find that these are the clients who remember you over the holidays with generous gifts and on Secretaries' Day with thoughtful reminders. And they are just generally the folks with whom you can establish long and mutually beneficial relationships. I always view each first-time caller looking to get a rush business letter or document produced as having the potential to become my next biggest client company. And more often than not, this is exactly what happens.

One of the "giveaways" I routinely present to my clients upon completion of a full brochure project—where I've developed the content, design, layout, and so forth from scratch—is a two-page synopsis of all the most creative ideas I can formulate for promoting their type of business. I find that after a brochure consultation, my head is spinning with great marketing concepts and promotional plans. I always schedule my appointments to allow fifteen minutes of time at the conclusion of a consultation to quickly prepare this listing encapsulating all my ideas.

And do you know what happens? The client is thrilled to receive "ideas for nothing." More often than not, the client follows up with me in developing at least some of these ideas. As I mentioned earlier, in one of my quarterly newsletters I offered a half-hour consultation free to every client booking development of a new brochure during the following thirty days. In just one month I completed four consultations for brochures. Yes, I gave away two hours of my time "for free" through that initial half-hour of consultation to each—but my billing exceeded $2,000 (not including printing costs), and I've got four happy clients now "hooked in" to a new service (from their standpoint).

I never hesitate to spend a few extra minutes off the clock talking shop with my clients. I've always found that doing so spreads tremendous goodwill—and comes back to me tenfold through increased sales. And even if a client doesn't need some ancillary service, chances are good that through the person's network of contacts, he or she will refer someone who does.

Over the past few years, this aspect of my business has really grown into what I now call business consulting. In many cases, a client will take advantage of the initial half-hour of complimentary consultation time I offer to discuss a full range of projects: development of a brochure, creation of corporate identity, design of letterhead and ancillary materials, *and* development of a marketing plan to accompany all these "goodies." Often, now, I'm able to charge for the marketing plan ideas that I previously "gave away." Best of all, I'm still able to generate these ideas and develop innovative and highly creative plans in a very short period of time, thus yielding maximum profitability for my business. If you're not initially comfortable with charging for this expertise, I would simply suggest that you allow yourself to do what I did in the beginning: Give it away for free while you hone your skills and become comfortable with the value of your knowledge. Then, gradually, break into charging for your valuable expertise and services.

Overcoming Prospective Client Objections

It's important for a business operator to prepare for the inevitable objections that will occasionally occur—resistance to price being the most obvious. A few years ago, when some of my colleagues mentioned using the phrase, "Oh, I didn't realize price was your *only* concern," I took note and have since added this to my "quoting vocabulary." Keep in mind that, for many callers, asking about price just seems like the natural thing to do *first*, but may not necessarily reflect that they are seeking a bargain. The important thing is to engage callers about their project requirements and your unique ability to satisfy their needs—professionally, promptly, and at a good value (not the same as cheap or inexpensive, but at a reasonable fee for the service—and perceived value or quality—rendered).

The longer you can engage a caller on the telephone, the more likely that person will either (1) book an appointment with you during that same conversation, or (2) call you back to book the appointment. Why? The greater the opportunity you have to demonstrate your understanding and knowledge, the easier it is to win this client's loyalty. In addition, I have found it useful—when speaking with someone I sense is still "shopping"—to *encourage* him or her to call others by stating, "I understand that you are probably checking around the area. Let me just add that I'd be happy to respond to any additional questions that might occur to you in a subsequent telephone call. I'd also like to point out that I've been in business seventeen years (I couldn't do this in my first year, of course, and instead quoted that I had worked successfully with a number of highly satisfied clients) and am keenly committed to customer satisfaction, as evidenced by the high number of repeat and referred clients with whom I work. It would be my pleasure to work with you, too, and I look forward to that opportunity. I'll look forward to speaking with you when you are ready to proceed with this project. Thank you very much for calling Absolute Advantage."

Develop and use your own unique attributes and qualifications to customize a response to the implicit prospective client query, "Why should I use your secretarial service?"

Developing Increased Sales to Existing Clientele

Let your existing clients know how good you are through testimonials. Always save letters and notes of appreciation received from your clients—even those quickly jotted notes at the bottom of your invoice thanking you for a super job. I freely use these letters (with the writers' permission) in promoting ancillary services and providing professional references. At the recommendation some years ago of Lynette Smith, executive director of the Association of Business Support Services International, Inc., I use an attractively laid out bulletin board to prominently display select testimonial letters and notes in my home office. It lets new clients know how satisfied my current clients are with my professionalism and commitment to service excellence.

A common occurrence is having a regular client suddenly discover, through glancing at the testimonial board, that I provide a certain service he or she didn't previously realize. The client will say, "Oh, you do that?" I quickly pull from my file not only examples of whatever the special type of work might be but also letters of appreciation from satisfied clients. It becomes an easy sell, and it reinforces the point that we help our clients—and ourselves—every time we remember to mention a service that might be useful to their business.

A new profit center I actively began promoting a few years ago is an individualized program delivered one-on-one with clients on "Interview Training and Techniques." I also teach this in an adult education program in my community along with a resume workshop (excellent visibility and great source of referrals). It was a natural add-on to my resume consultation service and taps into my professional background before running Absolute Advantage. I pulled the complete pilot program together in just a few hours and have sold a number of these packages to very satisfied resume clients who (1) had never heard of such a service, and (2) were thrilled to know such a product was available to help them prepare for interviewing.

It's been especially useful for clients who've been with one company for a long time and haven't interviewed in ages—or for people reentering the work force after a lengthy absence. Like most of you, I'm sure, I absolutely love meeting with and talking to my clients. A product such as this allows me to spend that time in an extremely profitable way that delivers tremendous client benefits. But if I didn't promote the service, most clients would never think to ask if it were available.

Strategies for "Working the Phone"

Highly Recommended Tip: Professional Coverage

This was mentioned earlier—and is important enough to mention again: Install a high-quality answering machine or professional voice-mail service as soon as your business telephone number is in operation. This is essential in order to maintain a professional office—*and* a private family life.

I do recommend an answering machine/voice-mail with Caller ID as the "first line of defense" in providing professional telephone coverage for the home-based office. This is because of the inherent flexibility in monitoring incoming calls (especially useful for the home-based entrepreneur with young children). I found that when my three children were babies, I simply couldn't answer a number of incoming calls because of the distracting and unprofessional-sounding (to prospective callers, not me!) background noise. However, with the ability to screen the calls through my answering machine, using the portable phone, I *was* able to pick up and speak with a number of regular clients who knew and were very comfortable with the fact that I had young children at home. First-time callers left messages, and I was able to return the calls promptly, but at my convenience (i.e., when the babies were napping).

In the early 1990s, I responded to complaints from clients that my line "was always busy" with the addition of call-waiting. After just a year or two of this service, however, I determined it wasn't solving the problem. When initiating a client call, I used the feature to cancel out call-waiting because I didn't want to interrupt my calls to clients; likewise, when clients called me, I didn't like having to place them on hold to respond to the call-waiting signal. The alternative, however, was no better: letting the call ring totally unanswered! Therefore, I canceled this service just a few years ago and, instead, added a voice-mail service available through my telephone company. With the use of Caller ID, I'm able to identify nearly every caller (except for some "private call" or "out-of-area" callers). This allows me to selectively answer the phone directly if I choose . . . or allow a message to be professionally left in one of my three "corporate" mailboxes in the voice-mail system (one for new clients, a second for those purchasing books or newsletters, and the third for folks interested in a Web site article link or magazine article). For those of you not familiar with voice-mail services, there is a special signal on the tele-

> ## Suggested Script for Your Answering Machine/ Voice-mail Message
>
> You've reached the offices of A–PLUS Office Services. This is Susan Jacobs speaking. Your call is very important to us. We're not available to take your call just now, but if you will leave a message at the tone, we'll be happy to return your call as soon as possible. [If applicable: If you'd like to transmit a fax, please dial 1–333–555–8888.]
>
> Thank you for calling A–PLUS Office Services.

phone line the next time I pick up the telephone alerting me to the fact that there is at least one new message waiting to be retrieved in the voice-mail system. I am able to record my own personal message on voice-mail—just as I did on the answering machine—and update it as frequently as I wish. I have the voice-mail service programmed to "answer" after four rings. The service is very inexpensive (less than $10 a month) and has totally eliminated client complaints of the lines always being busy or calls ringing unanswered. An added benefit is that the voice-mail system works around the clock without interruption—which is important since I have a fair amount of interruption to electrical service because I live in the country.

It is unlikely that you'll ever be available at all times, Monday through Friday, 8:00 A.M. until 5:00 P.M., when the majority of initial callers will try to reach you. Just taking into account brief breaks for lunch and coffee, trips to the restroom, and runs to the post office will mean that you are unavailable at some time each day. Therefore, it is critical that an answering machine or voice-mail handle these calls. Expect many hang-ups—nonetheless, the world is more accepting than ever of answering machines, and the majority of first-time callers (with the exception of price-shoppers or resume clients concerned about confidentiality) will leave a message for you to return their call.

Please notice two things in the suggested script, which should be tailored to meet your needs and sound like you: (1) you immediately identify the company name, and (2) you give the impression, through the use of *we,* of being a larger company. This conveys an important picture, especially to corporations. When recording your message, be certain there are no background noises (washing machine, kids, television, or radio). This may require you to make the recording at midnight!

Answering Machine Features

If you decide against a voice-mail system and are shopping for an answering machine, the following features are important:

- **Tape of unlimited length,** to take lengthy messages/dictation from clients. If you plan to offer microcassette transcription, you might consider obtaining an answering machine that utilizes microcassettes. These can then be transferred to your transcriber unit after clients use your answering machine to "phone in" their dictation.

- **Ability to set the answering feature to pick up immediately, after two rings, and after four rings.** Why? You'll want to set it to answer immediately or at the second ring when you are away from the office or on vacation; having the machine answer after four rings is the setting you'll want it on at all other times—this way, if you're at the other end of your house (e.g., if you have a baby you are putting down for a nap) but know you are in a position to answer, you'll have a chance to do that before the fifth ring. And when you are out of the office delivering completed work to a client, picking up office supplies, or even going grocery shopping, you will always know that the machine is automatically set to answer after two rings without having to remember to turn on the unit each time you go out the door. When you're in your office, you can, of course, answer the phone after the first ring regardless of the setting.

- **Portable phone feature** as part of the answering machine. This is invaluable if you have small children and equally useful if you simply want the ability to be accessible by telephone even if you're not physically in your office (e.g., when you're taking a much-needed break, outside retrieving the mail, or proofreading out on your deck). If, for example, you're relaxing with your children and they're playing quietly or perhaps watching a videotape and you have your portable phone with you (and your children are old enough to be safely out of eyeshot for a few minutes), you can answer a call at your discretion, walk to the doorway of the adjacent room, and still sound professional without your client picking up background "kid" noises and without having to disappear from your kids completely.

  I'm not suggesting that you be a slave to the phone; however, as a result of my own three start-up experiences (my family has relocated twice to different states since I first started my business), I recommend that, in the beginning, you try to personally answer the telephone as much as possible in order to begin to get that important first-time business. Once you have an established client, he or she will know that you are managing multiple priorities, perhaps with a family, and will freely leave messages for you to return phone calls. It's the first-time caller who, many times, will hang up and try the next listing in the Yellow Pages. You want to try to be as available as possible by telephone during business hours, Monday through Friday. And I've long advocated that, as much as you possibly can without totally disrupting your family life, you should try answering your business phone after hours and on weekends in the critical start-up months and even years. This is when first-time callers *really* need you. (Having Caller ID will ideally let you distinguish between a true first-time caller and, shall we say, a "pesky" ongoing client who doesn't respect your business hour parameters.) Your availability to respond to a first-time caller's immediate need in answering the phone after hours almost assures you of capturing this new business. Of course, you don't have to schedule the actual appointment and/or work until a more convenient time during your regular business hours. Keep in mind that this prospective client wouldn't be calling at 8:30 P.M. on Tuesday or on a Sunday afternoon if not truly in need of your services!

- **Hold button.** This, too, is an important feature because it allows you to place a caller on "hold" at any point during your telephone conversation. You would do this not only for the obvious reasons (e.g., your house telephone line is ringing, if it isn't also on an answering machine, or the UPS delivery person is at your door) but also for unexpected emergencies. A hold button is especially useful in households in which there are young children: They get into a squabble right when you're in the middle of closing a prospective new client by telephone, the baby masters climbing out of the playpen for the first time and is in fast pursuit of the family kitten, and so on. By politely asking your caller if you may place him or her on hold and then quickly pressing the button, you give yourself a minute or two to resolve whatever the situation is, while at the same time appearing professional. Think of the number of times you contact other places of business and are placed on hold. Provided that you are courteous, it's a very accepted practice—and a home business owner's saving grace!

As your business develops and you find yourself acquiring more clients and getting busier, don't feel obliged to always drop everything to answer your phone. At the point that your business has a regular flow of work and you have a two-hour stretch of uninterrupted time in which to work away on several projects having aggressive deadlines (for those with children, this might be while the kids are napping), don't always interrupt your work to answer the phone—just let the answering machine or your voice-mail service pick up. As your clientele becomes established, you'll find that you know which clients are receptive to a returned call in the evening—maybe when they are in their home office (again, if you have young children, it might be after the kids are bathed and in bed) and which clients can be called early in the morning (once again, if you have children and they are late risers). This gives you a little more flexibility in managing your day—another asset to a home-based business.

Of the many electronic "gadgets" designed for the home-based business market, a portable telephone with either an answering machine or a voice-mail system and Caller ID are probably your best investment.

CHAPTER FIVE

GETTING DOWN TO BUSINESS

ESTABLISHING THE PHYSICAL LAYOUT FOR YOUR OFFICE

You're in business (or about to be)! You've hung out your shingle and purchased your equipment. You're ready to organize your office setup. Home-based businesses are operated from nearly every room in a typical house, condo, or apartment: spare bedroom, dining room, today's often unused living room, closed-in breezeway, closed-in porch, room over garage, converted garage, and finished basement room, as well as an office constructed for that specific purpose (both attached to one's actual dwelling and unattached). How to determine the best use of space? Traffic pattern is probably the single most important factor. Ideally, you don't want to escort clients into a home office situated in a spare bedroom that must be accessed through your home's bedroom wing; however, nothing precludes your doing client work on a computer located in the bedroom office but using a more centrally located dining room or living room in which to conduct client appointments. Likewise, if you have a beautiful basement office but it is accessed through your laundry room or some other area of your house that you prefer clients not use, meet with them in an area nearest the doorway.

If you do establish an office location that is not client-accessible, you'll need to carefully manage how you conduct business. For example, it is a fairly typical practice for clients to return to your office to pick up their completed work—and proofread it "on the spot." This is especially the case with resume clientele; before having you print final originals on their choice of stationery, your clients will first want to inspect the document carefully. Consider how comfortable you will feel leaving the client in your meeting area while you run down to the basement or bedroom to make revisions while the client waits. These are considerations and, of course, point to the ideal situation of being able to work in the area in which you meet your clients. If your dining room or living room is not heavily used, you might convert one of these rooms to your office/conference area.

It is also ideal if the doorway into your office area is not the only entrance into your home. That way, if you have young children, for example, and meet with clients on Saturdays, whoever is caring for your children can still leave and enter the house without disturbing you.

No matter what space you decide on for meeting clients, it will help boost your professional image and self-esteem to furnish it as professionally as possible. Position your furniture in a manner that's comfortable for clients while they're waiting for you to finish their work. Also keep in mind that you'll want to be able to talk with clients at a table or desk area (e.g., for a resume consultation), take notes, and be able to face them (instead of sitting side by side). Rearrange furniture groupings and test various scenarios until you feel comfortable. Check and recheck lighting—both general and task lighting—to be certain you have optimum working light as well as ambient lighting that creates an attractive work space in which to meet clients. Remember that you will probably be working as much in the evening hours as you will during conventional business hours and that, therefore, night lighting must be a consideration.

Another thought with regard to office placement is proximity to the nearest bathroom. Inevitably, there will be occasions when clients ask to use the restroom. I know some people in this business who simply do not make that "option" available to their clients and direct them to a public restroom located within a few miles of their home office. I believe, however, that it is imperative to make this amenity available to clients, in spite of the slight inconvenience to you. (Maintaining an attractive, spotlessly clean restroom facility well-equipped with appropriate supplies is one more "janitorial" task you will have in addition to vacuuming and dusting your office daily.)

It is, of course, ideal to have a lavatory or powder room located right near your office that clients can utilize. If this is not possible or if your home has only one bathroom that is for the family's use, you may want to consider decoration and storage so that a streamlined appearance is maintained (with young children's bath toys, for example, stowed out of sight). I liken the availability of a restroom at a professional secretarial service to that at the offices of any other professional—all accountants, attorneys, and medical professionals have restrooms available . . . as do hair stylists and other service providers.

Assuming you have selected your office space, consider redecorating the area to suit your personality and the image you want to convey. Select a wallpaper and color that feel good to you—you're going to be spending a great deal of time in this area, and you should enjoy entering it! Add a few fresh flowers for accent color and enjoyment when you can. Use stacking bins and file trays to neatly arrange work in progress and other papers in your desk area. If you are a naturally clutter-oriented person (as I am), try to step back from your client meeting area before each client appointment and appraise it with fresh eyes. Clear as much clutter and maintain as open an area as possible—even if you are in a tiny work space. Always keep tablets, extra pens, extra business cards, and file folders available in the area where you actually meet with clients.

If you have determined to have a work area separate from where you'll be meeting with clients and the "client meeting" area is in another portion of your home shared with the family, establish a box (or even a laundry basket) of items that can be quickly moved into this area in advance of a client appointment (and just as quickly cleared away at the conclusion of your appointment). Items to have on hand include professional publications, any handouts you may have prepared (e.g., particularly relevant articles related to interviewing skills for your resume clientele), steno pads or blank tablets, pens, copies of your brochure, business cards, empty file folders, and blank Client Work Orders. If it is convenient, you can have up-to-date news magazines (*Time, Newsweek, Fortune,* etc.) and/or that day's newspaper available.

A final amenity you may wish to provide to clients is a beverage. I nearly always have a pot of coffee on in my kitchen (immediately next to an office and lavatory adjoining my house) and offer a cup to clients who are (1) regulars or (2) going to be in my office for more than just a five-minute pick-up. I also make ice water available. Some service providers keep a candy bowl filled in their reception/meeting area, while others offer homemade cookies, particularly during the holiday season. While these extras aren't essential, they certainly can add to the inviting atmosphere you create for clients entering your office and working with you.

IRS Guidelines—Business Use of Your Home

Once you've determined the optimum location for your home office, you'll want to calculate the applicability of the home office deduction for income tax purposes; there are stringent guidelines with regard to exclusive and sole use. Publication #587, *Business Use of Your Home* (see the Bibliography in the Appendix), explains use tests and deduction limits to use in determining your legitimate deduction for business use of your home. Detailed instructions, formulas, and a completed sample Schedule C form ("Profit or Loss from Business") and Form 8829 ("Expenses for Business Use of Your Home") are included.

Organization

With your office location determined, renovation and/or decoration complete, and furnishings in place, you'll next want to consider organization. Let's spend a few minutes discussing some of the recommended forms and procedures you may wish to establish. Please refer to the Client Work Order form (immediately following this section as well as discussed in chapter 4). This document (or one you tailor to suit your specific business requirements) should be utilized for every single new client transaction as well as each new project for repeat clients.

Client Work Order

As the sample form indicates, the following information should be obtained:

- Date and time of initial appointment (be sure to include year)

- Client's name

- Client's company (if relevant; not necessary for resume clientele)

- Client's home (or business) address (include e-mail address, if applicable)

- Client's office telephone number (also note fax number, if applicable)

- Client's home telephone number

- Brief project description (business proposal, mail-merge letters, resume, cover letters, etc.)

- Source of the business

  If from a Yellow Pages ad, include directory name and the applicable category

  Referral (include name of client or person making referral)

  Repeat client

  Other source (specify)

- Selection of font (if discussed in initial client meeting; some clients are very knowledgeable as to the exact font style and size they are seeking. If you make the selection during the actual typesetting of work, note here for easy reference).

- Selection of stock (paper) (typically used for resume work; the client generally makes the decision at the time that the proposed resume is presented for proofreading and approval. Specific color choice and name of the stationery should be noted for future reference).

- Number of copies, whether or not they should be stapled, number of originals—all as mentioned in initial appointment, if applicable; this would also be the area where number of originals and/or copies a client receives with a given project should be noted (e.g., if you determine to offer ten original laser prints of a resume with each typesetting project, you would place "10" on the "# originals" line).

- The minimum or maximum number of pages desired (sometimes relevant, particularly for student term papers where a paper must be "at least ten pages long" or "no longer than fifteen pages"; always determine from the client if he or she wants you to "play with type size" to expand or condense text to fit the requirement. I usually use Times Roman 14-point, double-spaced text for theses unless instructed otherwise or asked by a client to enlarge or reduce to meet a size restriction).

- Title or cover page, if not already provided by client (this would be for term papers, business proposals, and presentations; frequently, clients will not remember this piece of information. This prompt reminds you to ask how they want this information to appear).

- Details related to the preparation of the project (any information not covered up to this point, including spelling of an unusual name, special style instructions, reference to a client-provided style sheet, etc.).

- Next appointment (agreed-upon date and time, whether the client will pick up the project or wants the completed project to be delivered, whether or not the client is to be called first upon completion of the project, perhaps with an actual cost quote, etc.).

- Development of a cost estimate for the project ("worksheet" area to outline applicable costs). For typesetting a one-page resume with one-half hour of consultation time and one-quarter hour of editorial time, the handwritten estimated cost information here on the Client Work Order form might look like this:

Typeset one-page resume	$49.00
.5 hr. consultation @ $95	47.50
.25 hr. editorial services @ $95	23.75
Subtotal	$120.25

A deposit should always be collected on first-time projects with the possible exception of corporate clients (i.e., when you are handling work for a company and not an individual; I have never requested a deposit from companies for which I handle work and have had only one small problem—a company folded before paying my invoice, which was a little over $100).

Determining the amount of the deposit is a fairly flexible "science." Generally, you want to ask for enough of a deposit so that the client will have added incentive to return. While the method is not entirely foolproof, most clients will not hesitate to put at least $50 or $100 down on a resume project and $100 down (or more) on a lengthy thesis or term paper. A policy should be established for your business whereby work is not released until payment is made in full (or arrangements made in advance to your satisfaction). The same holds true for faxing or mailing work out on a client's behalf. Except for very trusted repeat clients, it is probably a good idea to request payment in advance of mailing out any completed work to a client. This is one area of business where I have been repeatedly lax—and gotten "burned" (e.g., mailing out revised resumes to clients who have relocated, "trusting" the assurance that payment would be "promptly sent" and never receiving a check; accepting credit cards has since become my solution). Much of what makes this business work successfully is establishment of trust and mutual respect, and to this end your own good instincts are important. As with any other business, however, it is equally vital to develop policies that are fair to *you* and your clients. (See additional information under Credit later in this chapter.)

■ Determination of the approximate balance due. Note the word *approximate*. This is because no matter how precise an estimate, it *is* only an estimate. You may find on a particularly lengthy resume consultation that while you estimated editorial time to be half an hour, you actually spent one hour and developed two addendum sheets to cover all of the client's professional publications. This may not have been apparent in the initial consultation and, therefore, affects the final balance due. Likewise, when you are handling business proposals or annual reports, additional information may be provided midway into a project that exceeds the original specifications—for example, a client might decide to utilize more graphic depictions of spreadsheet information you have prepared than initially planned.

You should obtain the client's signature on this form—and provide the client with a copy, circling the correct purpose at the top of the form: Client Work Order, Service Waiver, or Deposit Receipt.

Once a project has been completed, the Client Work Order should be part of the permanent paper file you maintain. For some secretarial service owners, a document of this sort is the only paperwork they maintain in a file; for my business, I prefer to keep a printout of the final original document (be it a resume, business proposal, cover letter, etc.) in my file for future reference when clients contact me for an update of their materials. The only exception to this would be a particularly lengthy document (manuscript for a novel or thesis); rather than waste the paper and devote limited filing cabinet space to such documents, these are retained only on diskette (an original disk plus backup on two additional disks). By the way, if computers are new to you and/or you haven't developed a consistent document backup process, I highly recommend backing up two separate disk copies of every document. You will probably want to keep separate disks for your large clients, but bulk together resumes on backup disks by letter of the alphabet. Resumes of clients whose last names begin with the letter A, for example, would all be filed on one disk. Zip disks for use on Iomega Zip drives are wonderful for backup storage.

Client Files

A secretarial services business requires filing space (at minimum a two-drawer file) to maintain not only the records of doing business but client information as well. Corrugated cardboard filing boxes provide an excellent means of archival storage. I have managed to keep my seventeen-plus years of business paperwork and client files confined to a two-drawer vertical file, a four-drawer vertical file, and five cardboard filing boxes (the last stored in a dry basement closet).

What Information Should Go into a Client File

- Initial Client Work Order
- Any style sheet provided by client or prepared by operator (see next section)
- Subsequent Client Work Orders (for new projects or continuations of extensive projects)
- Original final printout of client's project (with the exception of particularly lengthy documents)
- Copy of each invoice generated for the client
- Notation as to disk onto which project has been filed (if not obvious)

Style Sheet

A style sheet will frequently be provided by clients asking you to handle preparation of their theses, novels, or lengthy term papers. Essentially, a style sheet includes spelling of unusual words or those with several correct spellings, techni-

BEST BUSINESS SERVICES

Celebrating 17 Years! · 1983–2000

P.O. Box 123
Anywhere, USA 88888
(333) 333-4444 · Fax (333) 333-4466

Date/Time _____

CLIENT WORK ORDER · SERVICE WAIVER · DEPOSIT RECEIPT

Client Name

Company

Address

Office Telephone   Home Telephone

Project

Source

Font Selection   Stock Selection

\# Copies   Stapled?   \# Originals   Min/Max \# Pages

Cover Page

Special Instructions

Deadline/Pickup Date

Estimated Cost: $

Tax $

Total $

Less Deposit –

Approximate Balance Due $

The above estimate is provided to the best of our ability following initial review/consultation. Final invoice is based on actual project requirements. Significant differences between estimated total and actual requirements will be discussed with the client prior to completion of the work. For resume projects, the total quoted above is a firm number except as noted in the following paragraph.*

A minimum nonrefundable cash or credit card deposit of $50 is required for all word processing/desktop publishing services; a 50% deposit is required for all resume consultations. *For resume consultations, the above-quoted total *includes* a return or telephone review appointment of up to 30 minutes in length; review discussion exceeding 30 minutes will be billed at an hourly rate of $95 for the actual time spent. Other project deposits would be as agreed upon.

All written materials and consultation services must be paid for in full upon receipt of completed product; completed work will not be released until full payment is made, unless alternative billing arrangements have been made in advance. Unpaid accounts over 30 days are subject to a $5.00 monthly late charge. **Final proofreading is the responsibility of the client.**

The client hereby agrees that any inaccurate, incorrect, or misleading information in the resume or other materials provided to the client by *Best Business Services* is not our responsibility and that the client had an opportunity to review the materials and approve its entire content prior to delivery and/or reproduction. This includes the responsibility of students to insure that all components of a paper, thesis, dissertation, etc. comply with the guidelines provided by their school. The client's signature below certifies understanding and agreement with all of the statements of this document.

Signature _____   Date _____

Professional Desktop Publishing, Promotional, Editorial, and Office Support Services

SAMPLE STYLE SHEET

A–F

acetylene

cast-off (adj.)

Foucalt

beet armyworm

endopolyploidy

dog-ear (n./adj.)

carcinomatosis

M–R

nosce te ipsum

Menominee

Ripuarian

perphenazine

G–L

kickoff (n.)

gill-netter (n.)

half # sister

S–Z

thyrocalcitonin

secundum naturam

way-out (adj.)

Vinson Massif

Zephaniah

cal terms or phrases that may be unfamiliar, special capitalization, words with and without hyphens, usage as it relates to the material being keyed, and any other preferences noted by the client.

If a style sheet is not provided, you should ask during the initial consultation if one will be forthcoming, or if the client is willing to spend a few minutes with you (on the clock; this is billable time) developing at least an outline for the style sheet. A style sheet is generally handwritten and is organized in rough alphabetical order.

I periodically review my files to weed out any material no longer relevant. For example, as my resume clients update their resumes, I try to ensure that only the most current resume is stored in the paper files. (All previous versions remain on disk, however.) In addition, I maintain the notes I take during a client intake for a resume consultation for about two months; these usually number six to ten tablet pages. After the arbitrary timeframe (and this, of course, follows the client's approval of the final resume), I will shred my original notes. This helps keep my files streamlined but still enables me to immediately access any given client's file while I'm on the telephone, providing an immediate history of the transactions I've had in the past with this client. I find that resume clients, in particular, are always impressed by my ability to seemingly recall instantly the type of work I've done with them, down to the color and type of stationery they selected for the original printouts of their resume. This contact might be five or six years after their initial appointment. Alphabetically filed records that are handy allow for professional, timely access without having to switch disks at your computer while the client waits.

Other Relevant Forms

A Client Production Schedule (sample follows) should be utilized for each client project. You may wish to establish for each regular client a manila file folder in which you maintain this log. This serves as a good means for subtotaling work on a given project and allows for ease in invoicing. This is also a useful tool for maintaining regular client activity for those accounts to which you offer biweekly or monthly billing (discussed in greater detail in this chapter under Credit). This blank form can be photocopied onto the back of the Client Work Order and creates a permanent record of activity for a given account. When the client signs the original Client Work Order, be sure to maintain the original in your files, while providing him or her with a copy of the front of the form only.

A manila file folder should also be used at the time that you are meeting with a first-time client. At the conclusion of the initial appointment, the Client Work Order, a Client Production Schedule, and the project materials can be placed into the file folder. The folder edge should be labeled with the client's name. Next, the project should be entered onto the ongoing Project Status/Deadline Sheet (sample follows). Of course, deadlines and follow-up appointments should also be noted in your calendar. (I like the Franklin Planner.) Finally, this packet of project information should be placed in your to-do, work-in-progress bin.

You will probably find it helpful to photocopy (or have printed) a large number of the Project Status/Deadline Sheet forms and affix them to a clipboard or staple them to sturdy cardboard. As business grows you will probably update and rewrite the list at least three or four times a week, so you'll need a good supply.

This form is the "lifeblood" of your business, in terms of being the one document used to track all work in progress at a glance. Long-term projects with distant deadlines should be included, usually with an entry near the bottom of the sheet to note the overall deadline for the project as well as interim deadlines for segmented portions of it. Obviously, at the start of any given week you will have an idea of your standing client projects that are ongoing in nature. But let's say that the phone rings at 9:00 A.M. on Monday and it's a new client in urgent need of a resume (opportunity to charge for rush service; discussed later). So, you schedule the appointment into the day and squeeze the return appointment into the following morning. In order to enter this onto your Project Status/Deadline Sheet, you'll probably have to bump some things down and move other things around. That business proposal you have been working on is not really going to be picked up by the client until Thursday. But you had scheduled it for completion on Tuesday, wanting to plan ahead. With an opportunity to earn extra money for a rush resume, you now shift the proposal to Wednesday.

Things progress well on Monday, you receive a few more phone calls from regular clients Monday afternoon—one with a request for one hundred copies of a form you recently designed (he needs to pick it up Tuesday morning) and one with two rush bids that need to be done by Wednesday (you schedule her for a Tuesday-afternoon meeting). As the week goes on, you've now pushed the business proposal to Wednesday evening (for final editing), just in time for that 9:00 A.M. Thursday pick-up.

It's now Friday and as you look back at your Project Status/Deadline Sheet, you realize that near the bottom of the list are two notations for your own business—one to do your bookkeeping for the month that just closed and one to write the draft copy of your client newsletter. Oh, well, there's always next week! Similar to saving money, wherein the experts in personal finance recommend that you "pay yourself first" out of each paycheck before paying any other bills, scheduling your own company's "work" can be challenging. It's always easy to let your own priorities slip, especially when you have a client in need—and willing to pay—on the other end of the line. This is one more advantage to being your own boss. With only yourself to answer to, *you* make the call—is it worth pushing off once again a deadline you

CLIENT PRODUCTION SCHEDULE

Company Name _____

Client Name _____

Telephone _____

Project _____

DATE	START	FINISH	TOTAL	DATE	START	FINISH	TOTAL

PROJECT STATUS / DEADLINE SHEET

Company Name _____

Date _____

	Client	Project	Do Work	Deadline	✔
1					
2					
3					
4					
5					
6					
7					
8					
9					
10					
11					
12					
13					

had self-imposed? Does it create client goodwill? Does it enable you to make more money because of a rush service uplift charge? Is it opening the door to a potentially long-term relationship with a prospective client you've been cultivating? These are all good reasons to readjust your "calendar"—and write a new Project Status/Deadline Sheet. The key reasons for maintaining such a log are as follows:

1. You'll never need to worry about inadvertently forgetting to handle a client project—if you exercise absolute discipline in immediately logging each client project onto the sheet at the conclusion of each appointment (or telephone call); even if you don't write in the project in actual order until such time as you are rewriting the sheet neatly, the record is there.

2. You'll enjoy a wonderfully satisfying feeling of accomplishment as you check off completed projects over the course of the business day.

3. As your business growth warrants, you'll probably find it effective to rewrite the sheet at the close of each business day. This helps you to reassess priorities, make appropriate alterations, and plan your mindset for the following business day. When the next morning finds you at your desk, you are well-organized with a clear "plan of attack" for that day's projects and priorities—as well as equipped with a good road map for fitting in "new emergencies" and rush projects.

DETERMINING PROFIT CENTERS/YOUR EXPERTISE

With the backbone of your business operation established, it's now an appropriate time to evaluate those profit centers in which you hope to be engaged while you are waiting for the telephone calls to flood your office. In reviewing your responses to the initial assessment information in chapter 2, attempt to identify product offerings that align with your expertise and experience. Some good examples follow. Keep in mind that you should probably have reviewed this information prior to arranging for any advertising, business card and brochure printing, and so on. Let's look at some of the more common profiles of typical secretarial service owners.

Secretarial/Administrative Background

If your background is primarily secretarial/administrative and you have excellent keyboarding ability and enjoy typing, manuscript and document preparation is a likely service offering for your business.

Suggested Client Types. Students (for theses and dissertations), writers/ authors, and companies with lengthy proposals and manuals to be typed.

Suggested Ways of Attracting These Clients (beyond the advertising methods suggested earlier). Post notices on college campus bulletin boards (recheck frequently to replace worn and tired ads); advertise in campus telephone directories and in campus publications; seek out any local editorial clubs as well as those appearing on any of the computer user group networks; prepare direct mailings (well-written cover letter, business card, and your brochure) to large companies in your area.

Hints. Print on brightly colored (neon/fluorescent) paper. Don't mention your business name—or your name, for that matter. In appealing to university students, you'll generally have more success if you *don't* appear to be a large "professional" company. (There is usually a big concern over cost, and you don't want to appear to price yourself out of the market.) Yet you obviously don't want to appear to be

SAMPLE CAMPUS AD

MANUSCRIPT, TERM PAPER, AND THESIS TYPING
LASERPRINTING / COMPUTER EDITING / STORAGE

Call today for a quote on your next paper or thesis. It will be professionally prepared by computer with laser printout (disk available, if desired). We provide highly competitive pricing, prompt turnaround (rush service available), and a professional document prepared to your specs.

Day · evening · weekend appointments available.
Only 10 minutes from campus

CALL 333–3333 TODAY!!

3	3	3	3	3	3	3	3	3	3	3
3	3	3	3	3	3	3	3	3	3	3
3	3	3	3	3	3	3	3	3	3	3
·	·	·	·	·	·	·	·	·	·	·
3	3	3	3	3	3	3	3	3	3	3
3	3	3	3	3	3	3	3	3	3	3
3	3	3	3	3	3	3	3	3	3	3
3	3	3	3	3	3	3	3	3	3	3

using an old clunker of a typewriter, either; stress the equipment and services you provide, don't mention cost, and make it easy for interested students to respond. Use the format with telephone numbers running along the bottom of your flyer—cut between the numbers vertically with scissors, creating an easy method for students to tear off a slip. Always print your telephone number in large type on the flyer itself so that if all tear-off slips are removed before you have an opportunity to recheck and replace your flyers, the number is still accessible.

Office Support Services Background

A strong office support/secretarial background also lends itself beautifully to providing complete office services.

Suggested Client Types. Independent businesspeople—many of whom probably operate from *their* home offices but lack the equipment, time, and/or expertise to handle their own correspondence and reports. Credit Unions, nonprofit associations.

Suggested Ways of Attracting These Clients. Check with your local town/city hall (as well as those in neighboring communities) to obtain a list of businesses in your community (often listed in a town report in a separate tax section). Also, obtain names of companies and small-business owners from your chapter of the chamber of commerce. Develop mailing lists of identified small-business owners and regularly communicate—telephone calls introducing yourself and your service, direct mail letters with promotional offers (plus brochure and business card), promotional single-sheet flyers, and your company newsletter.

When I meet a prospective new client (or learn of a new business owner in my county), I immediately add the person's name to my newsletter mailing list and send him or her material for two years (eight issues of my newsletter, plus intermittent direct mail pieces). A number of years ago, I received a project from a prospect with whom I had initially communicated more than *four years* earlier (but from whom I'd heard nothing in the interim). Because I had continued to send him my newsletter, he remembered me when his regular support person—a secretary from the company at which he'd formerly worked—was on vacation. She had prepared a proposal for a major client he was meeting with in Washington, D.C., later that week; however, there were several typographical errors (and he did not have disks available). To ensure completely matching style and font, he wanted me to redo the entire proposal—for same-day service. I was able to help him out in a critical deadline situation, and he has since used my service exclusively (going on ten years now!).

In another instance of time-delay response that underlines the importance of regular communications with your clients and *prospective* clients, many years ago I

Dear [contact name]:

I am writing this letter to introduce myself to you and the department. [In my case, I next stated, "I have recently relocated from the Boston area to Connecticut and am seeking . . ."] I am seeking freelance work as a typist/word processor, in particular, of theses.

In addition to experience typing student theses, I have extensive background in the publications field, as my attached resume attests. This includes [I detailed three editorial positions I'd held in the "professional world" prior to starting my business; substitute whatever is most relevant from *your* personal experience]. Furthermore, as the owner of a freelance word processing and proofreading service, I have handled a number of manuscripts for clients [mention any local or well-known clients for whom you have worked, provided that they have no objection to this].

I utilize [list equipment work will be handled on]. I accurately type approximately [number] words per minute, and, [if relevant] as a proofreader, I possess strong editorial skills. I offer quick turnaround of material, and my rates are extremely competitive. Pick-up and delivery of work can be arranged.

Enclosed are several notices that can be posted for student convenience, as well as a number of my business cards. I would be pleased to answer any questions you may have and appreciate any referrals.

Sincerely,

[Enclose resume, business cards, brochure, flyer, and, optionally, professional references.]

had prepared a direct mail piece (a one-page letter of introduction describing my services, plus several business cards) addressed to all the department heads (about twenty, as I recall) at a nearby university. It wasn't until nearly *two years* later that I received a telephone call from a publishing company in close proximity to the university, seeking editorial assistance. After booking the business, I asked my usual question (at that time, before my business name change), "How did you find CSP?" The editor I was working with had contacted the English department of the university to which I had sent my one-time mailing two years earlier, and the *secretary* who had opened the mailing was impressed enough with the content to retain my business card in her desk drawer . . . and was able to provide this editor with my name and telephone number as a possible source of editorial services. That single contact led to a very lucrative client relationship wherein I provided freelance editorial services for nearly four years. For my $5.00 expenditure in postage for that single mailing, the cost of stationery for letters and envelopes (minimal), and my business cards (I enclosed about five in each letter), I had thousands of dollars in billables from this one client referral.

Hints. Call to obtain the actual names of the department heads for this (and any other mailing); you'll have better success sending personalized letters. All marketing experts will advise that you can greatly enhance your direct mail results if you follow up each contact by telephone within a week. I must confess, though, that cold calling or even semiqualified cold calling is not a strong suit for me, and I've never followed up my direct mail pieces with a telephone call. I'm much better making my outreaches *in writing*—and I'm very comfortable doing all the selling and closing by phone *when prospects contact me.* In spite of this, I continue to have good success with targeted direct mail.

Here are some additional ideas related to reviewing the newspaper, an excellent source of business leads:

- Subscribe to and *read* all local newspapers (weeklies and dailies), scouting out any information you can glean about prospective clients.

- Search for news of someone starting a business in your area. (Congratulate the person and offer your services, including an introductory discount; enclose your brochure and business card; add the name to your mailing list for newsletters.)

- Look for news of someone being promoted within a company for which you'd like to work, ideally someone involved with administrative and/or office management responsibilities. (Congratulate the person on the promotion and offer your services, including an introductory discount; enclose your brochure and business card; add the name to your mailing list for newsletters.)

- Try to locate an interesting or effective advertisement. (Comment on how effective and well done or attention-getting a particular ad might have been and let the prospect know he or she can have the same impact in printed materials with you providing assistance; include an introductory discount; enclose your brochure and business card; add the name to your mailing list for newsletters.)

- Especially in the beginning months of starting a business, read all want ads for positions matching your background, interest, and experience (transcription, secretarial, office support, clerical). Develop a response letter template so that you can easily reply to every ad *quickly*. (The next day is ideal.) Write the letter from the standpoint of an individual seeking freelance or subcontracted work, mentioning your company in a somewhat understated manner. Enclose a resume. I recommend against including your business card and brochure—you don't want to turn off the reader, who at this point is seeking an *employee*. You can always send a second mailing of your brochure and business card at a later point.

In attracting clients through advertising, some of your responses will be immediate and clearly linked (e.g., a prospective client telephoning you and arranging for your services as a result of seeing your ad in the Yellow Pages when the person was searching for an appropriate business to handle his or her needs). Many of your clients will contact you as the result of referrals by satisfied clients. But a sizable percentage of business will ultimately come your way that may not necessarily be aligned to any single thing you did. This also emphasizes the importance of really querying first-time clients to find out some of the underlying reasons for their contact. Do this at the conclusion of your first transaction when they have reviewed the completed project you handled, have expressed satisfaction, and have paid you.

For example, we've already discussed pursuing further those clients who say they located your business in the Yellow Pages ("Which directory?" "What category?"). It's also important to understand *why* they selected your company. Unless you're the only company listed under the category they consulted, try to find out why they made the choice they did. Sometimes it's location ("You were the only company in my hometown" or "You're located near where I work"). Often, however, you'll be provided with valuable feedback:

- "You were the only one who actually answered the phone, and I didn't want to leave a message on an answering machine" (frequent with resume callers who might have concern about confidentiality).

Dear [contact name]:

This letter is in response to your recent newspaper advertisement for a [position title].

As my attached resume attests, I have professional editorial experience and am a very skilled word processor, editor, and proofreader. I am seeking to provide word processing/freelance editorial services through my home-based business, ABC Typing Services. I have extensive experience handling manuscripts; my resume details some of the background I have acquired at the publishing companies of [etc.]. In addition, I have handled a number of manuscripts for clients [mention any local or well-known clients for whom you have worked, provided that they have no objection to this].

I utilize [list equipment work will be handled on]. I accurately type approximately [number] words per minute and, [if relevant] as a proofreader, I possess excellent editorial skills. I am also an experienced transcriptionist.

I can offer quick turnaround of material, including pick-up and delivery services, as well as handle "rush" assignments. My compensation requirement is negotiable and very competitive, considering the quality of my work, my background and experience, and the computer/word processing equipment that I own. If you employed me as a subcontractor/freelancer, you would not need to add to your payroll, provide costly fringe benefits, or handle Social Security/withholding deductions.

If you would like to explore a possible working arrangement, I'd be pleased to meet with you and discuss this further, in particular, if you are not successful in finding qualified administrative candidates to work in-house. At that time I would be happy to present a portfolio of my work. I am a very motivated and hardworking professional and believe that I would be an asset to your organization. I can be contacted at 777-7777. Thank you for your consideration.

Sincerely,

[Enclose resume and professional references.]

- "Your ad looked professional and listed the services I was looking for." (It can really pay off to spend a little more on your ad to detail specific *benefits* to your prospective clients.)

- "The free offer attracted me" (free copies, free resume guidelines, free pick-up and delivery, free ten-minute review of resume, etc.).

- "The fact that you offered appointments at times other than strictly 9:00 to 5:00."

- "I called a lot of places, but you really sounded interested, professional, and able to help me."

- "Your prices sounded fair" ("the best," "the lowest," etc.) or "Even though your prices *weren't* the lowest, you sounded like the person best able to help me."

Great stuff! And very valuable marketing information to have—and utilize—in growing your business. Never overlook, too, the spin-off effects of some of the other types of advertising you do. While a recent flyer with a promotional offer you send to prospective clients may be what spurs them to respond and book an appointment, the fact that you have regularly run an ad in the weekly tabloid newspaper, have an ad or two in the Yellow Pages, and have recently been featured in a local newspaper story have all helped to assure this client that you are a viable business with "staying power." Occasionally, in spite of the grilling I professionally and quickly do with my new clients, some will neglect to mention until later, sometimes many months later, that they noticed a story about me in the newspaper or also checked under different headings in the Yellow Pages before contacting me, noting that because I advertised in so many places, I really appeared to "know my stuff."

I liken this type of advertising response to the manner in which many of us view new businesses—for example, the new restaurant in town. See if some of these points don't apply to your actions too:

- Before you consider going to a new restaurant, you ask around to see if others have tried it—and liked it.

- You watch the newspaper for an ad to appear, or a special discount or offer (the popular "two-fers")—or you look for a direct mail piece with an offer to appear in your own mail.

- You watch the newspapers for early reviews and publicity articles.

- You want to make sure the restaurant stays in business, irons out the bugs, and so on, before trying it.

- You are too busy to get around to visiting the restaurant until many months go by.

Well, all of these points can apply to the way in which your community (all potential client prospects) may first react to your business—they hopefully read the press release about your start-up business in the local newspaper; they see a flyer under their windshield or at the local supermarket; they think, "Yeah, it might be a good idea to have my resume updated"; they read another story about you in a different local newspaper; they see your ad regularly in the papers; they recall that they'd initially thought about finding that old resume and getting it "polished up"; they receive a direct mail piece about a special offer you're running; they lose the ad but remember you're right in town, so they look in the Yellow Pages and there you are: They call and book the appointment. Which form of advertising actually caused the client to contact your business? *All of them!*

Now that we've explored profit center possibilities for those with a heavy typing/secretarial background, let's move on to the next area of potential service offering.

Transcription and/or Medical Background

If you have Dictaphone experience and enjoy transcription and/or have a medical background, this can be an excellent profit center—or be your sole business, if you desire.

Suggested Client Types. Doctors and psychologists (for medical reports, psychological and custody evaluations, etc.); companies (that wish transcripts made of VCR tapes: transfer to audiocassette tapes first); and town and city commissions (to provide transcripts of meetings and hearings).

Suggested Ways of Attracting These Clients. Most of these prospective clients will find *you*—usually in the Yellow Pages. (Be certain to include the word "transcription" in your ad.) But, by closely watching the employment classifieds *on a regular basis*, you can ensure immediate responses to those companies and practices seeking help. Use an introductory cover letter (as shown in the earlier sample).

Recording Secretarial Background

If your secretarial background includes experience with providing meeting minutes, this is a very profitable business to offer (*if* you enjoy providing this type of service and *if* you enjoy having "evenings out" on a fairly regular basis; for those with young children, you must be able to arrange for child care in your home evenings while you attend meetings—for example, "Dad's time with the kids"). Plus, if this is a service area you think you'd like, you'll probably find that you will especially enjoy the chance to leave your home office on a regular basis—while getting paid and "being professional." For any home-based business owner, it's imperative to "get your nose out of your office" on a frequent basis and talk with other people. Isolation is important to guard against.

Suggested Client Types. Condominium associations (for meeting minutes; usually requires attending a meeting one evening per month to take minutes and then providing typewritten minutes within a week); town and city commissions (again, for meeting minutes; many of these groups meet twice monthly, and most are happy to tape meetings for you when you're not able to attend; you simply "transcribe" the tapes [not verbatim] to create minutes); board of education meetings; and company annual meetings. (This, however, would require your availability during daytime business hours, which means time away from developing your own business, answering the telephone directly, etc.—there are always trade-offs in any business!)

Suggested Ways of Attracting These Clients. Contact property management companies and/or realtors in your area for a listing of contacts at local condominium associations. Check with your own town as well as neighboring towns; the town/city clerk's office is probably the best source of leads for opportunities with any local commissions or boards. Check with the central offices of any school districts in which you might have an interest to determine schedules of meetings for the boards of education. Think of every "job" you accept in this area as a method of networking. You will probably find that the hourly rates offered are not comparable with your own rates and are perhaps even laughable. If you become affiliated with a medical/psychological practice, for example, handling the work of a group of professionals, your opportunity for networking is multiplied. Likewise, if you become a recording secretary for a professional group or commission in or near your community, each member of that group represents a networking opportunity *and* is a potential client. In addition to all of these "future prospect possibilities," you greatly enhance your visibility within any community for which you provide support to a community-based commission or board. Your mailing list of prospective clients increases and will inevitably produce business for other aspects of your service that are likely to be more profitable than simply generating minutes.

I have provided minutes preparation services (attending meetings, then generating minutes) for a number of years for two condominium associations and my town's board of education and planning and zoning commission. (I have since been elected as a full commissioner to the planning and zoning commission, but continue to provide meeting minutes [for pay].) For the condominiums I set rates that are commensurate with my hourly fees for creative/editorial services but are substantially discounted because of the informal continuity of the service contract. For any governmental or school work, however, you can expect to be offered significantly less than your typical hourly fees. (In most cities and towns, budgets are set that provide a specified rate for services of this type, and, unfortunately, the value is significantly underestimated, in my opinion.) Nonetheless, I personally love participating in activities within the community and being informed as to what is going on in my own town, and I enjoy the visibility. In addition, these relationships have cultivated many spin-off assignments—from project management to complete resume package development for a number of members, to interesting transcription work (memoirs), to complete newsletter and brochure development. All of these adjunct services are booked individually by various commission and board members and are priced using my regular fee schedule.

Legal Secretarial Background

If you have a legal secretarial background, seek out attorneys and planning agencies for their overflow work. Also consider becoming a notary public and offering this as an adjunct service (useful regardless of your specialty). Advertise notary services as "no charge." This builds goodwill and opens the door to other business. It's easy to pass the simple examination. The fee varies from state to state but is usually $40–$100 for a four-year term. The cost of a stamp and seal is generally $30 or so. You can obtain information from your local governmental office (town or city clerk) or your secretary of state's office.

Suggested Client Types. Attorneys, legal assistants, and governmental agencies form the likely candidate pool.

Suggested Ways of Attracting These Clients. Direct mail pieces, with regularly planned follow-up correspondence (your company newsletter is perfect) to a prospective client database you develop after consulting the Yellow Pages, are ideal.

Human Resources/Editorial Background

If you have strong interpersonal and editorial skills, and particularly if your background includes human resources/interviewing experience, a resume service is a very lucrative and challenging business for which there is an especially great demand (and if this field interests you, I strongly recommend reading a separate book I have written on this topic, *How to Start a Home-based Resume Service* [Globe Pequot Press, 1997]). A listing in your Yellow Pages is a prerequisite here because, besides referrals, that will be primarily your sole source of new business in this area.

Suggested Client Types. From about-to-graduate students to white-, blue-, and gray-collar professionals and workers, to teachers, physicians, business owners, and day care providers, nearly every person from age eighteen to eighty is a potential candidate for a professionally developed resume or CV (curriculum vitae). My oldest client to date for a resume was 74; my oldest secretarial service client was 93. Even people who are not in the job market benefit from having a well-prepared resume. (Those starting up a business will need one for their business plan; civic leaders and those who volunteer in the community will need one, particularly if they are seeking elected office on a local commission or committee; company owners and individual contributors who wish to be public speakers will need one—the list goes on and on.)

Suggested Ways of Attracting These Clients. Beyond your all-important Yellow Pages advertising in *both* Typing Service and Resume Service categories, be certain to encourage referrals through coupon offers to your current resume clients. Include a "dollars-off" coupon in the folder of their completed work, offering them a future discount for every referral that turns into closed business for you.

If you possess expertise and interest in this area, plus are a skilled public speaker, offer to give a lecture or miniworkshop on writing and updating resumes and cover letters in your community. Adult education programs, public libraries, and the like are always looking for good speakers on this timely topic. (I've picked up some nice visibility, while earning a stipend, by teaching in an adult ed program; information about my fully packaged program can be found in the Appendix, "Resume/Personal Marketing Workshop Kit.") You typically will earn a small fee through adult ed programs, plus enough to cover any expenses incurred (e.g., for copying costs of handout materials). Most libraries will offer you publicity in exchange for the time you provide at no charge. These are great ways to gain visibility for your expertise and service in these areas. Be certain to include a description of your services in any handouts you prepare, and offer a discount to any participant in these programs who books a consultation with you.

Basic requirements for success in the resume service business include your ease in meeting with many clients of diverse backgrounds and your ability to *quickly* ascertain salient points through face-to-face consultations and then concisely and relatively quickly assemble a well-written resume that is distinctive, professional, and attractively formatted.

Also important is the ability to offer appointments to meet the needs of clients who may be unavailable during business hours. If you can offer one or two evenings of appointments each week, plus perhaps Saturday mornings, this is a *big* competitive plus—and is something you should mention in your advertising. Not so incidentally, this happens to be a perfect profit center to specialize in at the onset of your business start-up if you are planning to continue a position on a part- or full-time basis during daytime business hours while grooming your own business at night. If offering evening and weekend appointments is not compatible with your own personal or family goals, however, you might opt not to enter this field. Most clients of this service will expect you to be available on a fairly regular basis at other than traditional business hours. If you do make a commitment to this profit center and hone your interviewing and writing skills, you'll find it's probably the single most profitable word processing type of service there is, with built-in residual business, since after having a resume prepared, almost everyone needs professional cover letters, follow-up letters, and, ultimately, updates to their resume.

I have offered resume services from day one, and at last count I have written and/or typeset more than 8,000 resumes. And while I haven't counted, I've written probably twice that many unique cover letters. I particularly enjoy this aspect of a secretarial services business because of the diversity of clients I meet, the rewarding feeling of providing a highly valuable service to clients very much in need, and the bottom-line profitability of this profit center.

Refer to the scripts related to promoting and selling resume services included in the Booking Business section of chapter 4. The following information details the techniques I've developed and use to conduct successful resume consultations. This is intended to provide a brief overview of the manner in which a resume consultation can be conducted by a secretarial service operator with expertise and interest in this field. It is by no means comprehensive or all-inclusive; again, my book, *How to Start a Home-based Resume Service,* focuses exclusively on this profit center. In addition, sample resumes will not be included, because there are literally thousands of professional formats and styles that can be used. Specific examples will be shown, and I'll try to share the key areas to cover for those secretarial service owners possessing the experience to appropriately deliver this profitable service offering.

Conducting a Successful Resume Consultation

- Have resume materials assembled in the area where the consultation will be conducted—blank tablets,* several pens, Client Work Order (partially filled in with information gleaned when the appointment was scheduled), appointment book (for scheduling a return visit to approve the resume proof), and any articles or handouts you may have prepared for resume clients. (Always

---

* Besides handwriting your notes, there are two other options for conducting a resume consultation. Some service providers will tape-record the entire consultation and either transcribe or listen to the tape later, when actually writing the resume. I recommend against this practice, for two reasons: First, you will expend at least as much time as, if not more than, you did in the initial consultation getting to the same point you could have had you taken concise handwritten notes in the beginning. This will greatly reduce your efficiency (and profitability). Second, I do believe most clients will respond more confidently, naturally, and comfortably if you do *not* tape-record their responses. You'll elicit better material to use in writing the resume.

The other option you may wish to experiment with is doing the consultation intake at your computer (either desktop or notebook). I have tried both methods. Before purchasing my Mac Powerbook, I would bring one of my client chairs right beside mine at my large desktop computer and type in the responses while the client talked. *I* wasn't comfortable doing this, because the client could see everything I was typing in—a lot of

give full credit to the writer or publisher of each article and also include a line like "Provided courtesy of Busy Secretarial Services.")

- I conduct client consultations at a conference table (sitting, again, at right angles to each other). I also have a large wraparound sofa in my office, but I've attempted conducting consultations using the sofa and find it's not as easy for me to take notes and doesn't feel as comfortable/professional. Once again, you have to find the location that's most workable and natural for you and your clients. In recent years, partly as a result of widespread use of the Internet's minimizing of "global barriers" and as a consequence of my now guesting frequently as a resume/career expert on radio programs nationwide, more and more of my clients are *not* from Connecticut; therefore, most of my consultations are via telephone as opposed to in-person in my office. I have found that while I still love direct people contact, I'm enjoying the flexibility of doing business totally over the telephone, have become very skilled in my listening ability (even more important when you can't read body language), and admit to liking days when no one is scheduled for an in-person visit (I can wear my most comfortable clothes and don't need to harass my kids to pick up their things in the office!).

- Back to in-person consultations . . . when a client arrives, I offer coffee or ice water before we get started. Once settled, I pull out the Client Work Order and review proper spelling of the client's name; use of a middle initial, *Jr., III*, or any other designation; address (permanent and school, for students); and telephone number. (Most clients wish to list only their home telephone number.)

- Then I launch into easily paced questions designed to elicit the relevant information I need to write the resume while at the same time allowing the client to become confident and comfortable in responding. I have not used a questionnaire for the past fourteen years, but I did use a simple form when I first started. A sample questionnaire follows this section and includes basic information you may want to use if you feel most comfortable starting out

---

what a client will discuss, while important to my overall understanding of a client's background, is superfluous when it comes to writing the resume—yet if the client saw me *not* typing in something, he or she sometimes became uncomfortable or possibly intimidated. ("Why isn't that considered important? It must not be . . .")

When I purchased a Powerbook, I could at least position it at an angle when working with a client at my conference table. (I never sit immediately opposite a client; instead, we sit at right angles to each other.) I found, however, that the Powerbook still created a barrier I was not comfortable with and simply found it more user-friendly to take notes on paper (a mix of shorthand and abbreviated English). At the time of writing the resume, I did not find it quickened the process to have five or six partial pages of double-spaced notes already in the system; I start with a blank page to create each new resume anyway. Certainly try various options to determine which method you like best.

with this. I recommend against asking clients to fill out the questionnaire; instead, use it as a tool to guide your questions and to ensure not overlooking any key areas.

- The main components of what is the most popular form of a resume (chronological) are name/address section, summary of qualifications (also called skills summary, key accomplishments, or, simply, summary [highly recommended in today's resumes to detail key strengths and core competencies]), professional experience, internships, licensure, educational background, military background, professional interests, special skills, recognition/awards, civic/community organizations, publications, speaking engagements, and mention of professional references (always an addendum, if used). Not all of these components will be on every resume, of course.

  Not included on a resume: Any personal information—marital status, number and/or ages of children (except possibly for a woman reentering the job market after a long absence raising a family), religious denomination, personal hobbies and interests (unless possibly indicative of perseverance, determination, and drive, as with a marathon competitor), height, weight, age, birthdate, Social Security number, or salary (current or anticipated). Considered dated today, an objective is better articulated in a cover letter than noted on the resume.

- The first area of questioning centers on the purpose for developing the resume. This is important because it's not always obvious. This knowledge allows for asking relevant questions and delving in appropriate depth into those areas of the client's background most related to the purpose of developing this resume.

  Sometimes a client will be updating the resume for internal use within his or her own company, possibly for promotion purposes. This type of resume has an entirely different slant and level of detail than one used externally from the company.

  Occasionally, a resume or CV will be developed for professional purposes, ranging in use from speaking engagements to membership in a professional association and from providing biographical information for a publication to submitting the resume to an alumni magazine.

  Clients will periodically want to have a resume written simply to have a professional documentation of their accomplishments and career background without any other planned purpose *at this time* (somewhat rare, as most resume clients need their resume "yesterday" to respond to an immediate opportunity).

Clients will also seek preparation of a resume to accompany a business plan, a law school application, or a myriad of other professional interests.

Finally, the majority of resume clients *will* be obtaining a resume in order to pursue employment for any one of the following reasons: They may be seeking a change in company, profession, or field; they may or may not be currently employed; they may be new graduates and never employed in their intended field; they may be newly discharged from one of the armed services; they may be newly laid off or newly released from an incarceration facility; they may have opted for a "golden handshake" agreement with a large corporation that's undergoing "right-sizing"; or they may be returning to the work force after a lengthy absence (childrearing typically being the most common reason for this).

- The order in which I prefer to ask questions, after establishing the purpose for writing the resume, is professional experience first (beginning with the most current or recent employment and working backward), then education. For new graduates we discuss educational background first, then employment.

Under the category of professional experience, I ask the name of each company and the town/state in which the firm was located. (Do not include street address, zip code, or telephone number; *do* advise clients to maintain this information in their permanent files somewhere, though, because it is frequently requested on job applications.) I obtain the title of each position held and the timeframe for each position. Depending on the individual's overall background, sometimes just the year is adequate (1993–Present); in other instances it's necessary to provide the month and year (either a format such as Apr. 1993–Mar. 1996 or 4/93–3/96, depending on the overall layout of the resume).

If the client has held more than one position with any company, the total period of employment with the company is noted next to the company name (formats vary), with the actual timing of each position noted in parentheses after each title. Example:

1985–Present   ABCD Corporation · Anytown, USA
Chief Financial Officer (1995–Present, Promotion)
[description of accomplishments, key responsibilities—
eight to twelve lines or so]

Controller (1991–95, Promotion)
[description of accomplishments, key responsibilities—
six to ten lines or so]

Staff Accountant (1985–91)
[description of accomplishments, key responsibilities—
no more than four to eight lines)

As the timeline goes backward, increasingly *less* space should be devoted to each position.

For students it is most likely that their "professional background" is really not (i.e., professional), and this section should be captioned "employment experience" or just "experience." For students and those clients possessing master's or doctorate degrees, educational background should be listed *before* professional background or employment experience. For almost all other clients, professional experience would precede educational background.

Concerning education, mention the most recent/advanced degree first, followed in decreasing order by other degrees held. As the person preparing the resume, you are not responsible for verifying the authenticity of any information provided by the client (hence the reason for a service waiver block on the Client Work Order form). If, however, the client asks your professional advice, I recommend responding that it is of utmost importance to be absolutely honest and accurate in providing information for the resume. Education is an area that will frequently come up in discussion with clients, typically those without any formal education beyond high school. It is perfectly fine to list a college attended (provided a degree is not mentioned) *or* to mention "pursuing studies toward a degree in business administration" (again, if this were in fact true). Occasionally, I will work with clients who have completed extensive training through various corporate workshops and the like—this is certainly appropriate for inclusion (if very lengthy, as an addendum to the resume). Generally, class standing and GPA (grade point average) are not included unless the resume is for a recent graduate or the ranking/number is significant. Mention of honors status (cum laude, magna cum laude, or summa cum laude graduate) should be included, as would status as the class valedictorian or salutatorian.

High school is mentioned only in the case of recent college graduates who have minimal work or internship experience. This information is dropped as soon as there is valid professional information to replace it.

For recent graduates extracurricular activities/athletics (collegiate and possibly high school) are listed. The list does not need to be all-inclusive, depending on space available; however, it should be representative as to breadth of interest and reflect election to any positions of leadership.

- Military experience should be mentioned briefly, unless you are working with someone with a full military career; if so, then expand this background, handling it exactly like professional experience.

- The breadth and depth of community and civic background varies extensively among clients. Typically, mention is made of any organizations to which a client has belonged or does belong. Also included would be any elected positions held and the years of membership in an organization. For individuals possessing extensive civic experience and minimal professional experience, accomplishments and highlights can be expanded in this section of the resume.

- Licensure, be it licensing in health care, special equipment operation, or real estate, would be briefly mentioned in one or two lines in this section.

- Professional association memberships are also listed, with usually one line devoted per entry, along with mention of election to any positions of leadership.

- Briefly mention any relevant awards, recognition, and honors received in this section of the resume.

- Special skills can include computer skills (particularly specific hardware/software familiarity and expertise), additional training in a particular field, foreign language fluency (written and oral), extraordinary typing speed, and so on.

- With regard to references *if* space allows, it is permissible to state at the very end of a resume "Professional references provided upon request" *or* "Excellent references available upon request." This is optional and space-dependent. I always provide a typed version of a client's references at no charge when they have been presented to me at the time of a full resume consultation. I match the format established for the name and address/telephone information at the top of the resume, repeating it at the top of the reference page, then list no fewer than three and generally no more than seven references (with no more than two "character" references). The name of each person is listed, followed by professional title, place of employment, address (home or office), and telephone number (indicating whether it is home or office). Clients should be advised that the reference sheet is typically not mailed directly with the resume, unless so requested. It is usually provided during the course of an interview.

- Discussion of a summary of qualifications is intentionally left until last. Once a full resume consultation is nearly complete, I'm in a good position to assess a client's strengths and accomplishments and can determine if the use of a

RESUME QUESTIONNAIRE

Date _____

Client Name _____

Address _____

City _____ State _____ Zip Code _____

E-mail Address _____

Telephone Number to Use on Resume _____
(also note business and fax telephone numbers)

Professional Experience

Place of Employment _____

Town/State _____

TOTAL Time with This Company (in Months/Years) _____

Title of Most Recent/Current Position _____

Timeframe in This Position _____

Key Responsibilities/Accomplishments _____

_____

_____

_____

_____

_____

_____

_____

_____

_____

_____

[Areas to address: number of direct/indirect reports; human resources responsibilities (recruiting? interviewing? hiring? training? supervising? managing? developing? terminating? assessing of performance? preparing/administering salary plans?); any programs developed/implemented; for sales professionals—performance to quota and time period, results, increase by X percentage, any cost savings or productivity gains (in $'s/%'s), etc.]

Place of Employment _____

Town/State _____

TOTAL Time with This Company (in Months/Years) _____

Title of Position _____

Timeframe in This Position _____

Key Responsibilities / Accomplishments _____

_____

_____

_____

_____

_____

_____

Place of Employment _____

Town/State _____

TOTAL Time with This Company (in Months/Years) _____

Title of Position _____

Timeframe in This Position _____

Key Responsibilities / Accomplishments _____

_____

_____

_____

_____

_____

_____

[Copy above 8–10 times.]

Education
[For recent graduate, GPA (if above 3.0) or ranking in class (if in the top 25% or better)]

College/University _____

Town/State _____

Degree Held _____ Year Earned _____

Major _____ Minor _____

College/University _____

Town/State _____

Degree Held _____ Year Earned _____

Major _____ Minor _____

College/University _____

Town/State _____

Degree Held _____ Year Earned _____

Major _____ Minor _____

Licenses Held

Type _____ Year _____

Type _____ Year _____

Type _____ Year _____

Type _____ Year _____

Type _____ Year _____

Internships

Institution/Company _____

Town/State _____

Position Title _____ Months/Years _____

Highlights _____

Institution/Company _____

Town/State _____

Position Title _____ Months/Years _____

Highlights _____

Institution/Company _____

Town/State _____

Position Title _____ Months/Years _____

Highlights _____

Institution/Company _____

Town/State _____

Position Title _____ Months/Years _____

Highlights _____

Military Background

Branch of Service _____

Locations (if Relevant) _____

Position/Rank Achieved _____

Years of Service _____

Honorable Discharge? _____

Key Accomplishments/Special Recognition/Awards_____

_____

_____

_____

_____

_____

_____

Special Skills

Computer? Hardware/Software _____

_____

_____

_____

Language? Fluency Oral/Written _____

_____

_____

Civic/Community Memberships

Organization Name: Years Involved: Positions Held:

_____

_____

_____

_____

_____

Professional Memberships

Organization Name: Years Involved: Positions Held:

_____

_____

_____

_____

_____

_____

Recognition/Awards

_____

_____

_____

_____

Publications

Article Title: Name of Publication Appearing In: Coauthor?   Year:

_____

_____

_____

_____

Speaking Engagements

Topic/Speech Title: Name of   Keynote   Year:
                             Organization Addressed: Speaker?

_____

_____

_____

_____

Ideas around Objective Statement (if used; recommend against this _unless_ client will not be using cover letter)

(Professional/Career Goals)

_____

_____

_____

_____

_____

Ideas around Summary of Qualifications (highly recommended for placement on resume *before* "Professional Experience" section)

(Characteristics, Traits, Attributes, Key Accomplishments)

_____

_____

_____

_____

_____

_____

References

Name _____

Title _____

Company_____

Address _____

City/State/Zip Code _____

Home Telephone _____ Office Telephone _____

Name _____

Title _____

Company_____

Address _____

City/State/Zip Code _____

Home Telephone _____ Office Telephone _____

[Copy above 8–10 times.]

[*Note:* Even if you are using a questionnaire form, you should always have a blank tablet available for recording additional information at the time of the consultation.]

summary of qualifications would be beneficial for a particular client; at that time, I make the appropriate recommendation; again, for most resumes, a qualifications summary is essential and recommended. This may not necessarily be the case, and if inappropriate, I, of course, do not mention it. Generally, an objective statement is used only for clients opting not to use customized, individual cover letters in a conventional job search. I usually advise against generic objective statements as they are typically so watered down as to be nothing more than a waste of valuable space. ("A challenging position utilizing my background and experience that will provide opportunity for growth based on demonstrated performance," etc. is all too commonly used.)

A caveat, however—and this relates to all aspects of being in the secretarial services business—*the customer is always right*. I will occasionally work with a client who wants things a certain way—if he or she is amenable, I will discuss professional recommendations. But I always allow the client to make the final decision, and this doesn't always match my suggestion. That's what this business is all about. More often than not, though, clients appreciate your professional opinion. Particularly in the area of career development and resumes, if you are an expert in the field, your recommendations will be appreciated.

With regard to the length of a resume, as a *general* rule (and there are too many variables to list here), resumes should never exceed two pages. For new college graduates and those with less than five to eight years of professional experience, a resume should not exceed one page. Although there is a perception that for anyone a one-page resume is *preferred*, an exception exists when a client's professional background numbers fifteen or more years, is with three or more firms, and/or reflects extensive community/civic or military experience, coupled with solid accomplishments and qualifications. A two-page format is perfectly appropriate and specifically indicated in such cases. For clients with extensive professional speaking experience and/or publications to their credit, this information can be developed on pages that form an addendum to the resume.

At the conclusion of a resume consultation (for a full consultation, this can be anywhere from forty-five minutes for a new college graduate to about two hours for an experienced professional with a significant background spanning a number of years), clients should be asked if there is any additional information they would care to provide. The follow-up appointment should then be scheduled and the client informed that at the time of the follow-up appointment, a draft of the resume, which will resemble the final product, will be presented. The client should also be made aware that any changes and revisions to the resume will be made during the follow-up appointment, and final printing of original resumes will be handled then as well. A deposit should be collected at the conclusion of the consultation, and the client should be advised of the approximate balance due (or an exact amount, if the client contracted for a package price). Finally, thank the client for the opportunity to work with him or her and encourage the person to feel free to contact you over the next day or two if he or she recalls any other relevant information that should be included.

PRODUCT MIX

Unlimited combinations of product offerings can constitute the successful desktop publishing, word processing, and/or secretarial service. Initially, you'll probably find yourself saying yes to nearly every request in order to begin to build your business. As time evolves, you may find that you enjoy certain areas of the business more than others or that specific products and service offerings are more profitable than others. These "revelations" will help you to determine the future direction of your business.

Some secretarial services specialize in only one or two service offerings and find that these are quite profitable and that they are satisfied with their business growth. I consider myself a generalist with expertise in a lot of different areas; I like the diversity that comes with working with various types of clients, ranging from corporations, small companies, and health care professionals to individual business owners and students. I also love the flexibility of having a broad spectrum of project types to choose from every time I sit down at my desk to work. If I don't feel particularly inspired and creative, I can put aside newsletter development for one client and instead handle a routine database development project or mail-merge a few hundred letters for another client. If my creative juices are really flowing, I can do back-to-back writing—a resume for a client, an article for my own company's newsletter, a marketing letter in response to a prospect call I received yesterday, minutes from a meeting I attended a few nights ago, a preliminary brochure design for a new client, or maybe a story to submit for possible publication in a magazine. If I have an especially high energy level and it's during a period of time when there's a low volume of telephone interruptions (11:00 P.M. or 5:30 A.M. are particularly good times for this!), I'll tackle transcription of a meeting in which there are many unidentified speakers and lots of background noise . . . or transcription from a doctor using extensive technical terminology. Were I to specialize in transcription *only,* however, I can safely say that there are days and times of the day when I would not feel inspired to tackle that kind of work, especially day after day after day.

Each secretarial service owner must establish the prototype of his or her own business service offerings. This will be dictated by market niche and need, interest, expertise, and price. Why price? Let's move into the next section, Establishing a Price Structure.

ESTABLISHING A PRICE STRUCTURE

How you price certain offerings will in large part determine how much of a particular type of work you want to handle. Let's use the transcription example again. In my own case, while I handle transcription occasionally for some of my clients for whom I provide lots of *other* services, I don't actively seek just transcription work alone with any given client. I don't price that particular product with any special discounts or promotional offers, as it's not in the area of creative editorial work that I vastly prefer. A service offering transcription services exclusively would probably offer all three varieties (standard, mini- and microcassette; I don't offer mini, just standard and micro); pricing would probably be very competitive (e.g., transcription in the medical world is usually priced by the line, the word, or the character, although there is an industry move to change this). My pricing for transcription follows the same method I use for any other word processing service—an hourly charge based on the actual time expended.

There are no hard-and-fast rules for establishing specific pricing, but there are some general guidelines to consider. First and foremost, *fairly* and *reasonably* price your services so that *you* make a profit. Many home-based businesspeople underprice themselves; while it's true that your overhead is significantly less than that of people with an office suite or center-of-town business office location, you will most likely be providing additional conveniences to your clients (via early A.M. or late P.M. drop-off and pick-up privileges, weekend appointments, etc.). Most important is that you want to be able to make a good salary, for you will undoubtedly be working harder (and enjoying it more) than you ever have before. Finally, you need to ensure a reasonable profit for yourself so that you can *stay* in business.

Refer to your initial analysis of your competition and develop a matrix of various service offerings you plan to provide. A good rule of thumb in starting out is (1) not to charge the lowest prices (unless you're really going after volume and plan to advertise that fact heavily—something most home-based entrepreneurs aren't in a position to do immediately, particularly if they're mothers with small children) and (2) not to have the highest prices (unless you're in a specialty niche area with no competition).

If you strike a balance between what's already being charged across your market area, you should have a good starting point. With regard to an hourly rate for word processing services, for example (probably the biggest profit center starting out), you should try to obtain pricing from at least ten competitors across your

Word Processing Services

Competitor	Location	Office/Home	Hourly Rate
ABC Word Processing	Middletown	Office	$ 32
Creative Services	Middlefield	Home	$ 22
Davis Secretarial	Middletown	Home	$ 26
Excellent Office Support	Middleville	Office	$ 36
Fisher's Secretarial Services	Middlefield	Home	$ 18
Home Office Services Plus	Middletown	Home	$ 28
Middletown Office Services	Middletown	Office	$ 34
Middleville Secretarial	Middleville	Home	$ 30
Taylor Editorial/Secretarial	Middlefield	Home	$ 28
WordPro Services	Middletown	Office	$ 26
	TOTAL:		$280

divided by 10 services = $28 average hourly rate among competitors in market area

Worksheets should be prepared in each product category you plan to offer (e.g., resume services, transcription, editorial services) for which you will have different hourly rates. These are purely hypothetical rates; my own hourly rate for word processing is $48.

COMPETITIVE PRICING INDEX WORKSHEET

Profit Center* _____

Competitor	Location	Office/Home	Hourly Rate

TOTAL: $_____

divided by _____ (# of services)

= $_____ average hourly rate

among competitors in market area

* Develop a worksheet for each profit center for which you will offer a different hourly rate (e.g., word processing/secretarial, resume services, transcription).

geographic area (including both home-based and office- or suite-based, if known/suspected). Total these ten hourly rates and divide by ten to obtain the average. This is a good double check that the amount you're planning to charge on an hourly basis won't cause sticker-shock or be too underpriced for your market.

Depending on your area of the country, you'll find there are different ways of charging for your services. The two most common methods are by the hour (utilizing tenth-of-an-hour increments) and by the page (usually based on double-spaced text). With the exception of certain flat fees (e.g., resumes—a flat dollar amount for a one-page typed resume and an uplift for the second page, not counting editorial or consultation time), charging on the basis of time is probably the fairest and most equitable manner of pricing for both you and your clients. It makes allowances for quality of input as well as complexity of project. One client's "basic document to be word-processed" could be significantly more involved (complicated tables requiring you to perform calculations) and difficult to read (smudged, very light pencil-written pages on both sides) than another client's.

You can count on being asked to provide an estimate over the telephone during initial client inquiries. You probably won't encourage business by choosing not to respond to these questions. By quoting estimates on the telephone ("I charge $XX per hour in tenth-of-an-hour increments; I can typically produce seven to nine double-spaced, proofread pages per hour, averaging $XX per page"), you can give a prospective client an *idea* of a per-page rate for comparison shopping. Always reiterate that the charge is calculated on the basis of the actual time to handle the work and that you can provide a more accurate estimate once you have inspected the incoming work. It's also good to mention your typing speed (providing it is fast, more than 80 or so words per minute), but mention, too, that the quality of incoming documents and materials varies considerably. Always stress, "I can work with any materials, however."

When determining your rates, you need to factor in hidden costs, such as electricity and heat, a portion of your mortgage or rent for space in your home, and your costs for equipment, software, supplies and advertising, *plus* your time, experience, and expertise! There are some good industry standards available through the ABSSI that are useful for establishing pricing, estimating, and factoring in your speed, skill level, and years of experience (see Appendix). Nothing, however, is better than your time and experience in this business for analyzing and assessing your rates, providing quotations, and understanding what works best for you.

Nina Feldman (see information about her publications in the Appendix) states that "using *Industry Production Standards* may allow you to bill 'in complete fairness to your client' for more than your actual time (rather than penalize yourself for efficiency). If you charge $30 an hour and each day you give away five minutes of each hour you bill, you've lost $3,000 per year; at $20 per hour, you've missed out on an extra $2,000!

"Don't assume you have to 'shave off time' even if you're doing something you've never done before. For instance, if you have a word processing service, you might find that in using an advanced feature of a program that is new to you (such as tables, columns, shaded boxes, etc.) you slow down. You may be tempted to refrain from charging your customers for your time, thinking that if they went to someone else, they wouldn't have to pay for that learning time. But if you've been in business as long as I have and have talked to as many other people in the same field, you'll probably find that because things in the computer field change so fast, chances are most other word processors don't know the program any better than you do, perhaps not as well! Use your own judgment, but be fair to yourself. If the technology is new, or you're one of the few folks in town who has it and your client is reaping the benefits of your special new service, he or she should expect to pay for that advantage.

"Another problem is charging too low an hourly rate. As someone who talks to more than five hundred people a year who are new to the self-employed word processing/desktop publishing world, I find that the tendency to underestimate charges is one of the main reasons people go out of business and have to return to the full-time working world. One of the biggest misconceptions is that, 'If I don't have the lowest rates around, people will go elsewhere.' To the contrary, I found that once I raised my rates, I added credibility to myself as a professional.

"The easy accessibility of computers has made for more competition for those of us who work in the computer trade. Everybody and her cousin wants to offer services on a computer! A tip: When calling around to compare prices among those in your field, call people who are in the Yellow Pages rather than those listing small classifieds. The latter are often just trying to make money on the side—they may have another source of income or they may be students or beginners. There are few reasons you should charge any less than someone who rents an office simply because you work from home, if you are providing the same services and level of professionalism. After all, you pay for your office space, too, even if it is just by losing that amount of household space. When you set your rates too low, you often end up with the people who haggle over every nickel, and those are often the most difficult to work with. The question is: Will the work you generate from these customers pay to cover your doctor bills while you try and cure your ulcer?

"Be sure that your hourly rates also incorporate cost-of-living increases, on top of all other costs of doing business. The Consumer Price Index has gone up over 50 percent since I went into business in 1981, meaning that the $15 an hour I charged as a beginner translates to close to $27 an hour now, without even raising rates to reflect increased experience and efficiency. To cover those, I charge $35 an hour. If you don't add all expenses and costs of doing business into your hourly wage (expenses and unpaid time often add up to 50–75 percent of your total billing rate), you will be making significantly less than someone working in an employer's office. Do you want your own (or your family's) earnings to subsidize your clients' expenses? When clients try to get you to compromise on your rates, that's essentially what they're asking! Remember, the buck stops with you, so cover your costs, or you may have to go back to calling someone else 'boss!' " *(Author's note: Nina Feldman publishes a resource package as well as conducts consultations by telephone based on her extensive business experience [for a fee]; see the Appendix for additional information.)*

The following exercise helps outline all the variables you should consider in determining the correct minimum rate you should charge. Keep in mind, too, that you, as the business owner, are not necessarily locking in to any of these rates (unless you sign a contract or promise a client a given rate for a fixed period of time). You are free to raise (or lower!) them at any time, as well as offer discounts and promotions whenever you choose. Remember, though, that raising your rates is something that should be approached with caution and awareness of timing. Obviously, you won't build a lot of client goodwill if your rates are going up every other month. It makes sense not to raise your rates any more frequently than once a year. During times of economic recession, service providers in many industries wait even longer than the typical year to "raise rates." You can advertise this fact if you choose to hold your rates flat over a period of a few years. This may not necessarily be in your best financial interest; you will need to continually invest resources in your growing business, and one way to do so is to increase profitability—most easily accomplished by a reasonable increase in rates at reasonable intervals of time.

Pricing Exercise

To arrive at the appropriate rate to charge, you must consider three basic variables: your expenses, your available time/billable hours, and your desired profit.

Expenses

First, assess all of your expenses. Fill in the actual or approximate *annualized* numbers for each category on the sample expense sheet. (A key follows, providing more detailed instructions for all footnoted items.) You will obviously need to estimate some of these numbers.

Billable Hours

After reaching an annual estimate for expenses for your business, you can then consider the amount of hours you intend or would like to work each year (and, from this, the amount of that time you can reasonably "sell"). If you plan to work forty hours a week and have three weeks of vacation per year, you would be projecting a maximum of 1,960 hours available. The amount of time you could actually expect to be compensated for, however, is considerably less than this amount. Why? Most business experts state that organized, productive entrepreneurs are doing well to be billing 60 percent of their total working time. (In other words, of the 1,960 hours available, 1,176 of them could be considered "billable.")

What this essentially means is that in any given forty-hour work week, you will realistically be spending about 40 percent of your time doing nonbillable work. Every time you answer the phone, the "clock stops ticking" on a project you may have been working on but had to interrupt to answer the telephone. You may spend ten or fifteen minutes on this telephone call responding to a prospective client's inquiries about your services, scheduling an appointment, and providing directions. That is "overhead" time that cannot be charged back to any one client; however, this type of downtime must be accounted for in your overall rates.

When you make your daily or weekly trip to the post office for replenishing supplies, to the bank for making deposits, to a client site for picking up or delivering work (providing you're not charging separately for this time), or to the office supply store for purchasing office supplies, you are expending time related to your business that cannot be billed to a client. Using a round number of $20 an hour, for example, you can quickly see that to cover your 40 percent downtime that's nonbillable, you really will be making only $12 an hour (and this doesn't take into account all of your other expenses).

For purposes of this formula, I'll use the aforementioned example a little bit later and then revise it several different ways to illustrate what can happen with just a few minor adjustments.

Profit

While many entrepreneurs in this field are happy with whatever is left over after paying all their expenses, it is smart planning to forecast, price for, and anticipate a reasonable profit. This amount could be a sum you decide to allocate to an individual retirement account, for example, or place in some other nest egg. This number is over and above the amount you've established as your salary in the expense portion of the exercise. We'll use $5,000 for the example. The number you arrive at is contingent on many factors and is also reflective of your initial reasons and goals for establishing a business. For many people, being in business for themselves brings its own rewards that don't always carry a dollar value. This book has assumed throughout, however, that as much as you will love being successfully in business for yourself, a key objective is to make money.

Calculating the Formula

The simplest and most common business equation used to reach a minimum, breakeven point (and set a baseline hourly rate) employs the three components developed earlier in the example:

Expenses ($31,350) + Profit ($5,000) ÷ Billable Hours (1,176) = $30.91 per hour.

Using all of the factors in this equation as detailed in the example, this says that $30.91 is the *minimum* amount you can charge per hour and cover all of your expenses *and* your salary and profit objectives. There are some important factors to take into account when starting a business. It is unlikely that you will start off working full-time immediately and billing twenty-four hours out of every forty-hour workweek. Even in an established, five-year-old business, for example, there are swings on a week-to-week basis. It is also highly unusual (but not impossible) for a start-up business to *turn a profit* in its first year. In other words, while it is reasonable to hope to earn a salary (again, not that common in a start-up business) in your first year of doing business, it may not be possible to provide for a profit. In addition, during your first year of establishing a business, you will probably need to inject a substantial amount of money (quite typically your own funds) in purchasing equipment and software you may not already own (a bonus if you do) and investing in "extra" forms of advertising (covered earlier) while waiting for your Yellow Pages advertising to appear in a new directory. You will *save*, though, on your telephone bill because the charge for the Yellow Pages advertising will not appear until the month the new directory containing your ads is published. Tax obligations are less as well, if your earnings are less than estimated.

Now, let's have some fun playing with the variables to see what happens. If you decide that a goal of owning your own business is to work fewer hours than you might have in a more traditional setting but still earn the same compensation, let's cut back by 50 percent of the billable hours to see what happens.

Expenses ($31,350) + Profit ($5,000) ÷ Billable Hours (588) = $61.82 per hour.

Realistic? Probably not. But, you might determine that while you can't expect to earn the same amount in half the time, you *can* compromise with a cutback in projected profit to perhaps $2,500, a slight decrease in compensation to $17,000, and work thirty hours a week (thus billing 18 hours using the 60 percent calculation). Run the equation again. (Remember to adjust the tax line item as well.)

Expenses ($27,510) + Profit ($2,500) ÷ Billable Hours (882) = $34.02 per hour.

SAMPLE EXPENSE SHEET

Your salary[1]	$20,840.00
Utilities/house expenses[2]	300.00
Equipment[3]	1,000.00
Software[4]	300.00
Telephone/Yellow Pages advertising	1,800.00
Fax line (if separate)	-0-
Other advertising/marketing/newsletter costs	400.00
Professional subscription costs	100.00
Professional membership costs	150.00
Printing expenses	200.00
Office supplies and materials	800.00
Postage	300.00
Professional fees[5]	200.00
Self-employment taxes and federal and state taxes[6]	4,760.00
Shipping/overnight delivery	200.00
TOTAL ANTICIPATED ANNUAL COSTS	$31,350.00

SAMPLE EXPENSE SHEET

Your salary[1] $ _____

Utilities/house expenses[2] $ _____

Equipment[3] $ _____

Software[4] $ _____

Telephone/Yellow Pages advertising $ _____

Fax line (if separate) $ _____

Other advertising/marketing/newsletter costs $ _____

Professional subscription costs $ _____

Professional membership costs $ _____

Printing expenses $ _____

Office supplies and materials $ _____

Postage $ _____

Professional fees[5] $ _____

Self-employment taxes and federal and state taxes[6] $ _____

Shipping/overnight delivery $ _____

_____

TOTAL ANTICIPATED ANNUAL COSTS $ _____

[1] For a starting point, begin with the salary you'd *like* to earn. You can adjust that upward or downward later on in the exercise.

[2] Determine the percentage of space your office uses as compared with the total square footage of your home available. Let's assume your office comprises 10 percent of the total area. Calculate your electrical bill for the year and then use 10 percent as that portion which your business should pay. If your electrical bill for the year totals $1,000, the portion to be assumed by your business is $100 for the year. In this example, because of the equipment you will be using, the percentage used may actually be higher; as you track your electrical bills in the first year of business, you may want to adjust this percentage upward to cover the "real" amount (perhaps 20 percent or even 25 percent for this utility).

Then, if you heat by oil or gas, take 10 percent of your annual heating bill and add this to the equation. If your heating costs are $500 for the year for your entire home, then $50 is the amount to be charged to your business. Don't forget to include the same percentage of any ancillary household services and expenses, including snow plowing (if you live in a section of the country for which this is relevant), lawn maintenance, trash removal, household cleaning, homeowner's insurance (provided you don't have a separate business policy or rider to your homeowner's policy, in which case the entire amount for a business policy would be added in), security/alarm system, etc. When you take 10 percent of each of these items and add them all together, this number becomes the amount to include on this line item in the formula.

Note: Not all of these expenses are necessarily tax-deductible business expenses (always consult with a representative of the IRS [see Bibliography], or review with your accountant, if you have one); however, they can be considered, for purposes of your pricing formula, relevant to the overall cost of doing business.

[3] Use the depreciation tables of the IRS schedules to arrive at the appropriate number to use for this line item. (For most electronic/computer equipment, three years is probably the maximum amount of time recommended, even though you may keep a piece of equipment in service beyond that time.) You should always be planning for replacement costs. For instance, if you already own a computer, you may be tempted not to include an amount for this line item. This would be a mistake because in probably the next two to four years, you will want to replace your computer with a more up-to-date system—and even if you lack the desire or discipline to be saving in advance for that expenditure, your overall pricing should reflect a certain amount to be allocated to the replacement of equipment.

[4] You should allocate a certain amount of money for the purchase of new or updated software each year.

[5] Professional fees would be the services of an accountant and/or an attorney if you've decided to engage such assistance.

[6] As a general guideline, self-employment taxes will run about 13 percent, federal/state will vary, but anticipate another 10–20 percent. (Here is where an accounting professional specializing in small business can provide valuable assistance in your first year.)

Company Name _____

Address/Telephone _____

Please be advised that the following prices will become effective

January 1,* _____:

Word Processing Services—$XX hour

Desktop Publishing Services—$XX hour

Editorial/Consultation Services—$XX hour

Minimum Charge—.5 hour at prevailing service rate

*[Also mention any change in pricing for ancillary services: stationery,
copies, fax, notarizing, etc.]*

We appreciate your business and thank you for the opportunity to provide
professional services. [Include business slogan.]

* Keep in mind that rate increases do not necessarily have to be the first of the year.

A small, laser-printed postcard is an efficient way to communicate price changes to regular clients; for clients you haven't seen in three or more months, price change notification is probably not necessary (the next time they contact you for a quote on a project, you'll simply quote at the rates in place at that time).

That's probably more reasonable! Experiment with the equation to assess the impact of any decision. As a final step in the exercise, compare this information as you are calculating with the competitive information for your market that you ascertained earlier. If you find that the hourly minimum you've determined in this exercise falls somewhere along the line you established for your competitors, you can confirm your placement on the scale. If you find that your minimum is way below the scale, then move the number up (total "profit" at this point!) to be more reasonable. If you are significantly above the competitor who charges the most, you might consider reassessing why your numbers look so high: Is it because you are projecting spending too much in the first year on equipment? (Maybe consider leasing in the first year only.) Are you anticipating too high a profit for a first-year business start-up? Or is your strategy to be the most expensive and provide the best service . . . and will your advertising reflect this stance? There's nothing wrong with being the most expensive, provided that you are patient, willing to work harder at bringing in first-time clients, and have the necessary reserves to fund a probably slower start-up. There are hidden perceptions to pricing: For some, higher price means higher quality. If you pitch to that belief, you may find a successful niche. This is not recommended, however, as the way to get a business going successfully in the quickest way possible. Striking a median position along the scale for your marketplace (while at the same time ensuring that your minimum costs to break even are covered, still yielding you a fair salary and a reasonable profit) makes the most sense for starting out successfully.

The form on the previous page illustrates a professional way to simply announce future price increases to your client base. Never apologize for increasing your rates.

CREDIT

Credit, particularly for a new business, should be extended judiciously. For those clients seeking to have you carry them "on account," an application should be completed. (See following sample.) With individual clients, their word and your mutual agreement are probably sufficient.

You will typically find that most medical practices, large companies, and corporations will pay your invoices according to their internal accounts payable policies (usually thirty days, sometimes forty-five days). With smaller accounts, generally individual business owners who utilize your services on a regular basis, you should discuss whatever terms seem most appropriate. The majority that want billing "on account" will expect to be invoiced once per month and have terms of anywhere from ten to thirty days. Attempt to stagger the billing dates of these monthly accounts so that you have an even division between those you bill at the end of the month and those that you bill on the fifteenth of the month. Why? *Cash flow.* One of the most important factors of any viable business that succeeds is appropriate cash flow. If you find that the majority of your regular, ongoing business is made up of monthly accounts all billing at the end of the month (and all paying, e.g., at thirty days), you're going to experience cash shortages the first two or three weeks of each month. If you stagger your billing cycle (simply in half), those accounts billed on the fifteenth paying at thirty days will provide an injection of cash at the middle of every month and those accounts billed on the thirtieth paying at thirty days will give the cash boost at the end of every subsequent month.

For extremely regular accounts where you're providing in excess of ten or fifteen hours of service per week, week in and week out, you may want to consider

Creative Secretarial Services

P.O. Box 111 · Anytown, USA 55555

(333) 777–2222 · Fax (333) 777–6666

Credit Application

Client Name _____ Title _____

Company _____

Address _____

Mailing Address (if Different) _____

City _____ State _____ Zip Code _____

Telephone (Area Code) _____ (Number) _____

Fax (Area Code) _____ (Number) _____

Type of Business _____ Years in Business _____

Number of Employees at Your Location _____

Dun & Bradstreet Number (if any) _____

Do you use a purchase order system? YES ___   NO ___

Bank References

1. Financial Institution _____

    Address _____

    City _____ State _____ Zip Code _____

    Telephone (Area Code) _____ (Number) _____

    Fax (Area Code) _____ (Number) _____

    Business Checking Account Number _____

    Person to Contact at Bank _____

2. Financial Institution _____

    Address _____

    City _____ State _____ Zip Code _____

    Telephone (Area Code) _____ (Number) _____

    Fax (Area Code) _____ (Number) _____

    Business Checking Account Number _____

    Person to Contact at Bank _____

The Very Best in Business Support Services!

Credit References

1. Company Name _____

   Address _____

   City _____ State _____ Zip Code _____

   Telephone (Area Code) _____ (Number) _____

   Fax (Area Code) _____ (Number) _____

   Account Number _____

   Person to Contact/Title_____

2. Company Name _____

   Address _____

   City _____ State _____ Zip Code _____

   Telephone (Area Code) _____ (Number) _____

   Fax (Area Code) _____ (Number) _____

   Account Number _____

   Person to Contact/Title_____

3. Company Name _____

   Address _____

   City _____ State _____ Zip Code _____

   Telephone (Area Code) _____ (Number) _____

   Fax (Area Code) _____ (Number) _____

   Account Number _____

   Person to Contact/Title_____

MUST BE SIGNED BY AUTHORIZED COMPANY OFFICER

I certify that all statements made by me in this application are for the purpose of obtaining credit and are correct to my knowledge. I authorize these references to release my credit status and to provide such other information as Creative Secretarial Services may require. The undersigned expressly agrees to make payment in full to Creative Secretarial Services for all purchases in accordance with Creative Secretarial Services invoice(s). At the discretion of Creative Secretarial Services, a deposit/project retainer may be required in advance of commencing work on a project. Applicant acknowledges that all accounts over ten (10) days old will be assessed a service charge at the maximum rate permitted by law. The undersigned agrees to pay a reasonable attorney's fee and all other costs and expenses incurred by Creative Secretarial Services in the collection of any obligation of the undersigned pursuant hereto. This application for credit, once accepted by Creative Secretarial Services, shall become part of every invoice to applicant and is incorporated herein. This application shall remain Creative Secretarial Services' property whether or not it is accepted and approved.

Signature _____ Title _____

Date _____

Credit Department Use Only

Date Application Received _____ Date Application Approved _____

billing twice a month; for accounts this active it's a good idea to establish terms at net ten days (vs. thirty). In fact, I recommend at least establishing your terms as "net ten days" on all accounts. Consider it this way: If a client first utilizes your services on May 1 and then continues to use services throughout the month, by the time you generate the invoice on May 31, you may be billing $1,000 (for purposes of this example). If the client takes thirty days to pay this invoice, you won't receive a check until perhaps June 30 or even the first week in July (almost two months after first providing the service). If you bill the client twice a month, that shortens your receipt cycle by at least two weeks, plus provides cash injections on a steady every-other-week basis thereafter.

INVOICING

Your invoices should include terms (whether "payable upon completion of a project" or "net due ten days from date of invoice"). If a client is tax-exempt (in a state where you are otherwise required to collect sales tax), the tax exemption number should be noted on the invoice. If you are handling work for a reseller (i.e., a printing company), the reseller should provide you with a copy of a resale certificate on which its sales and use tax registration number appears; you do not collect sales tax on this work because the reseller will be incorporating your charges in *its* invoicing and collecting sales tax from its customer. If a client is with a corporation that uses a purchase order system (this should be ascertained upon acceptance of the first project), be certain to reference the appropriate purchase order number. If a client requires that your invoices bear numbers, you should develop a numbering system within the invoice template on your computer, unless you use an invoice program that generates numbers automatically. A simple system I use for those clients requiring it is B00 · 03; the B denotes the first letter of the corporate name (e.g., Brown Corporation), the 00 is for the year in which the invoice period occurs, and the 03 indicates this is the third invoice I've generated for this client in a given year. Because the invoice is also dated, there should never be a duplication. I've never had more than about a half-dozen clients at any one point that required an invoice number on their invoices, so this easy-to-use method works well.

RECORDKEEPING

Depending on your computer software, you may wish to try one of the many good bookkeeping/accounting packages. (I especially like Quicken.) While an accountant can set up books for you to follow if you so choose, you'll readily find a plethora of good information in your public library as well as through the Small Business Administration (see the Appendix).

Whatever method you develop, attempt to keep it as simple and easy to use as possible—once your business really begins to be *busy,* you won't want to spend precious time on complicated entry tasks. Your goal with recordkeeping should be twofold: (1) to provide timely information for managing your business and understanding its cyclic peaks and areas for growth, and (2) to provide accurate reporting information for city and state government agencies and filing of tax returns.

In addition to maintaining financial forms (discussed in chapter 3) tracking my company's financial health, I use Quicken to keep track of several key things for my business: accounts receivable (the amount of money due me that's still outstanding—unpaid client invoices), overall billings of all clients (I'm able to view this information in a variety of formats: I find monthly, half-monthly, and weekly reports the most useful), and breakout of my charges. (I separate my labor time from such client-charged expenses as Federal Express fees, paper costs, copy costs, postage, etc.) My typical ratio of labor hours to total billing has been consistently 70 percent for a number of years. (In other words, if my annual billings to clients totaled $10,000 for purposes of this example, $7,000 of that total would be in my directly billable hours; the remaining $3,000 would be allocated to copies, paper, postage, supplies, etc.)

Over the years, I've modified my recordkeeping system and vastly simplified it. This has resulted in two positive things: (1) I *maintain* my records regularly, and (2) I have up-to-the-minute financial data for my business whenever I wish to look at them. I find it personally motivating to "compete" with myself from month to month and year to year to see if my billables are going up (as well as my profits!). At the repeated urging of my dear friend and colleague, Louise Kursmark (author of *How to Start a Home-based Desktop Publishing Business,* Globe Pequot Press, 1999), I finally disciplined myself to open Quicken on my desktop at the start of each work day and *immediately* record invoices for clients as I generated them. I'm usually able to log the information into Quicken while waiting for the client's invoice copy to print. With this system, I never need to allocate specific "bookkeeping" time to building clients' invoice records.

A horror story I'll share (in the spirit of "if I can keep just *one* person from committing this mistake, it's more than worth my personal embarrassment in telling you this"): A few years ago during an especially frantic period when I was working some seventy to eighty hours a week, I allowed myself the "luxury" of stacking up invoices for entry into Quicken "at a later, more convenient time, when the pace slowed down." Well, the pace never slowed down and it wasn't until April 10 of the following year (yes, just days before the tax filing deadline!) that I finally *had* to build a full year's records into Quicken in order to create the appropriate reports that would enable completion of my tax return. Because I generate

Allen's Secretarial Services

123 Main Street

Anywhere, USA 89888

(444) 444-4444 · Fax (444) 444-3333

Invoice for Services Rendered   Date: _____

Company Name   Purchase Order #_____

Address

Invoice # _____   Billing Contact: _____

Date of Service	Project Description	Hours/Rate @ $XX.00	Subtotal

Payment is due upon completion of project.   Subtotal $

Sales Tax $

Thank You!   **Total** $

Professional Secretarial and Office Support Services

between 250 and 300 invoices *per month* (many highly detailed), this was a formidable task. You may ask: "How were you able to meet your quarterly filing requirements for both self-employment taxes and remittance of collected state sales tax?" Using my checking account statements (tracking all deposits for my business), I was able to quickly get quarterly totals from which to calculate the appropriate amounts due. A sloppy system at best and, unfortunately, during a spectacular year businesswise, I had absolutely no sense or handle on just "how well" I was doing—no numbers to look at in the dark of night to inspire me . . . no numbers to analyze and show areas where I probably wasn't making money . . . and, worst of all, *no method by which to keep track of accounts receivable!* I'm sure there are *still* probably clients out there from that year who owe me money because other than the original invoice provided to the client at the conclusion of a project, I conducted virtually *no* billing—or tracking of payments! After that awful year, I vowed to listen to Louise's advice about simplifying my system and doing it on a real-time basis. I'm happy to report I've followed this good counsel for more than five years— and am very pleased with the results!

Using Quicken, I'm able to prepare a wide variety of informational reports in seconds with just a keystroke or two. A partial listing of those reports I find most helpful are: A/R (Accounts Receivable) by Customer, Cash Flow, Income Statement, and Summary. Each of these reports can be "cut" in a number of ways; as mentioned before, I like viewing running monthly totals in all categories across a year, then looking at weekly and half-monthly snapshots. I review my client billing numbers to tell where my biggest client is this year and how the numbers compare with those of last year (and of the year before). I always chart the information graphically, as well, at the end of each month, to see at a glance where my clients rank as a percentage of my business. The old 80-20 rule almost always applies. That is, you can expect 80 percent of your revenues to come from 20 percent of your base. Apply to this some good common sense for running a successful business: Those clients forming the 20 percent of your base that yields 80 percent of your revenues should be your top priority and receive your consistent attention. By tracking numbers in this manner, you can quickly spot downward trends and attempt to reverse them.

For example, if you note that one of your top clients over the past year begins to have a downward spiral in terms of generating less and less work from month to month, you might want to inquire as to the reason. It may be a perfectly natural business cycle, but it might represent an opportunity for you to provide enhanced services or address a problem you might otherwise not have known existed. By watching your numbers on a regular basis, you will also observe those once infrequent clients spending more time—and money—with you. These may be the next "stars" on your top 20 percent list and deserve extra attention as you cultivate their business!

Tracking Costs

By building records into Quicken that capture detail off each client invoice, I'm able to watch specific cost centers. For instance, if your largest account is ABC Company and its monthly invoice amount is $1,271.03, the invoice will detail how this amount was derived. (This is a fairly typical itemization for an account's invoice.) Use the example on the following page to break it out (all fictitious numbers).

In recording this information in Quicken, hourly rate categories are separated and the respective amounts are entered under each category. Each of the other entries has its own category—office supplies, fax charges, delivery charges, miscellaneous (e.g., for the special airport pick-up, which is not a commonly billed service), postage, and so forth. Once all invoices have been broken out into these respective categories and totaled for the month, you will have an excellent picture as to where your time is spent (vis-à-vis the different hourly categories) and where you are selling additional services. Some items may be strictly "pass-alongs" to your clients (i.e., you may choose not to add any extra charges for providing overnight delivery; e.g., the company you select charges $22.50 for an overnight letter and you pass this cost to your client without adding any additional markup) and, therefore, not represent any profit to you. Other items may be nearly "pure" profit. (If you charge clients to receive faxes, once you have absorbed the cost of the machine and separate telephone line, if applicable, your only cost to receive faxes is the paper charge; this can be highly profitable.)

Most secretarial services add on a small amount for ancillary services to cover their time in handling them. Use of overnight services is a good example. While clients might choose to make their own arrangements, for their convenience you handle complete arrangements, from telephoning for a pick-up and completing the accompanying shipping document (which requires you to maintain an adequate supply of materials, provided at no cost by the various shipping companies) to wrapping a package securely and presenting the package to the delivery service person when he or she arrives at your office later in the day. All of this takes time on your part—and it's reasonable to add a small markup for this service (perhaps $2.00–$5.00) to the actual cost charged by the shipping company before passing it along to your client.

Tracking numbers on a month-to-month basis is valuable in terms of spotting trends in the way your business is growing. If you experiment with offering a new service, for example, editorial services, at a higher hourly rate than your word

3 hours of editorial services @ $75/hour	$ 225.00
5 hours of desktop publishing @ $65/hour	325.00
5 hours of word processing @ $50/hour	250.00
Office supplies (Pentaflex file folders, manila file folders, and labels to complete "Smith" project)	75.00
Postage for "Jones" mailing	58.00
FedEx charges (7 @ $22.50)	157.50
Special pick-up at airport (flat fee)	50.00
Fax charges	70.00
Subtotal	**$ 1,210.50**
Sales Tax (assuming it's 5 percent)	60.53
Total	**$ 1,271.03**

processing services (which it should be), you can observe how this category of business is growing from month to month. If you determine that it is well-received in your market area, you may opt to concentrate more time and resources in further advertising and developing this segment of your business. The flip side would be a decision to offer transcription services keyed at a different hourly rate from your word processing rate (even if only a $1.00 difference). Let's suppose you take a separate Yellow Pages ad under Transcription Services for a year and track an hourly rate of $22. (For purposes of this example, we'll say $22 as compared with $20 for your regular word processing rate.) By observing activity for the twelve months your advertising has appeared in the Yellow Pages under this new category, you may note that your billing was zero for the first two months (June and July); $50 a month for August, September, and October; zero again in November; $75 in December; and $25 for each month January through May. If your additional advertising expense in the Yellow Pages is $40 per month for this ad, it would be a reasonable conclusion that this is not a viable profit center unless you choose to do something different. This might be analyzing of your competition to discover that *their* hourly rate for this service is only $18 (hence, you are overpricing for this service, something you should have checked before deciding to offer transcription services). It might also be that you can assess from your different clients in this area a potential surge of business coming in the next year. Engage in open discussion with these clients. Let them know you are considering specializing in this area—are they willing (or likely) to provide additonal business? Is additional business even available? Are they growing in this direction? All of these factors can influence whether or not you spend even more money advertising this service the following year—or pull your ad out of the book and do not seek to further develop this area of business.

MANAGING ACCOUNTS RECEIVABLE

With individuals you should collect payment upon completion of a project at the time of pick-up. Depending on your own philosophy, you may wish to establish a cash-only policy or determine that personal checks are acceptable. It's always a good idea to collect a deposit (usually 50 percent) up front when a project is first delivered to you (again, from first-time, individual clients, especially students and resume clientele); with established clients this shouldn't be necessary.

You may want to investigate offering clients the option of paying by credit card (Visa or MasterCard). It is somewhat costly, however (initial fees of up to $200, plus a percentage of each sale, usually between 2 and 4 percent), and many banks frown upon offering this through new home-based businesses. If you decide that the protection of not getting bounced checks is worth the cost of providing this option, you may wish to check with an independent sales organization (ISO) for assistance in obtaining merchant status. These businesses exist to help other businesses apply for accounts, and they charge a fee on top of whatever the bank would normally charge you. Information regarding ISOs can be located in the Bibliography section of the Appendix.

If you determine that offering the option to clients of charging to a major credit card makes sense for your business, you might wish to structure your pricing to provide a discount to those clients paying cash, as it is not permissible by law to add a surcharge for use of a credit card.

I acquired "merchant account status" (enabling me to accept credit cards) in 1994 and find that in addition to making it easier for my clients to do business with me, my accounts receivable problem nearly disappeared. The cost for obtaining an electronic processing terminal (in which to swipe clients' credit cards—or key in their account numbers, for over-the-phone or e-mail sales) was about $300; I share a telephone line with my home telephone number. (Each transaction takes literally seconds to complete and, therefore, doesn't warrant a dedicated telephone line.) The "discount rate" (a misnomer, because it's the fee charged by the credit card processing company) is in the 2 percent range, based upon my annual volume. Especially with resume clients, being able to accept credit cards allows me to take revisions and updates to existing resumes over the telephone and promptly mail out completed originals—without having to wait for payment to arrive (usually a check) or, worse, trusting that the client would send a check upon receipt of the package. My initial system accepted Discover, MasterCard, and Visa cards; several years ago, I also added American Express for a small installation fee. I find that a number of my sales managers have corporate-issued American Express cards to pay for their secretarial services.

While being credit- and, now, debit-card ready is not essential at the onset of starting a secretarial service, you may wish to consider this offering as the years go on and you become more established. As with any projected new service offering, it's always a good idea to poll your clients to test their interest in a new service!

Many secretarial services, including my own, accept personal checks; however, you must be especially careful when taking checks from transient clients—that is, clients you may see one time only. You obviously want to limit your exposure to bounced checks as much as possible. Unfortunately, it is the rare secretarial service (or any business, for that matter) that hasn't been the recipient of a bounced check at least once or twice.

If you are working with a client who after a few months has the potential of being a "regular" (most sought after, naturally!), you might want to extend credit over the course of the month using a log to record time on that client's projects on an ongoing basis. (See the Client Production Schedule earlier in this chapter.) A summary invoice is prepared at the end of the billing period. Establish payment expectations with a client at the onset (e.g., that billing will occur once monthly, with payment due within ten days of receipt of your invoice).

It's also a good idea to have the client initial each entry on the log as completed work is picked up throughout the month.

How you track your ARs will partially be a function of how you establish your books and how you like to organize your files.

Over the years I also have found that it is important to keep somewhere in my files a copy of every invoice generated for each client. Occasionally (and this is generally only with large companies), I am required to resubmit copies of actual invoices for payment in instances where staff may have changed, paperwork may have been misplaced or lost at the company, and the like. By having physical copies in my file, I don't have to recompose actual invoices in the system—and I don't need to use valuable disk space to keep the copies in a running disk file. I simply update the template invoice that appears in each client's "file" on his or her disk.

Once again, if you decide to automate your financial records and the program you utilize provides for invoicing, you may want to experiment with an automated system on your computer.

COLLECTIONS

Managing collections is a necessary aspect of any business and is probably one of the more unpleasant activities in which you'll need to engage at least periodically. If you have established good credit guidelines, invoice your clients regularly, and stay on top of unpaid accounts, you shouldn't have too much difficulty.

There will, however, inevitably come a time when a client's check bounces. You immediately contact the client by phone upon notification from your bank that the check did not clear (usually, because of "insufficient funds," although I have had instances where an account was no longer open). You pleasantly explain to the client what happened. Always assume at the beginning that it was an honest error. Give the client a chance to apologize/explain and then ascertain a commitment for resolving the situation. Unless it is a regular client for whom this really was an honest mistake, I recommend requesting cash payment or a certified bank check for the amount due, *plus* the amount the bank charges you for the problem as well as any administrative fee you wish to add ($5.00 or $10.00 seems typical in this industry to add on to the bank's charge to cover for the inconvenience). Also, be sure to add on any amount you may be charged for checks you write that do not clear because of this check's not clearing.

Hopefully, you're able to sustain a reasonable balance in your business checking account at any one point to provide for this occurrence. Keeping a $500 or even $1,000 cushion available at all times in your account is not a bad idea and helps cover for situations of this type, which usually are rare. Using the Client Work Order form from the original project for which this situation has occurred, record briefly the notes of your conversations held throughout the collection process. Note the date you received the bank notice and the date/time of your call to the client. Note the commitment made by the client, with a specific date. If the client does not follow through on the commitment, immediately contact the client the next day to inquire about the status, restating what the original commitment was. You will probably find that the majority of instances in this category are resolved within a week or two.

Unfortunately, there will likely be a time when either a company goes out of business before paying your invoice or an individual client moves but leaves no forwarding address and closes his or her bank account (after writing you a check that bounces). The experience of most people in this business that I've talked with is that you will have to write some business off each year; that is, chalk it up to bad business (and take it as an expense, "bad debts from sales or services," which is an expense item on Schedule C of the federal income tax form). You can attempt to obtain amounts due your business through small claims court, depending on the amount of time you have available to warrant the accompanying headaches of pursuing this action. I have found a reasonably successful method of collecting on unpaid accounts (or accounts for which checks have bounced) that costs little in terms of time or money. I initially telephone, following the steps just outlined. I record all conversations and note on my desktop appointment calendar when a commitment should occur. If it does not, I will call again, even several times.

If thirty days pass with no payment, I then briefly document the telephone calls, dates, and commitments in a letter, attaching a copy of the invoice, and formally announce in writing that "if full payment in the amount of $XX isn't received by a certain date [I give ten days at this point], legal action through small claims court will be taken." If day ten arrives with no payment, I call one last time—and then promptly mail the delinquent client a copy of the small claims court's "Small Claim and Notice of Suit" document, fully completed with the relevant facts of the case. These forms are available free of charge from the superior court in your county. I do *not* mail the form to the small claims court (which entails a filing fee of about $25 or $30). I have found that simply sending such clients the copy of the form is enough to spur many of them to pay.

ALLOCATING FUNDS FOR TAX OBLIGATIONS

As you are managing your income, expenses, and cash flow, you should establish a means for saving aside monies for your quarterly tax obligations—self-employment tax, state sales tax (if relevant in your state), and so on. If desired, an accounting professional can advise the best means for doing this, in addition to advising the proper way for reporting your income (cash or accrual basis). A simple way to ensure proper savings is to allocate on a monthly basis the appropriate percentage of all that month's business. If, for example, 5 percent is your state's sales tax percentage that you are required to collect on all sales, at the end of the month total all the taxable business you've billed, calculate the 5 percent amount, and set that aside until the quarter in which the payment is due. Likewise for self-employment, federal, and any state taxes: You should set aside a given percentage (conservatively, 25–30 percent). This may seem like a lot of money to set aside for payment of taxes, but if you don't plan for this on a regular, monthly basis, filing of quarterly returns will be difficult if not impossible.

CULTIVATING CLIENT RELATIONSHIPS

This next aspect of "getting down to business" assumes that you have clients beginning to come to your service. Nearly every marketing publication in existence advises that it is much easier and less costly to retain a current client than it is to find a new client to take a former client's place. In addition, there is an informal rule of thumb in business today stating that a happy client will tell three to four people about your business (all prospective clients), and an unhappy client may tell ten to twelve people about your service! Therefore, it makes sense to satisfy and take good care of your valuable clients. Besides providing excellent service and quality, for which you are charging (hopefully) at the appropriate rate, having computed a reasonable and fair salary, plus profit, you should invest a small amount of time as well in going the extra mile to always thank each client for his or her business upon the conclusion of a transaction. Sending greeting cards is a thoughtful and appropriate gesture that isn't excessively costly. Instead of or in addition to communicating at Christmas, consider sending a thank-you to clients around Thanksgiving—to thank them for being your clients. You can use other seasonal events to create a theme for client communications: Valentine's Day (to let clients know how much you "love" the opportunity of providing professional services to them) and April Fool's Day (to tell your clients they're "the best—*no foolin'!*"), for example.

Developing a newsletter for your business (discussed fully in chapter 4) is an excellent way to subtly keep your company's name in front of regular and occasional clients as well as prospective clients. It also can effectively advertise the newsletter writing/production service you offer. The format can be as simple as a one-page, three-panel self-mailer. A quarterly or bimonthly schedule is usually manageable and affordable. It's also an ideal vehicle for spotlighting new products or services you may be adding as well as demonstrating your skill and expertise in writing, layout, and design. My clients repeatedly tell me how much they enjoy my newsletter—from reading my chatty column to finding helpful tips they can use in their own business pursuits.

Managing client relationships successfully and effectively is an important skill for any business owner. When you're in a business providing strictly services, as obviously is the case with a secretarial service, clients primarily will do business with you because of you. While price, location, or an initial satisfaction of their need for a particular service may have attracted them to you in the first place, repeat client business will be a function of how well you serve your clients' perceived and actual needs. What do I mean by this? Let's say a client contacts you to prepare a small mail-merge project of twenty-five names. You are given the responsibility of typesetting a cover letter (handwritten reasonably well by the client), creating the small base of twenty-five names and addresses from various newspaper and telephone directory clippings, and printing individual letters and matching envelopes. Not a big deal—maybe, all told, one hour's worth of work or so. But this is the first time that this client has contacted you. So what can you do "above and beyond" to help pave the way for future business with this client?

When typesetting the letter, objectively consider the message being delivered. Can you offer any suggestions on how to improve the language chosen, the way in which the message is delivered, the use of a dynamic opening or dramatic close, the use of an effective "eyebrow?" An eyebrow is the use of a short, distinctive phrase—placed above the salutation—that is created to capture the reader's attention. It is typically set in a larger font size than the body of the letter, is usually in boldface, and is frequently set in a different font from the body of the letter. An eyebrow replaces the more conventional subject line, or "RE" line, on a cover letter. For a company marketing a new service that promises to save its client companies money, an effective eyebrow might be: "Our Company Is in the Business of Saving Companies *Like Yours* Big Bucks." See the example on the next page.

Merely making well-considered recommendations to a client demonstrates that the client is not dealing with just a typing clerk but a professional committed to the success of his or her business. This type of "team thinking" provides comfort *and* confidence to clients in cultivating an attitude of caring about their work. Clients begin to see you as a business partner, someone who is really working on their side to help them achieve their goals. As your opinions become valued, clients will turn to you more and more for advice on matters ranging from how best to write a sales letter to how a proposal can be effectively developed. Once you demonstrate your expertise in "thinking like a business partner," your advice will be sought in other areas and on other projects. This many times leads to additional projects . . . often coming from suggestions you might have made. For the large numbers of individual small-business owners throughout the United States who utilize secretarial and office support services, there are literally hundreds of opportunities for suggesting add-on projects. There is hardly a businessperson who couldn't benefit from a well-developed brochure or newsletter. Most simply lack the time and expertise to develop their own . . . or, even more likely, haven't considered what such a piece could accomplish for their business.

As the provider of professional secretarial and office support services, you are in a unique position to deliver many ancillary services to your client base beyond the obvious word processing projects. Use your expertise and captivated client base to your advantage—open new profit centers and sell add-on services to your regular clients who will truly benefit from them. A significant by-product is the higher rate you can—and should—charge for such creative work.

PROFESSIONAL ASSOCIATION

A membership in both the Association of Business Support Services International, Inc. and its local chapter in your county or state is highly recommended, especially at the local level, if you have a strong chapter (see the Appendix), and particularly

XYZ Company

123 Main Street · Your City, USA 55555
(800) 343–3434

Date

Addressee
Title
Company
Address
City, State, Zip

Our Company Is in the Business of Saving Companies *Like Yours* Big Bucks.

Dear _____:

I'll bet that captured your attention . . . want to learn more about how XYZ Company can save your firm a substantial amount of money . . . (etc.)

during the start-up phase of operating your business. You'll have an opportunity to network with others experiencing some of the same challenges as you—acquiring clients, getting repeat business, and effectively managing a business from your home. (Although you'll find a number of members are based in retail offices or executive suites, many are home-based.) You can benefit from the experiences of others as well as possibly develop a referral network for overflow work. This can work both ways: In the start-up phase, you'll most likely be hoping to obtain overflow from someone else's business, but as your business grows, you will appreciate having cultivated a network of professionals to whom you can confidently refer client projects you simply lack the time for . . . or whom you can contact for assistance in a possible subcontractor arrangement.

The National Association of Secretarial Services (NASS) was originally founded in 1981 and was renamed in 1998 as the Association of Business Support Services International, Inc., or ABSSI. Lynette Smith, who became the executive director in 1997, was the owner/operator of Qualitype, her own home-based secretarial service in California, for sixteen years. Lynette was eminently qualified to take the helm of this trade association and position it for growth in the next century. A strong supporter of entrepreneurs, she spent significant time volunteering throughout the 1980s and '90s for such key projects as developing and growing local colleague networks, teaching start-up workshops for business support services, giving presentations at then-NASS conventions, writing for publication in Industry Focus and other industry trade journals (including my newsletter, The Word Advantage), and self-publishing her own line of industry pamphlets. She shares some of her insights and background here.

"In the summer of 1980, shortly before my son Byron was born, I left a nine-year career in the corporate world, where I had most recently served as an administrative assistant. That fall, I established Qualitype.

"Originally, I had meant to work at home for three years and then return to the corporate world. However, in 1983, I reassessed my situation. As a business owner, I had freedom to make my own decisions, scheduling flexibility, income commensurate with my skills, frequent positive feedback from clients about what a good job I was doing, and no office politics! As a parent, I found it beneficial to be more available to Byron as he was growing up. Clearly, the benefits of self-employment far outweighed the risks, so I decided to remain self-employed.

"My first clients had been students and people who needed resume retypes. Later on, my client base expanded to include writers, an attorney, a couple of consultants, a few sales reps, and a business owner or two. Had I chosen to offer transcription services, I'm sure I would have had even more types of interesting clients.

"Advertising initially was through a semester-long classified ad in the local university newspaper. Soon after, I paid for a combination of one-line listings and boldface, boxed, in-column ads in a privately produced but popular edition of the Yellow Pages that was distributed within an eight-mile radius of my home business. I avoided Yellow Pages display advertising, believing it would generate more calls than I could easily handle. Eventually, positive word-of-mouth became my strongest source of new business, with my Yellow Pages listings running a close second.

"Changes in technology caused my business to take turns I never would have suspected. Starting out with a typewriter alone, in 1981 I began to offer word processing on a home-brew CP/M computer ('You know you're getting old when you talk to someone who never heard of eight-inch floppy disks') with a daisy wheel printer. In 1984, I started working with PC-compatible systems and laser printers and began to offer copying and faxing services as well.

"Between technological changes and personal preference, the scope of my business services expanded from typing to word processing to low-end desktop publishing and higher-end copyediting. It seemed that the clients who stayed with me were those who needed and appreciated my copyediting services. Occasionally, I found that I was hired just to red-pencil manuscripts or catalog pages—never even powering up the computer!"

In addition to sharing details of her own start-up, Lynette offers the following recommendations to consider when starting your own home-based secretarial service. (These supplement my ideas and those of your colleagues sprinkled liberally throughout this text; don't overlook the "top five recommendations" of all your colleagues in chapter 8.) By the way, Lynette highly encourages consideration of your Yellow Pages deadline as being pivotal to your start-up success—and, as I suggest, timing your start-up to be coincident with Yellow Pages publication.

- Research your target market area. Most clients visiting your business will travel no farther than 3 to 5 miles. On a map, draw two circles around your business— one at a 3-mile radius, the other at 5. What ages and types of prospective clients live and work within these circles? What types of services will most of them require? What nearby competition do you have? What are they charging for similar work?

- If you want clients, you'll have to market. A listing or ad in the Yellow Pages is vital. To select the right Yellow Pages directory, conduct a survey in your neighborhood, asking people two questions. First, "If you needed to have [an example of one project only, e.g., business letter or resume] professionally done, which Yellow Pages directory would you reach for first?" Next, "Which classification would you first try to look under?" After visiting a small number of homes or businesses (rotating different "projects," e.g., business letter at every third house or business), you'll have a good sense of where to place your listing or ad.

- Also become active in one or two organizations that contain a high percentage of prospective clients, e.g., trade groups, chambers of commerce, service organizations, and even leads clubs (as long as the business mix is promising and members regularly generate quality leads). Tell everyone what you do and ask for referrals. If you offer a specialty, such as psychological transcription, consider mailing and then phoning target prospects, offering to drop by to show examples of your work and explain how you can help them save time or money.

Have a "you" rather than an "I" focus in all marketing efforts. Direct mail marketing can also work, but usually only if you mail to the same people five or six times in succession. (It generally takes that long to be noticed by readers.)

- Price wisely to guarantee profitability. To underprice will put you out of business; instead, decide what the market will bear. If you have good employees or subcontractors, your profit potential is greater than if you operate alone. Another factor is how much time you spend at your business. Alone, expect to bill no more than 75 percent of your available business hours. Thus, if you operate your business full-time for 50 weeks per year, you could bill (at 30 hours per week) 1,500 hours a year. Multiply that by a typical hourly rate in your area to calculate potential gross income. From this, deduct your average annual expenses (probably several thousand dollars); what's left would be your net profit, or personal earnings.

- Make sure your financial backing will carry you through the early months and years. Typically it takes three to twelve months before your income outweighs your expenses, depending on how specialized your service is, how aggressively you promote your business, and how great your expenses are. And even if you're a highly motivated, aggressive marketer, it could still be one to three years before you can bill at least 30 hours a week (typical of a 40-hour-per-week business). Some new business owners accept short-term temp assignments to help bridge the financial gap until their own business generates enough income to be self-sustaining.

- Befriend your competitors. Take time to meet your colleagues. Show one another samples of your work, and explore the similarities and differences among the services you each offer. There are wonderful opportunities to share large projects, refer inappropriate or extra projects, or even have a trusted colleague care for your business calls or clients during an illness or vacation. Working together gives you added independence and greater workload stability, and you gain a confidante for sharing business problems and devising solutions.

- Market during the busy times, not just the slow ones. If you market only when business is slow, the results will start to come in later on, when you're already busy with other work. Therefore, make time to market regularly. If you have more time than money, pound the pavement, write letters, make calls, and network with prospective clients. If you have more money than time, send direct mail pieces and follow up by telephone or in person.

- When meeting or conversing with prospective clients, do more listening than talking. If prospects don't know they have problems, they won't care about what you have to say. Therefore, the best way to get a prospect's attention is to ask about his or her situation or business. Listen and probe as necessary to learn (and help your prospects identify) what their greatest business communication challenges are; then tell them how you can help meet those challenges head-on.

- "Show and tell" is good. A samples portfolio and an attractive bulletin board are excellent ways to "show" your expertise, and written testimonials and references from satisfied clients is a comfortable and credible way to "tell."

- Exceeding "Model Operator" skill levels will enhance your profitability. According to the Industry Production Standards (IPS) Guide (co-published by ABSSI and the Executive Suite Association [ESA]; see information in the Appendix), a Model Operator (owner or employee) keyboards at 70 WPM, has two to three years of administrative experience, and good English grammar skills. Model Transcriptionist Operators have another two to three years of transcription experience, above-average English grammar skills, and exceptional listening skills. ABSSI and ESA suggest that you use the IPS Guide to bill your time as if the Model Operator had done the work. This protects clients from overbilling when slower operators do the work, but it also rewards faster operators for their efficiency!

- Continuing education is vital. Face it: Your clients either have or soon will have their own computers. But they'll stick with you as long as you're more efficient at accomplishing tasks than they are, or can accomplish tasks that they could not hope to tackle with their limited software or learning time. This means you have to be proficient in the latest hardware and software. Read trade journals, take software classes, and make appropriate purchases for your business. Also, for greater professional credibility and to better serve clients in a wide variety of fields, strive to achieve the Certified Professional Secretary (CPS) designation through the Institute for Certification, a department of the International Association of Administrative Professionals. (See information in the Appendix.)

ABSSI Membership Benefits: Strength in Numbers

"The best thing about being an ABSSI member? It's hard to pick just one! Professional resources, information, encouragement—not being 'alone in the boat' or having to 'reinvent the wheel' constantly."
(Georgia Adamson, Adept Business Services, Campbell, CA; business started in 1991, ABSSI member since 1991; home-based)

■ Professional credibility and identification. As an ABSSI member, you receive an ABSSI Membership Certificate and Code of Ethics for display in your work area, plus camera-ready "Member of ABSSI" logos in various sizes that you can reproduce on your letterhead, brochures, and other printed materials. (A membership pin is also available for a nominal charge.) Rather than appearing to be "just a local business," you convey to your clients and prospects that your business is part of a professional, international industry. Annual ABSSI membership is $132 (which includes the newsletter); a six-month trial membership is offered for $75 (including six months of the newsletter); an annual subscription to the newsletter alone is $48. (All information is current at time of publication; contact information appears in the Appendix.)

"I display my ABSSI membership certificate with pride and always tell all my prospects and clients that I belong to ABSSI. That gives me and my business greater credibility, because then they know I conform to certain high standards and ethics."

(Laurie Larsen, Renton Secretarial Service, Renton, WA; business started in 1984, ABSSI member since 1996; executive suite)

■ On-line presence and potential referrals. ABSSI's new Web site, www.abssi.org, has many exciting features, including a searchable directory of ABSSI members showing name, company, location (city, state, and zip/postal code), phone and fax numbers, and automatic links to E-mail address and URL. The ABSSI Web site is visited by not only your colleagues, but also potential clients, thanks to hypertext links and other publicity. Who knows? Your next client could find you there!

■ ABSSI Annual Membership Directory. The ABSSI Annual Membership Directory is published each January. (Deadline for inclusion is the prior October 10.) Your listing includes your name, business name, address, county, phone number, fax number, email address, URL, operating system, software used, services provided, and length of ABSSI membership. This directory helps you and other members in a wide variety of ways. One current directory is included with membership.

- Complimentary toll-free consulting line. With over eighteen years of experience as this industry's only international trade association, ABSSI has offered guidance to thousands of business-support service owners. Consulting topics include how to get started, how to price different services, how to get new clients, how to expand upon existing services, and how to improve your marketing materials. Nonmembers pay $75 per hour for this expert advice, but it's free to you as an ABSSI member.

- The monthly *Industry Focus* magazine. Every month, you'll receive ABSSI's sixteen-page *Industry Focus* magazine, packed with ideas, information, and other members' experiences to help you succeed in your own business. Articles address every facet of the industry: pricing; marketing; dealing with clients and employees; and adding new profit centers or improving your existing services in such areas as executive suites, mailroom operations, multimedia presentations, on-line services, resumes, telephone answering, transcription, and more. (Nonmembers pay $48 for an annual subscription to *Industry Focus*.)

- Deep discounts on industry publications. Written solely for the business support services industry, these valuable and affordable ABSSI publications are a wealth of information on how to run your business more profitably. Some of these publications are unavailable to nonmembers at any price. On nearly all the rest, ABSSI members receive substantial discounts. (See Appendix for a partial listing.)

- Discount of $25 to $50 on the annual ABSSI convention. Every spring ABSSI conducts a three-day convention consisting of presentations and panel discussions on profit centers, pricing techniques, sales and marketing, business operations, equipment, and related topics. Each ABSSI convention is held in a different part of the United States.

- Discount of 10 percent on New Horizons classes. Survival in this industry depends, in part, on keeping your computer skills current. Your 10 percent ABSSI-member discount on all New Horizons Learning Centers classes and products, obtained through our special contract, helps you reduce this continuing-education expense!

- Local support from/for ABSSI chapters. In geographic areas with enough ABSSI members and *Industry Focus* subscribers, an ABSSI chapter is often established to provide further networking and other benefits at the local level. ABSSI provides full support for establishing and building such chapters through a detailed, example-filled manual and individual chapter consultation. ABSSI currently has fifteen chapters.

"While ABSSI puts the power of an international organization at your disposal, your local chapter has its finger on the pulse of your local business community. Together, you have an unbeatable combination—the best of both worlds!"

(Jenny Rhodes, Rhodes Secretarial Service, Phoenix, AZ; business started in 1982, ABSSI member since 1986; home-based)

Joining ABSSI does make a difference! Joining connects you with other business-support professionals throughout the world who realize the great benefits ABSSI offers and recognize ABSSI's contribution to the success and growth of their industry. ABSSI and its members continually strive to enhance the image and prestige of their industry, which results in individual prosperity for each participant. This truly is "Strength in Numbers," as Executive Director Lynette Smith says. Be a part of it!

CHAPTER SIX

RUNNING A HOME-BASED BUSINESS . . . AND A HOUSEHOLD

F or many home-based operators of desktop publishing, typing, and word processing services, the lure into this field of work is the ability to *be* home-based and thus manage the multiple responsibilities of earning an income—often while being available to one's children. I wouldn't be totally honest were I to say that it's easy to run a home-based business with small children—but it is possible and it's highly rewarding.

For those without children and/or empty-nesters, you'll find sprinkled throughout this section recommendations that will apply (and maybe find yourself thankful not to have small children underfoot). I've noted those sections especially applicable to individuals with small children. No matter what your circumstances, operating a home-based secretarial service will, in all likelihood, be one of the most satisfying and rewarding ventures you'll ever undertake. Among many other benefits, it certainly beats the rat race of getting yourself (and possibly kids) out the door by a certain time every morning and coming home exhausted at the dinner hour with groceries and a briefcase (and maybe kids in tow also) each night. As a home-based business owner, you may still find yourself exhausted at times, but the *big* difference is that *you're* in control (or you can be, if you so choose and if you possess good self-discipline).

The beauty of a home-based business is that you dictate the workload and the hours, not someone else. If you find yourself running to the beat of many demanding clients, that's a challenge for you to address; however, that's not likely to occur in the first year of starting up and operating your own business.

Here, then, are some time-proven techniques and suggestions for successfully maintaining a profitable home-based business that doesn't infringe *too* much on your family's life.

ACCOMMODATING YOUNG CHILDREN

Many home-based mothers balance their day through the use of some form of partial child care—be it an after-school high-school-age sitter for their children, part-time (and sometimes full-time) placement in nursery schools and day care centers, or summer camp programs. Keep in mind that whatever works best for you is what is important. Even if your business grows to the point where it is full-time (and this is what you want) and you determine that full-time day care is appropriate, you still have the wonderful flexibility of shuffling your work schedule and client appointments when your children are ill and need to be at home or when you decide to take an impromptu day off and head to the beach with your kids or accompany them on a school field trip. This compares very favorably with a mom working full-time at a company with perhaps a hectic travel schedule that keeps her away from home for days and nights at a time. If you manage to work around your children's being home full-time with you, you'll still have to juggle work when they are ill and demand your complete attention all day long. But you have the option of working late at night or early in the morning (or both, during busy dissertation deadline time!) while they sleep.

SCHEDULING APPOINTMENTS

My recommendation is to work by appointment only and not permit drop-ins. I've had several persistent clients over the years who failed, at times, to adhere to my appointment-only policy and dropped in at inconvenient times (e.g., when I was in the middle of nursing a baby). These occasional occurrences have actually provided many laughs over the years.

A little side humor here—the funniest moment in this area occurred when I was eight months pregnant with my youngest child. Although it was during February and cold and snowy in New England, *I* couldn't get cool enough or comfortable enough sleeping and found sleeping au naturel to be the most convenient. Because I had not yet installed a laser printer, I was using a daisy wheel, letter-quality printer. For those of you with experience on these, you know how noisy they are when printing. I had a 200-page document (all statistical pages filled with bars, columns, numbers, etc.—lots of tiny type) to print one morning. Because I knew it would take literally hours to print and I couldn't stand the noise while it was printing, I decided to get up early and—before even showering or dressing—go get the printer started. That way, by the time the twins were up and we were out in the office area, it would perhaps be half-completed.

I dashed as quickly as an eight-months-pregnant woman can out to my desk and started up the computer. (Now, bear in mind, my office is of a contemporary style, surrounded by floor-to-ceiling windows, no curtains; the office is next to the garage and faces the driveway.) I had just about queued the document to print when up my sidewalk, from the driveway, walks a client. It's 6:00 A.M.! I'm wearing nothing, very pregnant—and completely vulnerable, sitting surrounded by all these windows and nowhere to hide. I shouted to my husband, who came running—not to my defense but to the door! I had no alternative—I hopped into the garage.

This client, with whom I'd worked for several years, was acquainted with my husband and began what seemed like an interminably long conversation in the middle of my office about his new car. I'm standing barefooted and bare-everything-else on a cold, cement garage floor; it was no more than 20° Fahrenheit! The client finally left . . . and I think I resumed speaking to my husband sometime that afternoon. I've never chanced it again by coming into my office naked, although a big benefit every home-based business owner has is working after hours in pajamas. The *importance* of scheduled appointments . . . .

By scheduling appointments, you have a luxury enjoyed by few in the corporate world of giving yourself time off when you want it. If you find with your schedule that you prefer doing your creative work during early morning hours, before the phones start and/or kids awaken, that's your prerogative. But unless you really want to be working twelve or so hours a day, it doesn't mean that you should write from 4:00 until 9:00 A.M. and *then* offer "conventional" business hours of 9:00 to 5:00! Likewise, if you are a night owl (as I am) and do your best work between 9:00 P.M. and 1:00 A.M., you probably don't want to be available to clients in your office at 7:30 or 8:00 A.M.

How you schedule your appointments is strictly up to you—and doesn't need to be the business of your clients. If you can meet with clients only in the mornings, for example (perhaps you have children in nursery school or kindergarten and they're home afternoons), you don't *have* to advise your clients that you can't meet with them in the afternoons "because the children are at home." Instead, as you're scheduling time, simply make morning times the only option. "Would you prefer to get together first thing in the morning or nearer to lunch?" If pushed for an afternoon appointment, simply state, "I'm completely booked afternoons this week. Would a morning later in the week work better for your schedule, or would you like an evening [or weekend] appointment?"

If you are involved in some other activity—from training for a marathon to attending classes mornings at a local university, or from serving on a committee at your children's school to volunteering with the elderly at a hospital—you have the flexibility to set your work schedule around these commitments and interests. Some secretarial service owners offer client appointments on just one or two days per week and reserve the balance of their time for handling project work without interruptions. They know that they have to "dress for business" only one or two days each week and can be entirely comfortable, productive, and free from distractions the rest of the time. Other business owners find that they are most productive in the morning; therefore, they let their answering machines pick up all morning calls and never schedule clients in the morning—instead, they meet with clients in the afternoons. The point here is simply this: It's *your* business, and you have the flexibility to create the schedule most suited to your needs at any given time. I do, however, recommend that you keep your regular clients posted of any changes. For example, when I was writing this book, I had to allocate time in my already very demanding schedule to work strictly on this project. I experimented with trying to allocate a few hours during each business day but found that client emergencies kept infringing upon that time. Then I hit upon the idea of booking the same day each week "out of the office" to write. I advised all my clients in advance, including via a brief note in my quarterly newsletter; added the information to my message on my answering machine; and scheduled accordingly. It meant the four other weekdays were more compressed than ever, with Thursday night's work inevitably spilling way into the wee hours of Friday before I could catch up on my sleep. But it worked. I had Fridays fully available to write. That same kind of scheduling discipline can be applied to any major project you might undertake—as well as be used for any personal objective you may set for yourself.

As a side note, long after the first edition of this book was complete back in 1993, I *continued* to let my answering machine and voice-mail messages announce that the "office is closed on Fridays." I liked the idea of having one day each week when I could feel free *not* to answer my phone, *not* to return phone calls, and *not* to meet with clients. I have used this day to good advantage . . . I write resumes and other lengthy projects on Fridays . . . amazingly enough, nearly all my three sons' field trips are scheduled on Fridays and I go on all of them . . . and having a three-day weekend built right into the schedule every week just "feels" good. Of course, there are occasions, especially wrapped around vacation time and the weeks away from my office for professional conferences, when I do schedule client appointments on Fridays and possibly even pick up the phone. But it's my choice, my prerogative. And I love it!

If You Have Young Children

Another suggestion in the area of scheduling: When your children are very small, stress the convenience of offering evening and weekend appointments to your clients, in particular, for resume consultations (if this is an area you pursue). Basically, unless you use a form of sitter/child care, evening is the only time when you'll be able to meet with clients uninterrupted if your husband/significant other can care for the kids at the end of the day. This is a big plus for clients, though, and you can market it accordingly. Most office suite services and dedicated resume companies offer appointments *only* during the hours of 9:00 to 5:00. With extended hours your business is more user-friendly. No one needs to know that it's to suit *your* convenience and lifestyle. When scheduling appointments, you need never explain any of your personal reasons for doing business the way in which you do— you can simply state, "Our appointment book is completely filled for the next few days [or week], but I do still have a few evening openings and one appointment left on Saturday."

Appointment Timing

Determining the proper amount of time to allot for an appointment, like many aspects of this business, is an imprecise science. As a minimum you should allow at least fifteen minutes per "appointment," even for a supposedly quick pick-up of completed work or drop-off of a project. If a client is picking up a lengthy project and your policy is to allow review/proofreading in your office, take this time into account. For a thirty- or forty-page proposal, an hour might be necessary. Provided that the client does *not* require your active attendance *and* you can work on other projects, you don't charge the client for that time spent in your office. (You charge only for the time in which you are actually working with the client on any revisions.)

For clients dropping off work, it is typical to allow between five and ten minutes "off the clock" (noncharged time) for the client to briefly review instructions. Any time beyond that should be added to your overall time charge for the project. At the point when you are scheduling an appointment, you should attempt to clarify the purpose of the meeting, nature of the project, and amount of time that may be required to review it.

When you are meeting with resume clientele (if this is a service offering), the time requirements for appointments will vary substantially. For basic typesetting of a resume that the client has already written, no more than five to ten minutes should be necessary (once again, charge for any time after that—or build it into your flat rate); likewise, proofing of a resume you've simply typeset should not take more than five to ten minutes. If a client who has contracted for this level of service begins a dialogue asking your opinion of how something is phrased, beyond a quick response, I would recommend mentioning that you'd be happy to provide consultation services at your appropriate hourly rate (and, if your appointment schedule allows, handling it at that precise point; otherwise, it would need to be scheduled for a different time).

Resume clients for whom you've booked a complete consultation would typically be informed in their initial inquiry telephone call to allow a certain amount of time for the appointment (commonly between one and one and one half hours). If my scheduling permits, I try to keep a two-hour slot open for full resume consultations; if the appointment wraps up in just an hour, I then have the next hour available to at least rough out my thoughts on how to present the client's accomplishments and background information. I find, as a general rule, that the sooner I can work on a creative project after the initial appointment (be it resume development from scratch or creation of a brochure or newsletter), the easier the ideas flow (before my notes get "cold"). My thoughts are fresh, immediately on the heels of the consultation, and I spend much less time trying to recall other points made in the consultation that I may not have written down.

In spite of best efforts to schedule appropriate appointment times, occasionally more than one client will show up at the office at a given time. The client who is within the scheduled appointment time has the priority; depending on the confidentiality of the work, I will advise the second client at the door that he or she is a bit early, and because I am meeting with another client confidentially, I ask if the person would mind waiting a few minutes in his or her car. If the initial client meeting is not confidential, I ask the first client if he or she would object to client #2 waiting in another portion of my office (where there is a sofa); there is usually no objection, and the matter is resolved. If a client is significantly late for an appointment and there is another scheduled to begin very shortly, I advise the late client of this situation and either offer to meet partially at that point, with a reschedule at the earliest available time, or offer to reschedule the entire appointment. I don't allow the second appointment to slip (if that client is on time) just because the first client was tardy. Using diplomacy, tact, and basic consideration, these are easily resolved situations. By the way, I don't charge late clients for the time they were late, nor do I charge for appointments canceled at the last minute or "no-shows" (relatively infrequent).

"TOT TECHNIQUES"

The following section was created strictly for those with children. Depending on the ages of your kids, some of the following suggestions may prove to be very useful:

- If your kids are old enough, try to "employ" them in your business. Obvious ideas: stuffing and sealing envelopes, applying postage, applying labels, operating the photocopier, collating, filing, and organizing files, cabinets, and bookcases. Preteen and teenage "computer whizzes" may be very helpful to you in doing simple typing tasks on the computer (this is ideal if you someday have a second computer system). Even the youngest children can "play office" and help organize drawers of safe contents (keep them away from staplers, correction fluid, rubber cement, sharp scissors, etc.) and "open the mail." (Save junk mail in a folder for this.)

  For older kids who can really perform useful tasks, be sure to pay them for their work on some equitable scale (age-dependent again, maybe 50 cents or $1.00 an hour). For younger children, have a good supply of interesting, fun-colored stickers on hand and make up a chart on your computer; award them stickers for jobs well-completed.

- You might consider setting aside a shelf or a drawer in your office filled with child-friendly "work" materials. Here is where the junk mail comes in handy for the younger children. If you order from some of the office supply catalog vendors, you'll soon be receiving lots of extra catalogs. Kids love to go through these looking for things. If you know you're going to be on the phone with a "regular" client (so that a little controlled background "kid" noise is not objectionable), assign your child the project of finding an orange file folder, a red pencil, a bulletin board, and so on in a large office catalog. If the catalog is no longer needed and your children are old enough to have and use rounded, child-safe scissors, you can have them cut out and tape or glue pictures to construction paper.

- With somewhat older children you can "negotiate" time. This works for perhaps the six- to ten-year-old category of kids: "If you will read quietly or work on your puzzle book for the next hour, Mom will be able to spend time with you at the park [going for a walk, going to the library, etc.]."

- In my family we're not TV-watchers, but I do have a small library of *Parent* magazine's "Kidsongs" videotapes and several Disney videotapes that we allow the kids to watch. If you are really under a deadline and cannot watch the movie with your children, you can perhaps plan to be proofreading (if you have excellent concentration) while sitting on the sofa with them while they watch a film. Or, perhaps, you can arrange to be doing your collating, filing, and the like with them.

- In designing my home office, which was built onto the home specifically for my business, I planned it to be large enough to include an area where we have a library of books, a TV with a VCR (in my business I help clients practice interview techniques through the use of videotapes), a children's plastic picnic/activity table, and a big wraparound sofa to separate that area from my work area. There are hundreds of children's books on the shelves, plus coloring books and crayons, for the use of not only my children but the children of my clients as well. The sofa is useful as a waiting area for those times when two clients are here at the same time. (As I mentioned earlier, I never deliberately schedule two clients at the same time, but it happens.)

- Child/pet gates are a useful investment, depending on the layout of your home/office. When my children were babies, I used the gates to keep them in my office with me (when they weren't playing in the playpen). As the older two (twins) reached three or four and were playing in their playroom, I'd use a gate to keep one or the other from dashing away from their dad or babysitter and interrupting me during a client consultation.

  For much older children who can safely be left unattended, a gate is a useful reminder that Mom is working and is to be disturbed only in an emergency. (This is particularly helpful if there is not a door to your office, only an open doorway.)

- If your office is separated from the rest of your home by a door, installing a message board on the door can make good sense. You can advise family members "Meeting with a Client [or On the Telephone]—Please Do Not Disturb." Simply closing the door can be a reminder to children that you are not to be disturbed. During times of the day when interruptions would be OK, you can establish an "open door policy"; that way your family will know it is OK to interrupt.

- Keep a large, attractive toy box in one area of your office (i.e., if your kids are permitted to play in your office) into which you can quickly stow toys prior to opening the door for an early arriving client. Always encourage your kids, from the time they are very young, to pick up their toys and games before getting out something new so that they'll have good, quick cleanup habits.

A DAY IN THE LIFE OF . . .

I think you'll find the information shared in this section to be of special interest. In responding to my research questionnaires, a number of colleagues took the time to detail a "typical day." At the start of each miniprofile, I'll note the year each person started her business and the number and age(s) of children at the time the questionnaire was completed, if applicable, to help you see where your "fit" might be. Updates to some of these folks' profiles appear in chapter 8 (including the fact, of course, that children are getting older!). By reading this information you can gain valuable tips on scheduling your work around your children—no matter what their age.

RENÉ HART, First Impressions Resume and Career Development Services (1993), Lakeland, Florida—one son, one year old

Typical Day

7:15 A.M.	Wake up, shower, and dress for the day. Get my son Christopher up, feed him breakfast, change his diaper, and get him dressed for school (our preferred word for the day care program he attends twice weekly).
8:30 A.M.	We're off to school!
9:30 A.M.	Return home to work—either to conduct scheduled consultations or to prepare for return appointments.
12:30 P.M.	Run short errands; pick Christopher up from school.
1:30 P.M.	Return home—play with Christopher (all the while listening for the phone!).
2:30 P.M.	Husband Greg comes home from work and takes over with Christopher, allowing me to head to the office to get some late afternoon work completed.
5:30 P.M.	Cook dinner, clean up afterward while Greg gives Christopher his bath.
7:00 P.M.	Christopher's bedtime! Depending on the evening's TV selections, I either return to the office for a few more hours or settle on the couch with something that doesn't require me to sit at the computer.
11:00 P.M.	If energy levels allow, watch the evening news, then go to bed.

JOYCE MOORE, Moore Business Services (1994), Hendersonville, North Carolina—four grown children

Typical Day

7:30 A.M.	Write thank-you notes for the previous day's clients and do any recordkeeping left over from the previous day. Go over scheduled appointments and recheck work if clients are picking it up that

day. Straighten up office and make the place presentable.

8:30 A.M.	Begin to work on any projects left over from the day before or work on my marketing materials. (The phone doesn't always ring as much as I'd like; however, calls are picking up at a rapid rate.)
NOON	Make the post office run. My husband gets the phone while I'm gone or sometimes makes the trip for me if I'm expecting a client or am working on a project. I usually eat lunch after returning with the mail.
AFTERNOONS	Meet with clients in appointments, do client work, think up article queries. If I have an article in progress, I usually work on it afternoons. *[Author's note: Joyce also does freelance business writing.]* I will schedule appointments whenever a client wants. Most of my appointments seem to be afternoon. Some clients use me because I can be reached early (before 8:00 A.M.) or late (after 5:00 P.M.). The only other secretarial service in town has an office location and keeps business hours. I have won clients away from it because of my availability. Once they use me, they keep coming back. I've been told I "do better work."
4:00–5:00 P.M.	I usually call it a day around four or five, after my last client appointment. I work late hours when needed. I have had very few clients request late appointments or weekends; most make their appointments between 10:00 A.M. and 4:00 P.M.

VIVIAN LEE ADKINS, Adkins Resume Services (1995), Erie, Pennsylvania— one son, sixteen years old; one daughter, nineteen years old (who doesn't live at home)

Typical Day

5:00–6:00 A.M.	Eat breakfast and dress for the day, in appropriate business attire.
8:00 A.M.	Usually spend time with clients seen by appointment for resume pick-up/refinements, resume consultation, or typing service drop-offs or pick-ups. Occasionally I spend time at companies on temporary job assignments.
NOON	Lunch, fast food or at home.

1:00–5:00 P.M.	Usually spend time with clients for resume/typing work and document preparation. If I'm by myself, I usually listen to talk radio.
5:00–7:00 P.M.	Dinnertime.
7:00–10:00 P.M.	On rare occasions I see clients in the evening. I consider my business "never closed."

KATHY MANDY, Select Word Services (1981), Chanhassen, Minnesota—one daughter, seventeen years old

Kathy looked back over schedule changes as her daughter—and business—have grown. "My husband, Peter, and I have one beautiful, delightful, and charming daughter, Becky, who will be attending Winona State University upon graduation from high school. I started my business when Becky was three and a half years old. She was in nursery school two days a week. She was also a great napper. She napped right up to the summer before she started kindergarten, and she would nap for about two hours a day. The times that she was gone at school and napping were the times that I worked in my office. I also did some work when she was up, but it would only last for about an hour, then she would need some attention. She was given the closet in the spare bedroom that I used for my office in our first house. She had the closet full of toys and paper and crayons. It's rather embarrassing when I tell people that she used to play in the closet. She'd close the door, turn on the flashlight, tape pictures to the closet door, and pretend she was at the movies.

"One of my favorite pictures is of Becky sitting in my office with her feet up on my desk, a steno pad in her lap, and pretending to 'work' like Mom. She learned from the very beginning that when the phone rang, she had to keep quiet. She loved to play records and music, and her bedroom was right across the hall from my office, so when the phone rang in my office, I would close my office door and take the call. When clients were at the house, she would play in the living room or her bedroom. Only one time did she climb all over my chair and the table with the client there, and I talked with her and told her she couldn't do that again. The threat of Mommy going back to the 'real office' and her going to day care was used to great advantage. Once clients knew that I was home-based and had worked with me, they were very accepting of the home situation and they really enjoyed Becky. They would bring her presents and talk to her whenever they came to the house. But she knew that when the phone rang, she had to be quiet and even trained her friends to the phone routine when they came over to play. She never knew that other people's moms didn't work at home and just assumed that everyone had to be quiet when the phone rang!

"As time has progressed and Becky has grown, it's been a very positive thing for her to see her mom working at home, growing a business, dealing with clients, handling tough deadlines, setting boundaries with clients and family. She is now working part time at Kindercare Day Care Center and immediately picked up on the marketing that they do, how they charge their clients, and what they need to do to keep clients. This was learned firsthand from watching my business and listening to discussions between Peter and me about the business. She has absolutely no interest in working for me or doing the type of work that I do. Her plans right now are to go to college and possibly major in business and marketing. She loves coming down to my office and sitting and chatting with me on days she doesn't work, and I love having her here. She loves the easy access to a computer, copier, and fax machine!

"I think one of the reasons my business has grown and is so successful is because of my wonderful family. Both my husband and daughter have been very supportive of what I do. They put up with some horrendous schedules and pitch in when I need extra help. Peter is always willing to listen to me talk about the business. I always run ideas and questions by him. I don't necessarily always take his advice per se, but I take it into consideration as part of the whole brainstorming process. And I've been so lucky to be able to be at home and work. We knew we were only going to have one child, and we felt it was so important to have someone at home for her, and I was the lucky one!"

The next comments from three veterans in our industry are, not surprisingly, similar.

NINA FELDMAN, Nina Feldman Connections (1981), Oakland, California

"No such thing as a typical day—each day is different! That's what I love about being in business for myself, but it certainly can create stress."

KATHY KESHEMBERG, Computron/A Career Advantage (1983), Appleton, Wisconsin—one son, sixteen years old

"There isn't a typical day! Workload and client appointments certainly dictate what my schedule will be. I see clients between 9:00 A.M. and 5:30 P.M. I get up at 6:30, get my son off to school, grab a cup of coffee, and head downstairs to my office. Around 8:00 A.M., I head upstairs to shower and dress for the day. If the schedule isn't too demanding, I'll take thirty minutes to exercise. Then I'm back in the office to work on client projects, interspersed with phone calls (personal as well as business—one of the pitfalls of working at home is that relatives and friends know you're home and call to chat).

"My work schedule will typically include: writing/typesetting a resume; transcribing a tape or two for a counselor; taking addresses for cover letters from a client over the phone and producing the letters; making revisions to a specification for an architect, making and binding copies; word processing a script for a cartoon writer. In between these jobs, I'll meet with new resume clients, visit a client's office to get information for its next newsletter, or attend a networking meeting.

"At 5:30 (or whenever client appointments are finished), I make dinner, take an hour break to read the paper, and then, three to four evenings a week, will return to the office to work on larger projects, such as proofing/editing reports for a management consultant, writing resumes, or catching up on whatever didn't get finished during the day. Saturdays and Sundays are spent catching up on client work, bookkeeping, developing marketing pieces, writing my newsletter, filing, and cleaning the office."

WENDY GELBERG, Advantage Resume Services (1978), Needham, Massachusetts—one daughter, fifteen years old; one son, eleven years old

Wendy's response to describing her typical day: "Yikes! I'm not sure there is such a thing! I tend not to be a creature of habit or schedule, which is one of the reasons this business works so well for me, because it's so unpredictable." Wendy adds that "while mine are no longer 'young children,' I'm finding to my enormous surprise that they actually require more time in some ways than when they were younger. With higher grade levels come more complex homework assignments, which require more help. The kids are also involved in more activities, which require parents to chauffeur and attend. And with the teen and preteen years comes a need to tune in to whatever issues they may be struggling with and to be available for guidance (assuming they'll listen!).

"My kids have grown up with my business and with my clients. When I recently pondered the possibility of beginning to specialize and scaling back some services, my kids made it very clear to me that I 'couldn't' get rid of certain clients whom they've come to know and like. In some ways, my clients probably seem almost like extended family to my kids, and vice versa. I have fond memories of my then eighteen-month-old son climbing into a client's lap and gleefully rubbing the client's shiny bald head—something my son had never experienced before! The client had a grandson close in age to my son, and he was as amused with this natural curiosity as my toddler was! While I've always worried that I might be conveying a less than professional image because my home office and work life so obviously were structured around parenthood, I seem to have hooked up with clients whose values match my own and who never minded being surrounded by kid clutter or being interrupted by impatient little people.

"When I knew it was important not to have the clutter or interruptions, I simply scheduled appointments accordingly. I feel that my kids' lives were well integrated with my work life, and I encourage other mothers to try to do the same, if that is what they truly want. It *can* be done. My office has also been a very kid-friendly office—when clients bring their kids, as they often do, unannounced, I always have appropriate distractions available for them (including my own kids, who have taken visiting children under their wing on any number of occasions). I keep stickers and scrap paper around for visiting children, as well as a small box of toys that my kids have outgrown. Children and parents are usually delighted that I've taken the kids' needs into consideration.

"Also, my kids have been a source of business leads. I've done a lot of work for parents of their friends and for the schools and clubs that they're involved with."

THE BUSINESS OF ACTUALLY GETTING THE WORK DONE

This section relates to planning your business schedule and arranging appointments. Based on your own circumstances, time clock, and preferences, you will quickly develop a sense of the best times to work on different types of projects.

As a general guideline, plan to accomplish longer, more involved projects (writing a resume, composing original cover letters, etc.) during "off" office hours and (if you have kids) when your children are sleeping or someone else is caring for them. Your productivity will be greatly enhanced (as will your concentration) if you are not interrupted by the doorbell ringing, the telephone ringing, or your children fighting.

Reserve projects that can be done with many interruptions and less concentration for during the day when you are between appointments or telephone calls and/or the children (if any) are in your office. Projects lending themselves to interruptions might include long typing assignments, thesis typing, and so on. Keep a small clock by your computer/typewriter. *Always* use a Client Production Schedule for each project to log the time on and off the project—this is especially important for times when there are telephone interruptions too.

Be sure to invest in a screen-saver program for your computer monitor. (After Dark has a great one.) A program with a "message" selection that displays the message you previously entered, "typing" (with the sound of an actual typewriter) it across the screen after a predetermined lapse of time when no activity has occurred, is very useful. This accomplishes two things: (1) It saves your monitor screen from having the image burned in, and (2) it simulates an "office" sound that is lightly audible over the telephone while you're on a business call and helps to muffle "family" noises. I set my screen saver to begin after one minute of inactivity. My message is one more promotional message (my clients can see the monitor from their seat at the conference table): "Absolute Advantage—Our Business Is Making *You* Look Good!"

As discussed earlier, when you are accepting a client's project, specific instructions should be recorded on a Client Work Order. In addition, all materials should be placed into a manila folder. (One hundred can be purchased inexpensively from an office supply warehouse—usually for under $4.00.) When a client picks up a project, present the completed work in the same plain manila folder with your label affixed to the front. Use a kraft envelope of the corresponding size for large projects. This is inexpensive and looks professional. If you decide to invest more in your personalized office supplies, you can order custom-printed file folders and envelopes from your printer.

Refer to chapter 5 for information about using the Project Status/Deadline Sheet. This form will allow you to organize and prioritize your work. I recommend preparing a new list at the end of each business day to reorganize projects that have come in through the course of the day that may take precedence over other projects previously recorded. When you begin your work the following morning, you'll have a clear picture of what needs to be accomplished and when.

YOUR IMAGE AND THE IMAGE OF YOUR BUSINESS

Much has been said and written about the importance of your own image to being successful in business. The "dress for success" mentality certainly permeated the corporate culture during the early 1980s, particularly for women, who were advised to dress for the job they *wanted* to have, not the job they *currently* had.

I have always believed home-based professionals have flexibility with this aspect of their business; however, you are as professional as the demeanor you convey. Even in a home-based situation, it is possible to create a very polished, professional, and businesslike setting and style if you convey absolute authority and confidence in your manner of interacting with your clients. You may want to give consideration to "dressing up" in more conservative business attire for meeting with first-time clients (imperative when you are meeting in their offices). This is a particularly good idea with *business* clientele, as opposed to students or even resume clients; you may feel comfortable in your sweats for most subsequent meetings in your home provided that your demeanor is absolutely courteous, polished, and professional.

Much of this will be determined based on your own clientele. I work with a number of health care professionals as well as sales executives—many of whom operate from *their* home offices. They arrive for appointments attired in shorts, jeans, or whatever very casual attire is appropriate for the season. I don't feel a need to "dress to impress" for these meetings. We're all professionals—and on equal ground, regardless of our apparel. Of course, this assumes that while you may be casual, you are not messy—nor are your clothes unclean! Good grooming rules are never put aside.

On the other hand, when I am meeting with someone during a time of day when I know the person is coming directly from his or her office or a business appointment, I will dress more professionally. I believe that allows both of us to be more at ease. First-time resume clients who are professionals are also met with me dressed in more office-appropriate attire. Clients who require (and pay for) a Saturday-night or Sunday-morning appointment, however, might just find me in gardening attire, regardless of who they are and what their business is; it's much the same as going into any corporate office on a Saturday—you won't see any suits, ties, or heels.

As in all other matters related to developing your business, use your own good judgment in determining dress for client meetings.

CHAPTER SEVEN

GROWING THE BUSINESS

MANAGING BUSINESS GROWTH

While you might be tempted to chuckle and inclined to overlook this section, it's probably worthwhile to consider what can happen to your business in terms of growth. Any entrepreneur should possess optimism as a characteristic. Assuming you are an optimist, then, we'll presume your business is going to be successful and grow. To what extent would you like it to expand?

While it is true that limits of growth are, to an extent, only those you place on it, it is important to recognize that *at some point* you will be required to assess the overall future of your business. If you grow at a conservative 10 to 15 percent per year, it will take you a number of years to "max out" in terms of your ability to handle all of the work of your business. If, on the other hand, you enjoy even faster success (my own has been nearer to 25 or 30 percent per year), you will quickly reach a point when you must make critical decisions. After all, if you do all the work yourself, there are only a certain number of hours available each day (even if you choose to work sixteen or eighteen of them!), a certain number of days per week available (again, even if you choose to work all seven), and so on. What's a successful entrepreneur to do?

Well, one of the obvious things that many first-time business owners neglect to consider is this: Perhaps you are not charging enough for your services. There is a thought in this industry that goes something like this: "If you are getting *no* complaints about your prices whatsoever, you are not charging enough." This is not to give permission to gouge your clients, but it *may* be a good idea, if you find you are working fifty, sixty, or seventy hours a week, week in and week out, to reassess your rates and those of your competition—and then implement a price increase. What's the worst thing that can happen? You may find yourself working fewer hours per week, being happier, and *making more money*. Not a bad result.

CONSIDERING OTHER PROFIT CENTERS/ SERVICE OFFERINGS

The other thing solid business growth does is permit you the option of specializing in those aspects of the business you particularly enjoy. When most secretarial services begin, they handle any and all work that comes their way. From typing student term papers to doing transcription, they'll "do it all." This is fine, for diversity is interesting, the clientele is unique, and the profits are there. But as your business really hits stride, you may want to rethink your service offerings. Do you really *like* typing student papers? Perhaps you've found, as have a number of people in this business, that term paper typing can be an area fraught with rush deadlines, last-minute (and usually unreasonable) requests, little appreciation, and, unfortunately, occasional bounced checks. Do you need this headache and hassle? Maybe not. Perhaps you decide to stop posting notices at local campus centers. Maybe you take a line off your business cards and from your Yellow Pages advertising that says you type "term papers, theses, and dissertations." The same holds true for any other profit center—even if it's profitable, if you don't really love it, now is the time in your business cycle to truly focus on the services that are profitable *and* that you enjoy. You'll find included in the profiles that appear in the next chapter significant updates to the information provided for some of the home-based business operators. This is because three years after furnishing their initial information, *they've* grown to the point of a) expanding their businesses (in one case, out of the home), or b) specializing in one profit center only—and eliminating secretarial services.

If writing is your love and you've enjoyed dabbling in newsletter, brochure, and cover letter development, build a specialty around this service offering. It should be billed at a higher rate than basic word processing services, and by cutting out some of the lower-end word processing work (e.g., student typing), you'll have more time to focus on further development of this niche. The bottom line is to evaluate your overall business, assess the projected growth, and make deliberate decisions about areas in which you wish to be positioned.

IS IT TIME TO GET HELP?

No, not of the psychological nature, but perhaps what your business needs when you're at a consistently frenzied state of "too much to do, too little time," *is* help—in the form of freelance, subcontracted assistance. By far a better alternative for the sole proprietor who wishes to remain a "small but profitable business," subcontractors, as compared with employees, offer unique advantages for the secretarial service business.

From a tax standpoint, it is necessary to understand the differences between having employees and engaging subcontracted assistance. (See related publication of the Internal Revenue Service in Bibliography section of the Appendix or confer with your accounting professional, if you have one.) In order for a person to legally fit into a true subcontractor status, he or she must possess his or her own equipment and handle work for you out of his or her own home setting (in other words, not perform the work in your office). In addition, a subcontractor determines when he or she will work (not following a fixed schedule as determined by you). As a practical matter, you can coordinate times suitable to a subcontractor when making the necessary arrangements. A subcontractor, not you, is responsible for ensuring that his or her own tax obligations are met.

A subcontractor arrangement is a good means by which to grow your business without turning work away yet still maintain control over quality and your client relationships. (Your subcontractors would never meet with your clients, and you would always be checking and proofreading any subcontracted work before presenting it to a client.) An employer or subcontractor relationship must work well for *you*. Beyond appropriate skills and equipment, there must be a "fit" in terms of working style. You can usually determine fairly quickly in the interview process if the arrangement might be a positive one for you both.

The following forms depict a sample advertisement for seeking qualified subcontractor candidates, an ad for seeking employees, an application form, a listing of recommended subject areas to discuss in interviews, a sample proofreading test, a sample typing test, a job sheet for tracking time on projects, individual job sheets, and a sample invoice form for the subcontractor to follow in preparing invoices.

SAMPLE CLASSIFIED AD FOR SUBCONTRACTORS

> **Typist/Word Processor.** Part-time, flexible hours, freelance/subcontractor position. Min. 75 wpm, Mac background, Word 6.0 preferred. Excellent opportunity and pay. Submit resume: P.O. Box 111, Anywhere, USA 88888

SAMPLE CLASSIFIED AD FOR EMPLOYEES

> **Typist/Word Processor.** Part-time, flexible hours. Min. 75 wpm, Mac background, Word 6.0 preferred. Excellent opportunity and pay. Submit resume: P.O. Box 111, Anywhere, USA 88888

A-1 SERVICES PLUS

P.O. Box 111

Anywhere, USA 88888

(888) 888-8888 / Fax (888) 888–8889

Applicant _____ Date _____

Address _____ Telephone _____

Town, State, Zip Code _____

Mailing Address (if Different from Above) _____

Social Security # _____

Equipment/Software Owned _____

_____

Macintosh Experience?	☐ Yes	☐ No
Microsoft Word 6.0 Experience?	☐ Yes	☐ No
Excel 4.0 Experience?	☐ Yes	☐ No
Adobe Pagemaker 6.0 Experience?	☐ Yes	☐ No
Ready-Set-Go Experience?	☐ Yes	☐ No
Quicken Experience?	☐ Yes	☐ No
Dollars + Sense Experience?	☐ Yes	☐ No

Special Skills _____

_____

_____

Typing Speed: wpm _____ errors _____

[Please do not complete this line: tested wpm _____ tested errors _____]

Shorthand Experience? ☐ Yes ☐ No wpm _____

Transcription/Dictaphone Experience? ☐ Yes ☐ No

Medical/Psychological Terminology Background? ☐ Yes ☐ No

Professional Proofreading Experience? ☐ Yes ☐ No

[Do not complete: # errors _____]

PROFESSIONAL DESKTOP PUBLISHING, OFFICE, AND EDITORIAL SERVICES

REFERENCES

1. Name _____ Relationship _____

    Company _____ Phone # _____

    Address _____

2. Name _____ Relationship _____

    Company _____ Phone # _____

    Address _____

3. Name _____ Relationship _____

    Company _____ Phone # _____

    Address _____

RECENT PREVIOUS EXPERIENCE

Employer _____

Address _____

Position Title _____

Employed from _____ to _____

Phone # _____

Employer _____

Address _____

Position Title _____

Employed from _____ to _____

Phone # _____

Desired # Hrs./Week: _____ Max. # Hrs./Week: _____

Availability: Morning (Hours?) _____ Afternoon (Hours?) _____

            Evening (Hours?) _____ Weekend (Day/Hrs.?) _____

Any seasonal unavailability (summers off, planned vacation, etc.) _____

_____

Date Available to Begin: _____

Signature of Applicant _____ Date _____

NOT TO BE COMPLETED UNTIL SUBCONTRACTED

In case of emergency, notify: _____

Phone # _____

Date contracted _____ Starting Date _____

Hourly Rate _____ *Subcontractor is paid only for hours worked.*

A-1 Services Plus will provide subcontractor with Form 1099 in January, to be utilized in completing subcontractor's federal and state income tax forms. A-1 Services Plus will not deduct Social Security or income tax from subcontractor's payments. Subcontractor is responsible for any and all Social Security and income tax payments that may be due upon completion of his or her income tax forms. A-1 Services Plus is closed four weeks each calendar year for vacation. Subcontractor understands that all client records, files, and materials are to be maintained and handled in strictest confidence.

Acknowledged and Received _____
(Subcontractor Signature)

Date _____

[The following questionnaire outlines suggested responsibilities to be covered during interviews with candidates for subcontractor as well as employee positions. The information presented in this example is tailored to my specific business.]

SUGGESTED RESPONSIBILITIES

- word processing (manuscripts, correspondence, cover letters, resumes, presentations)

- typewriting (graduate school applications, employment applications)

- mailings (minutes, newsletters)

- transcription (two-person interviews, one-person dictation)

- courier (depending on time of year and work schedule, may be morning and/or afternoon; town[s]; vehicle provided; drive standard?)

OTHER KEY POINTS

- client confidentiality—most important factor! (i.e., resumes—all client contacts handled through this office must be held in strictest confidence)

- noncompete/confidential disclosure agreement

- execute agreement for subcontractor services (for subcontractors only)

- subcontractor to submit weekly summary of hours (for subcontractors only)

- Form 1099 provided (for subcontractors only)

- appropriate documents provided to employees

- flexibility in scheduling

- diversity and variety of work

- ideal background: a professional executive secretary with highly polished word processing skills (esp. Mac)

EXPECTATIONS

- selected candidate will be brought in at an agreed-upon hourly rate

- performance will be evaluated in 4–6 weeks, at which time—based on productivity—an adjustment will be made

- thereafter, performance evaluations will be conducted every 6–9 months, with increases as appropriate based on performance and productivity

IMPORTANT

It is vital that this process work for me in terms of overall productivity.

INTERVIEW NOTES

Date of Interview _____

Candidate Source _____

Approximate Days Available _____

Approximate Hours Available _____

Weekends? _____

Evenings? _____

Comments: _____

_____

_____

_____

_____

_____

_____

_____

_____

_____

_____

_____

_____

_____

_____

_____

_____

December 13 199

Joan Smith
General Business Copmany
144 Main Street
Anywhere, USA 66666

Dear Joan:

Thank for meeting with me yesterday to to discuss the upcoming regional sale meeting. The purpose or this letter is to outline the plans we made and ot pose some questions. We decided that the overall theme for the meetting wil be "Win with the Best". I will ask The marketing Department to design a logo to be used no all correspondence related to the meeting. The social evening will feature a "Breakout Bash I will coordinate with the hotel to arange decoartions and dance music.

I have come upwith more questions which need answer:

 —What is the budget for the social evening?
 —Will we provides breakfast before departure?
 —Will their be transportation for guests?

Please giv me your response by NOvember 20. I am anxious to implement all of these exciting plans.

Sincerely

Karen Rider

December 13, 199

Joan Smith
General Business Company
144 Main Street
Anywhere, USA 66666

Dear Joan:

Thank you for meeting with me yesterday to to discuss the upcoming regional sale meeting. The purpose of this letter is to outline the plans we made and to pose some questions. We decided that the overall theme for the meeting will be "Win with the Best" I will ask The marketing Department to design a logo to be used in all correspondence related to the meeting. The social evening will feature a "Breakout Bash" I will coordinate with the hotel to arange decoarations and dance music.

I have come up with more questions which need answer: that

—What is the budget for the social evening?
—Will we provides breakfast before departure?
—Will their be transportation for guests?

Please give me your response by November 20. I am anxious to implement all of these exciting plans.

Sincerely

Karen Rider

I am interested in seeking the Master's in Health Administration (MHA) for five primary reasons. First, I am very interested in actively working in the health care field and promoting health, prevention, and education.

Second, I have my Bachelor's of Science Degree in Social Work from XYZ University. I believe this degree is a strong asset to blend into the public health field. In the social work program, I developed skills in the areas of networking, advocacy, education, group work, and organizing activities.

Third, I am specifically interested in health care in the areas of drug and alcohol prevention/education, nutrition services, health advocacy, family health services, and gerontology. I feel that one of the greatest strengths of the MHA program is the concept of prevention and education. I am a strong advocate of this innovative philosophy.

Fourth, I have worked for the past four years as a residential counselor in a drug and alcohol treatment center for adolescents. I have seen the pain, anger, and havoc substance abuse has caused adolescents and their families. These clients often do not realize they even have choices as they become more and more immersed in their addiction. I strongly feel that health education, prevention, and promotion will have a positive impact on these social issues.

Fifth, I would value the opportunity to continue to develop my skills and education in the public health field. I am confident that I have the appropriate ability, dedication, and creativity to offer to the MHA program.

[Use your computer's word count and clock features to conduct a three-minute timing; allow the applicant time to "warm up" first.]

SAMPLE INDIVIDUAL JOB SHEET

[Use one per client project.]

Subcontractor/Employee Name _____

Date of Project	Nature of Project (Client Name, Type of Work)	Start Time	End Time	Total Time (In Hours, Minutes)

Copy multiple times.

SAMPLE SUBCONTRACTOR INVOICE FORM

Subcontractor Name _____

[address/telephone information]

Invoice for Services Rendered to: Date _____

A-1 Services Plus

P.O. Box 111

Anytown, USA 11111

Date of Project	Nature of Project	# of Hours @ _____/hr.*	Extension

Total Hours: _____ Total Due: _____

Subcontractor Signature _____ Soc. Sec. # _____

For A-1 SERVICES PLUS USE ONLY: Date Paid _____ Check # _____

Agreed-upon hourly rate

ASSESSING A MOVE OUT OF THE HOME

Because this is a book about establishing and operating a successful home-based secretarial service, I won't devote much space to this topic other than to say it may become a point of consideration in your long-range business planning. As you carefully assess your overall objectives, you may realize that becoming a corporation with a number of employees and having a retail storefront or executive suite location are appealing. You may eventually decide that a separation of your work and your home is important. Still, for many home-based secretarial service operators who have been successfully in business for a number of years, *staying* home-based is a primary objective.

If you are considering moving your business out of your home, be aware of the following points. Beyond the expenses of office overhead and changing your business cards, stationery, and Yellow Pages advertising (as well as any other advertising you do), there will be a commute and its associated costs. You will be tied down to maintaining regular, storefront hours typical of most executive suite or retail space secretarial services. Because you will be "susceptible" to walk-in traffic, you'll need to consider, almost immediately, having at least one employee to serve as receptionist and cover the front of the office when you can't be there (for the entire day, as in illness, or for a half-hour while you have lunch). This brings up immediate concerns about having employees, perhaps providing insurance and benefits and the like, in addition to another salary to support.

For many entrepreneurs starting their own home-based businesses, including secretarial services, a motivating factor was to leave the corporate pressures, the lengthy commute, and a less-than-satisfying environment in exchange for being the boss, setting one's own salary *and* hours, and developing an interesting client base. For those with young children, starting a business often represents an alternative to full-time child care and rarely seeing their children as they grow up.

Considering the explosive growth of home-based professionals in nearly every industry, home-based secretarial service operators are receiving more recognition, respect, and envy than ever before. With the significant technological gains in just the past five years alone, a home office can compete on equal footing with any executive suite or retail setup. Quality is a characteristic, as is professionalism, that can be provided from nearly any office setting, including home-based.

A final point to consider in this evaluation: Do you enjoy the flexibility and advantages available to you in working from your home? Are you willing to give these up and—if so—in exchange for what advantages that executive suite or retail storefront space would offer? Once you've really examined your business objectives and personal goals, you'll be in a good position to assess if a *physical* move is the right move for your business.

PROFESSIONAL AND PERSONAL GROWTH

Establishing and operating a successful home-based secretarial and office support service will bring greater rewards than you can possibly imagine—and in this success you will realize tremendous personal and professional growth. But the learning never stops, and the opportunities for even greater success (however you define this somewhat intangible term) never cease to present themselves. The directions you chart for your business will be a function of your own interests, personal objectives, and desires.

Through membership in professional associations and community organizations, you will have many opportunities to promote your business and your success in establishing and operating it . . . if you so choose. Concerning professional growth, I have found my memberships in the Association of Business Support Services International, Inc. and its "sister" organizations, the Professional Association of Resume Writers and the National Resume Writers' Association (see Appendix for additional information) to be invaluable as they relate to networking, building wonderful collegial and personal friendships, learning strategic business planning techniques, and refining/enhancing my professional skills. Over the past ten years, I have attended many national conventions of these associations, including serving as a major speaker at a number of these conventions. I can say without doubt that this participation has clearly provided me with the tools to continue to build and shape my business in a direction that is most rewarding and satisfying for me.

Many owners of secretarial services move into such interesting and lucrative areas as public speaking, teaching, writing, and consulting. The opportunities are truly limitless, limited only by your own set of objectives and expertise. Good luck, and *enjoy* growing your business!

CHAPTER EIGHT

PROFESSIONAL PROFILES

A CLOSER LOOK AT YOUR COLLEAGUES

The following snapshots offer you additional insight regarding some of us who have been in this field anywhere from one to more than twenty years. All of us originally home-based, many with families (some seeing our families nearly grown while watching our own businesses grow at the same time), we share numerous commonalities, yet enjoy distinctive differences. From rural to city locales and "traditional" two-parent households to single moms, we represent the many diverse ways in which a home-based secretarial service can be operated. In addition to the technical information presented in the profiles, you'll find valuable nuggets, including each entrepreneur's top five recommendations to someone starting his or her own secretarial service business. Most of the professionals profiled here accepted an invitation to update their information because of major changes in their businesses over the past three years (since the time they were first profiled). Others continue to operate in much the same manner as they did three years ago, and still believe their initial comments and recommendations to be salient. Where relevant, you'll see new information subtitled *1999 Update*.

Name: Vivian Lee Adkins

Company: Adkins Resume Services

Location: Erie, Pennsylvania

Description of Location: single-family home in a city of 100,000 residents

Year Business Started: 1995

Primary Focus: resumes and desktop publishing

Percentage Breakdown of Business: resumes 50%; secretarial/office support services 30%; desktop publishing 20%

Hours Per Week Worked at Business: 50–60 hours

Start-up Cost/Investment: $10,000 (credit cards)

Children at Home: 16-year-old son (also has 19-year-old daughter, not at home)

Biggest Challenge: Finding adequate time to rest with a very successful and busy business.

What She'd Do Differently: "I'd buy my computer system from a source that has excellent customer service capability. I bought an excellent system at a great price, but the service from this company's rep is terrible to nonexistent. I'd have given more thought to a computer system backup. We had a power outage here one night and I thought that six months' work had been erased. That turned out not to be the case, but it was very scary until I figured that out!"

Top Five Recommendations:
1. Know your software thoroughly.
2. Take as much time as is necessary to know your computer hardware and all of its connections.
3. Make customer service your business's top priority.
4. Make the success of your business your personal top priority.
5. Have enough savings to live on while you get started or some other source of income available.

Name: Sue Faris

Company: Word Processing Plus

Location: McFarland, Wisconsin

Description of Location: single-family home in a bedroom community of 5,000 residents near Madison

Year Business Started: 1987

Primary Focus: legal and medical transcription, resumes, desktop publishing, general business support services

Percentage Breakdown of Business: word processing 50%; transcription 40%; desktop publishing 5%; resumes 5%

Hours Per Week Worked at Business: 40 hours

Start-up Cost/Investment: $1,500 (cashed in life insurance policy)

Children at Home: 13-year-old daughter, 16-year-old son

What She'd Do Differently: "If I were starting my business today, I would probably go about it more methodically. I would have assembled a business plan and done more research into the entire process of starting a business. Initially I resigned from a government position due to personality conflicts at work, and the next week I started my business. No real preparation!"

Top Five Recommendations:

1. Be sure you really enjoy doing secretarial work and are comfortable wearing many different hats: marketing director, word processing operator, bookkeeper, inventory manager, etc.

2. Read all you can about this type of business. Talk to others in this business to get an idea of what a typical day is like.

3. If you have a young family, plan when your "work" production hours will take place so you can still spend quality time with your husband and kids.

4. If you're going into this as a one-person operation, plan ahead for how to take care of business when you are sick or an emergency comes up.

5. Join an organization like ABSSI or a support group of some kind for inspiration and support when you're feeling down and out.

Name: Nina Feldman

Company: Nina Feldman Associates

Location: Oakland, California

Description of Location: an apartment in a seven-unit building (surrounding a courtyard, with a lawn in the middle) in an urban city of 300,000 residents

Year Business Started: 1981

Primary Focus: computer and office support referral service

Percentage Breakdown of Business: referrals (to other secretarial/word processing services, for which fee is derived) 90%; word processing 10%

Hours Per Week Worked at Business: 40 hours

Start-up Cost/Investment: $10,000 (borrowed from family)

Children at Home: none

Biggest Challenge: "Separating my work from the rest of my life."

What She'd Do Differently: According to Nina, her "worst mistake when starting out" was rounding down her time on the hours billed clients so that she gave away time for free.

Top Five Recommendations:

1. Learn how to use your word processing software "backwards and forwards" until there is virtually nothing it can do that you are *not* familiar with.

2. Read manuals cover to cover, subscribe to a software magazine, and/or join a user group. It's quicker in the long run to learn and use "real" shortcuts that were designed to be used with a program.

3. Take a copyediting class and read style and secretarial manuals (*Chicago Manual of Style, APA Manual,* Kate Turabian's *A Manual for Writers of Term Papers, Theses, and Dissertations* and *Gregg Reference Manual*).

4. Charge enough and be comfortable with your hourly rate—and charge for *all* the time you spend.

5. Don't run your business in a vacuum. Sharing/networking with others in this industry has been the single most important thing I have done to maintain my success over seventeen years. Join ABSSI, create a local chapter, go on-line (AOL has a wonderful "Office Services" message board where secretarial service owners ask and answer each other's questions), read, research, ask, talk, write!

Name: Lisa Freeman

Company: Advanced Office & Resume Services

Location: Florence, South Carolina

Description of Location: apartment complex just outside city limits of a suburban area of 30,000 in hub of Pee Dee region (overall population of 130,000)

Year Business Started: 1994

Primary Focus: transcription, resumes, and desktop publishing

Percentage Breakdown of Business: transcription 50%; resumes 40%; secretarial/office support 10%

Hours Per Week Worked at Business: 40–60 hours

Start-up Cost/Investment: very minimal (already owned equipment/furniture); Lisa notes, "I have saved a lot of money in equipment costs by purchasing used, refurbished, and clearance items: for example, a used desk for $50 from a salvage shop; an ergonomic, high-back desk chair for $56 from Office Depot (it was a display model); a refurbished standard cassette transcription machine for $100 from Damark; and a refurbished copy machine for $350 from Damark (both items ordered from the factory-refurbished section of their catalog)."

Children at Home: none

Biggest Challenge: "The biggest challenge I've had as a self-employed individual is time management. When I worked for someone else, there were immediate consequences if I procrastinated, so I usually didn't. However, since starting my own business, I have had to learn a lot of self-discipline to make myself do work when I have the time instead of 'later' when I think I'll still have time. After getting way behind on projects I was putting off and staying up till 4:00 A.M. because I didn't finish something that could have easily been done earlier in the day, I started to learn my lesson. There are still days that I let myself be slack, but I try not to let it get out of hand. I work better on a deadline, but there's something to be said for not having work hanging over your head!"

What She'd Do Differently: "I was very unfocused during my first year of business, using the excuse that it was a 'learning' period for me. It was a learning period, but I wasted a lot of valuable time that I could have used to more aggressively market my business. I believe the growth of my business would be much farther along now had I been more focused in the beginning. Also, I set my prices on the low end when I first started out, and now I've got ongoing transcription accounts that are getting an incredible deal. Unfortunately, if I were to increase their rates now, I would likely lose their business and I can't afford that just yet."

Top Five Recommendations:

1. Read anything on self-employment and operating a secretarial service, in particular, that you can get your hands on *[Author's note: Lisa recommends this book, having used the first edition published in 1994 to help build her business]*. Ignorance may be bliss, but it doesn't pay the bills!

2. Try to find a group of secretarial service owners that you can network with and learn from. AOL has been that source for me.

3. Learn as much as you can about marketing. Running a successful secretarial service is as much dependent on adequate marketing as it is on providing excellent service.

4. Research your competition thoroughly. Try to find out what their rates are and listen to how they handle your requests as a "client." If they've been in business for a while, they're probably doing something right (which is not to say you can't outdo them).

5. To generate some immediate business (i.e., before your Yellow Pages ads come out), place flyers at the local colleges. My most successful flyers have been ones that were very simple in design with tear-off tabs for my telephone number and were printed on the brightest paper I could find. College students can be trying (late for appointments, impossible deadlines, sometimes they just don't show up), but they do have a need for both term paper typing and resume services. Also, when first starting out, they're a great group of clients to help you get your feet wet.

Name: Wendy Gelberg

Company: Advantage Resume Services

Location: Needham, Massachusetts

Description of Location: single-family home in an upper-middle-class bedroom suburb of Boston with about 30,000 residents

Year Business Started: 1978

Primary Focus: "I haven't had one primary focus in terms of defining a specialty—I *have* had one in terms of providing outstanding service! I do, however, draw heavily from the category of mental health providers and other small business owners/sole proprietors."

Percentage Breakdown of Business: secretarial services 45%; transcription 25%; desktop publishing 15%; resumes 15%

Hours Per Week Worked at Business: 50–70 hours (Wendy adds, "Sometimes I think there's *never* a time when I'm not at least *thinking* about some aspect of my business, so it's hard to know what the actual cutoff is. And in terms of my actual work habits, I've never been one to open up shop at 8:30 and close up at 5:00 or in any other way work predictable hours, even though I now see clients only during those hours, except under unusual circumstances. So, again, it's hard to give a precise total of hours.")

Start-up Cost/Investment: $300–$400 (in 1978 [!] for a "brand-new, cobalt blue, nifty IBM Correcting Selectric II typewriter"); Wendy adds, "When I reluctantly graduated into the world of word processing and decided to make this a business, we bought a shiny new Vendex-XT computer, loaded with Q&A software, which allowed me to do basic (and very primitive, by today's standards) word processing and database management. We bought the Panasonic dot matrix printer, too, along with a daisy wheel printer—all for a total cost of between $2,000 and $2,500."

Children at Home: 11-year-old son; 15-year-old daughter

Biggest Challenge: "For me, it's probably setting boundaries. It comes up in many different ways. In the early stages of the business, I was happy to take any work that came my way, day or night, weekday or weekend. When there's not much work, that's easy to do. As the workload has increased, it's been hard to wean people away from expecting 'round-the-clock service. Boundaries are also an issue when people show up without an appointment (as in, 'I saw your car in the driveway and figured you were home . . .'). I hate those awkward moments when you need to tell people that they've overstepped a boundary, and it's been a growing process for me to find the voice to do that. Finally, boundaries are an issue for me when the workload spills over into the time that I want to be spending with my kids and I find myself putting their needs second to a client's. Not the message I mean to be giving them, yet, in reality, it's the one that I do sometimes communicate."

Solutions (or attempts *at solutions):* "I have learned to tell people very clearly what my hours are. I may still work during my 'non-business' hours, but I don't answer the phone or meet with clients then, except under extraordinary circumstances and only when we've prearranged it. I am very forthright with all clients about the fact that my kids are an important part of my life. I've found that people respect my wish to be involved with my kids, and they learn early on that their work will always be ready on schedule. I also find it helpful to minimize client visits after school (although I've chosen not to completely block off that time—after all, some days, the kids don't come right home after school and the time is free, so in those instances I'd just as soon accommodate clients if possible)."

What She'd Do Differently: "This goes back to setting boundaries, for me. I'd set regular hours and policies and be clear with clients from the outset. Now that my kids are older, I would do one other thing differently. I would get a computer and printer exclusively for home use so that the kids didn't use my 'spare' computer for their school assignments. Having them doing homework while I'm doing client work can be distracting. Having them switch printers without telling me can be infuriating!"

Top Five Recommendations:

1. Read everything you can and talk to everyone you can about the industry to make sure you understand the unpredictable nature of the business so you're not taken by surprise when hordes of clients don't come charging through the door right away. This is not a "get-rich-quick" business. It's not even a "get-a-steady-reliable-income-quick" business. It's more typically a "slow-to-get-off-the-ground" business.

2. Definitely invest in Yellow Pages advertising—and make sure your ad is visible among the competition.

3. Use the early, quieter months to develop a portfolio of sample materials (give yourself some assignments, if need be, to generate samples; for example, find some documents others have created and improve them), create marketing materials, and learn all the ins and outs of the software you plan to use.

4. Find out the going rates in your area and be prepared to price your services competitively.

5. Develop a long-range marketing/public relations strategy that starts to develop name recognition for your business, which will ultimately bring more business your way. This includes networking (in groups such as professional associations, chamber of commerce, women's business groups), regular press releases, good works, and involvement in the community. Many of these activities are done with a relatively small investment of money, although perhaps a large investment of time. It's useful to begin this strategy in the early stages of your business when time is more readily available than money.

1999 Update from Wendy Gelberg
"It was interesting to look back on how things were three years ago. As for the update, in my case it's probably more dramatic than in many others' because I've pretty much abandoned the secretarial side of things. About two years ago, I decided to phase out the secretarial services side of my business (which is now known simply as Advantage Resumes—I've dropped the Dependable Office Services name) and focus mostly on resume writing and related tasks. I selected about half a dozen key clients from the secretarial realm that I wanted to retain and notified the rest that I was changing the focus of my business and would no longer be offering the services

I had been providing to them. I suggested some other places where they might get their work done. I also developed an arrangement with another ABSSI member in which she gave me a percentage of her billings from my client referrals for a fixed period of time, which was a three-way win: for my clients (who got their work done); for my colleague (who gained new clients); and for me (who got some ongoing income from the business I had built up over the years).

"An interesting thing happened: When it was apparent to the few 'privileged' clients (those that I chose to keep) that my secretarial services were becoming more scarce, I got a large check from one of them along with a lovely note thanking me for all the work I had done for him over the years. Others who were not in the privileged group (and who didn't even know there *was* such a group) offered to pay me at a higher rate if I would continue to work for them. Supply and demand—the supply of my services had gone down and the demand for it, along with the *value* of it, had gone up. I think there's an interesting lesson there for those of us who are hesitant to raise our rates for fear of losing customers. From their perspective, the fear is losing *us*!

"As for the biggest change in my business—that would have to be my internal decision to concentrate on resumes, as opposed to external forces having an impact on the business. The change has been very positive—fewer hours, better control over boundaries with clients, less of a sense that the business is running me rather than me running the business.

"I have not yet developed a Web site, although I intend to do so, and presently the Internet has no impact on my business in terms of direct profits. It is a wonderful resource for information that indirectly benefits my business. The recommendations I provided three years ago relative to starting a secretarial service business are just as relevant today."

Name: René Hart

Company: First Impressions Resume / Career Development Services

Location: Lakeland, Florida

Description of Location: single-family home in a city of 76,000 residents

Year Business Started: 1993

Primary Focus: development of resume and career search materials for individuals

Percentage Breakdown of Business: resume 95%; general secretarial 5%

Hours Per Week Worked at Business: 60 hours

Start-up Cost/Investment: $3,000

Children at Home: 1-year-old son

Biggest Challenge: "The biggest challenge I have faced as a business owner has been my effort to project confidence and assurance to the clients that they have made the right decision in coming to me to assist them. They rely on me for expert advice, and I find that most people just need someone to make the bottom-line decisions for them. In the beginning, I felt uncomfortable telling people what to do, but now I recognize that they're paying me for my training and experience in this area and expect me to advise them accordingly."

What She'd Do Differently: "If I could start all over again . . . I would immediately begin pursuing the resume aspect of the business. Writing resumes allows me to use my creativity while being rewarded at the same time. I also would have gone full-time a lot sooner than I did. Conducting a business on a part-time basis is very difficult and can be very discouraging. If you must do it part-time initially, invest in an answering service or a 'live' employee who can serve as a receptionist when you can't. There is *no* substitute when you're first starting out!"

Top Five Recommendations:

1. Read—everything you can get your hands on. Find out all you can about your profession, the competition, etc.

2. Plan—your marketing strategies, your pricing structure, your approaches to clients (both in-person and by telephone).

3. Save—every penny you have. It's not written in stone that you have to have a stockpile of money in the bank before striking out on your own, but it can't hurt. Don't go overboard in the beginning. There's no sense spending money on things you don't need yet.

4. Learn—recognize that we all are learning . . . we're just at different stages of the experience.

5. Have faith—believe in yourself and your abilities and you'll succeed!

1999 Update from René Hart

"After two years of struggling against well-established secretarial services, I decided to change directions and head in more of a career-oriented direction. Initially, I only typeset resumes, charging an average of $25 or $35 for the service. As my confidence grew, I began to realize that this was an extremely profitable niche. The local market was ripe for someone with my writing talents, so I spent the next two years aggressively growing the career services aspect of my business and phasing out the secretarial services. As word spread of my new focus, clients who had used me in a secretarial capacity gradually filtered in to take advantage of my resume-writing services. Now the focus of my business is entirely resume/cover letter development and Internet job search assistance. I work about 20–30 hours a week (and my son is now four years old!).

"In mid-1998, I woke up one morning and decided I didn't want to meet with clients anymore. I'd worked hard to cultivate an Internet presence: 80% of my business was conducted long-distance, and the local folks just didn't see the value in paying a premium price for a dynamic resume. So I took a few days off and developed a strategy for transitioning my local clients into a 'long-distance' mindset. As a result, my business has grown by leaps and bounds, and I no longer have to worry about making it home from the grocery store in time to meet with a client. If I have a standing appointment while I'm away from home, I simply grab a phone and a quiet corner, and I'm set. My business is completely mobile!

"Looking back over the past few years, it's clear that if I were to do things differently, I would have pursued resume services immediately and not focused at all on providing secretarial services and light typing for individuals and small businesses."

Name: Kathy Keshemberg

Company: Computron/A Career Advantage

Location: Appleton, Wisconsin

Description of Location: townhouse in city of 70,000 residents

Year Business Started: 1983

Primary Focus: "My focus is threefold: I target small businesses for transcription, correspondence, and daily/weekly secretarial services; the second target is desktop publishing jobs for these and other small business and large companies for overflow projects; and the third area is resumes (the most lucrative source of income but unpredictable from month to month)."

Percentage Breakdown of Business: secretarial/office support 55%; resume 28%; desktop publishing 12%; other (including publishing *Resources!*—see Appendix) 5%

Hours Per Week Worked at Business: 50 hours during slow periods to 70–80 hours during busy periods

Start-up Cost/Investment: $10,000 (bank loan)

Children at Home: 16-year-old son

Biggest Challenge: "Finding enough clients and generating the income necessary to keep my household running." (Kathy is a single, self-supporting mom.)

What She'd Do Differently: "I would have joined my local business women's group years ago. I was in business twelve years before finding that wonderful source of networking and support. I would have joined ABSSI sooner than I did and started attending conferences regularly. I joined five years after being in business and only started regular conference attendance four years ago. The ideas, support, and friendships are invaluable! I would have started doing press releases sooner (first one was sent in 1992!) and become more visible in the community."

Top Five Recommendations:

1. Charge enough. Don't give your services away just to get business.

2. Be prepared to wear many hats. Although your secretarial skills are vital, you will also need to be able to keep books, develop a marketing plan, trouble-shoot technical problems, and handle customer relations.

3. Be patient. It takes time to build a business.

4. Don't buy equipment until you have a paying client.

5. Subscribe to an online service. (I prefer AOL.) A wealth of information is available at a nominal cost.

1999 Update from Kathy Keshemberg

"Over the past few years, I have transitioned to not seeing clients and adapted to my new townhouse home and office. I have not yet mounted my Web site but am determined to get something out on the Internet this year!

"Compared with three years ago, my resume service is all done via telephone interviews, E-mail, and fax for both local clients (secured through Yellow Pages advertising and networking) and national clients. I also continue to provide business support services for several small businesses as well as association management. Resumes now account for 40% of my business, with business support at 35%, association management at 20%, and other profit centers (including publishing ventures) at 5%. Work hours hold fairly steady at 50 to 60 hours per week. My son is now grown and off on his own.

"My biggest challenge today? Staying motivated and focused. It's very difficult to juggle time schedules to meet the diverse needs of my client base."

Name: Cindy Kraft

Company: Executive Essentials

Location: Valrico, Florida

Description of Location: single-family home in an urban area of 116,000 residents

Year Business Started: 1994

Primary Focus: legal secretarial services

Percentage Breakdown of Business: secretarial/office support 50%; transcription 40%; desktop publishing 5%; resumes 5%

Hours Per Week Worked at Business: 40–60 hours

Start-up Cost/Investment: $5,000

Children at Home: 13- and 16-year-old daughters

Biggest Challenge: Marketing self and overcoming lack of self-confidence.

What She'd Do Differently: "Two things I would do differently: have more cash on hand for the slow times and I would have taken some marketing classes. I think selling a 'service' is more difficult than selling a tangible product someone can see." Cindy also notes, "I am a single mom with two teenage daughters. They have been wonderful this past year—supportive and helpful. They are even willing to work for free when times are tough! This has been a good experience for all of us. I know they are proud of me, and I am so happy to be home more with them."

Top Five Recommendations:

1. Network, network, network.

2. Don't expect instant gratification. Have enough cash on hand to get you through the slow times.

3. Read everything you can, including all the posts on AOL. There is a wealth of information available.

4. Join ABSSI. The newsletters and hotline are invaluable to any secretarial service owner.

5. Think through projects before quoting prices. Invariably I cut myself short because there was something I forgot to include when giving quotes over the phone. I do a much better estimating job when I take down the information, including the caller's name and phone number, think through the job, and

then call back with a quote. Perhaps this short-changing myself is due, in part, to my inexperience.

1999 Update from Cindy Kraft

"What has changed over the past three years? *Everything!* Following two rear-end collisions (them hitting me) in early 1997, I was forced to reevaluate how many hours I could tolerate sitting at the computer in pain from two bulging disks. By this time, more and more of my telephone calls were career development related, and it seemed like a synchronistic event! As a result, I changed the focus of my business from secretarial to career development.

"That same year, I met a colleague from across the bay—close enough for us to work together but far enough away so we were not in direct competition. Together, we set goals and resolved to grow our resume businesses through joint marketing. We had notepads printed as giveaways; developed a seminar entitled 'The Internet, A Gold Mine of Opportunities,' which we presented at job fairs, the library, and other organizations; created bookmarks; and wrote a Job Search Strategies resource book for our clients. We will be adding job coaching as an additional service for our clients upon completion of Dick Knowdell's Job Coach Training seminar. With regard to the Internet, given the statistics released almost daily, I truly believe every one of us needs to have an Internet presence.

"The Professional Association of Resume Writers' venture into America's Promise (a career assistance program) brought me into the Hillsborough County public schools as a business partner, and EPIC 21 was born. My technology partner and I developed a Web site to promote career awareness and list entry-level jobs for students (www.epic21.com), allowing students to use technology to find an interesting career and get a job. I was recently nominated for a Zone Award for my contributions in the school-to-careers arena. More recently, I was nominated by the chamber president for Ernst & Young's Entrepreneur of the Year Award for this project.

"From there, EPIC 21 expanded to develop a Web site for 'people who live and work and play in Tampa Bay' (www.tampabaycareers.net). We are linked to the Brandon chamber relocation page and are in the process of partnering with MacDill Air Force Base to provide a resource for the spouses of enlisted service men and women.

"Most recently, we have launched an on-line community in collaboration with the local chambers and community newspapers. This Web site (www.the-burbs.com) is exploding with interest from all segments of the community—businesses, non-profits, youth organizations, clubs. One "burb" (an online community or "suburb") has already opened, with three more scheduled to open later this year.

"My biggest challenge is time management. Juggling the resume side of my business with setting and making sales calls on the Internet-advertising side of my business and getting it all done is a constant battle. I have found that I really need to utilize Covey's method of scheduling my week every Sunday in order to best utilize my time.

"In December of 1998, I hired a coach to help me manage my time more effectively with a goal of doubling my income. We meet every three weeks to analyze what I've done in the prior weeks, talk about challenges and how to overcome them, and set new goals for the upcoming three-week period. In 1998, I realized a 31% increase in my business over the prior year. That growth is phenomenal—and I anticipate doing even better this year. Am I having fun? You bet!"

Name: Brenda Lorencen

Company: Word/Pro Connection

Location: Parma, Michigan

Description of Location: new single-family log home in rural town of 1,000 residents

Year Business Started: 1991 (initially); returned to full-time employment in January 1992, then restarted the business (on a full-time basis) in March 1995

Primary Focus: "Providing quality customer services!"

Percentage Breakdown of Business: secretarial/office support 50%; transcription 25%; resumes 15%; desktop publishing 10%

Hours Per Week Worked at Business: 35–40 hours

Start-up Cost/Investment: $3,300 (home equity loan)

Children at Home: 13- and 20-year-old daughters; Brenda notes, "The best strategy for my younger daughter (since my eldest is employed at a full-time job) is getting her involved in my business. She stuffs envelopes for me, affixes labels on the envelopes, folds letters, staples pages, etc. I find that when I give her this opportunity, it teaches her about what I actually do and she has an appreciation for what is involved."

Biggest Challenge: "Not letting my home-based business take over my entire life and neglecting my family and friends."

What She'd Do Differently: "I officially started my secretarial and word processing service back in November of 1991, but went back to a full-time job in January of 1992 after not enough money was coming in regularly. This shattered my dreams. I hadn't really given it much of a chance, but the bills were coming in and the money wasn't, so I went back to full-time employment. However, I still had the passion for my home-based secretarial business. I worked another three years as office manager in a law firm but still could not get this idea out of my head. I wanted another attempt at my business. I wanted to give it one more chance; I was totally determined to give it my all. On March 6, 1995, I quit my job in the law firm. On March 13, 1995, I began my second chance at my business, and my first client was my previous boss (an attorney). I convinced him he could actually save money hiring me as an independent contractor with no Social Security/withholding deductions, fringe benefits, and vacations to worry about." Brenda notes, "*This time* [in restarting her business], I really feel I had all the bases covered!"

Top Five Recommendations:

1. Read *How to Start a Home-based Secretarial Services Business* by Jan Melnik. ("Excellent advice, Jan!") This has helped me in my business tremendously, and I refer to it often.

2. Read any and all other publications you can get your hands on dealing with this topic.

3. Find a niche that you can specifically offer your clients.

4. Join ABSSI and other local professional organizations. Get involved in their programs.

5. Develop a "can-do" attitude and *believe*. The sky's the limit in what you can do. Persevere!

1999 Update from Brenda Lorencen
"Business is indeed flourishing! The biggest change in my business over the last three years has been in the volume of my workload. I have landed some large accounts in the medical transcription area for hospitals and clinics—doing their overflow work. This seems to be the majority of my workload.

"I am utilizing the Internet for a variety of small business resources and information that is available; however, I do not have a Web site as of yet. I'm still doing some research to see if this would be beneficial for my company. So many of my new clients come from referrals from previous clients with good results. I still have my Yellow Pages advertising, but I have substantially decreased the size of the ads which, in turn, lowers my advertising expense. I find my business name listing in bold print does just as well. I am hearing very often from a lot of new clients that I am the only one who actually answers my phone. Some of the other local services have an answering machine or voice-mail. This turns prospective clients off. They want a real, live person to talk to when they need assistance with their individual needs.

"My company's name is still Word/Pro Connection, but it has relocated to my new log home in Parma, Michigan. It's great to be able to build a new home and to actually enjoy spending a significant amount of time there and still make a living! The fringe benefits are outstanding in being home-based.

"The one challenge that I still face is to be disciplined enough to turn the business off for the day, and sometimes getting started for the day. The hours I work have significantly changed from three years ago. I now put in 50–60 hours per week but love what I do, and that is so important—to have the ability to truly enjoy your work. Thank goodness for a very understanding and helpful family. My husband does periodic pick-up and deliveries, and my 17-year-old daughter is employed part-time as my office assistant. It involves them in the business and gives them a better understanding of what actually goes on daily. I also have tripled my income since my first year in business full-time (1995). I wouldn't want to be anywhere else in my career and probably will never retire.

"My current percentage breakdown of business is transcription: 50%; business office support: 25%; resumes: 25%. My primary focus now is providing customized service for each client. Each client has his or her own specific needs. Being flexible in meeting those needs is essential. Go the extra mile for your client—you will definitely reap the benefits!

"By the way, I typed this on my laptop on my porch swing. The birds sound just marvelous today. Ah, the joys of being home-based!"

Name: Kathy Mandy

Company: Select Word Services

Location: Chanhassen, Minnesota

Description of Location: single-family home in a suburban town of 12,000 residents

Year Business Started: 1981

Primary Focus: Working with businesses and also individuals who work from their home-based offices

Percentage Breakdown of Business: transcription 66%; secretarial/office support (including some desktop publishing) 29%; resumes 5%

Hours Per Week Worked at Business: 40–50 hours

Start-up Cost/Investment: $4,500 ($1,500 of personal savings; $3,000 bank loan)

Children at Home: 18-year-old daughter

Biggest Challenge: Seeming credible to other people and setting boundaries.

What She'd Do Differently: "Two mistakes I made when I started up were under-funding and not having a separate phone line for the business from day one. I wish that I had had some slush funds to do some higher quality printing. I really skimped on the printing for my brochures; if I had just spent another measly $50 on them, they would have looked a lot better. My letterhead and business cards looked good, but the brochure I used looked pretty bad.

"When I first started, I used my home phone line as my business line. Because of this, people would call me at any time of day and night. The final straw came when my first regular client called me at 10:00 at night to dictate a letter. The next day, I called the phone company and got a business line installed. At the time, it cost me $75 a month, and this was 1981 dollars. My phone was my biggest expense, but it was also the most valuable investment I ever made. I now had regular office hours of 8:30 to 5:00 and didn't answer the phone at any other time. Clients soon learned that they couldn't drop in on me at any time of day and night, and a much more businesslike relationship developed. I also put a drop box on my house, which meant they could pick up and drop off at any time of day or night. I guess in hindsight what the business line did was set boundaries for the business in terms of hours and image."

Top Five Recommendations:

1. Take a course on how to start a business offered by a local vocational technical school or community college. I used to automatically tell people to join APOSS or MN-ABSSI, but I find that they come to these meetings with only the concept of wanting to "work at home." People really don't have a concept of what a business is. So I try to stress the difference between "working at home" and operating a business.

2. After attending a how-to-start-a-business class, join a local secretarial association and call and check out ABSSI. Order the ABSSI publications, order Jan Melnik's book, order Kathy Keshemberg's *Resources* package, and order Louise Kursmark's book. *[Author's note: Information about all these publications appears in the Appendix.]* When someone calls me about starting up a service, I send them information on these materials and tell them to invest $100 in reading and see if it's really what they want to do and do it right the first time.

3. Have a financial plan that allows you to live for at least a year without a steady income. I stress the need for planning some funding for good marketing

materials, Yellow Pages ads, a laser printer (not a dot matrix or bubble jet), a separate phone line, and all the other miscellaneous stuff that hits you during the first couple of months.

4. Make sure you know your software and equipment. Be as proficient on your programs as possible. Have at least one to two years of experience using the program, and really be able to sell your skills to your prospective clients.

5. Know that the first year is going to be a challenging year, but it will be fun and rewarding. It's going to take a lot of work, more than you had ever anticipated, to get your business up and running. Do some planning and don't let the negatives discourage you. Consider everything a learning experience and move on. Getting the first client is the hardest thing you'll probably ever do in your life, but once you get that first one, it's all downhill from there!

1999 Update from Kathy Mandy

"Yes, my business is flourishing—in the midst of a meltdown here with work coming from too many clients at one time. This feast-or-famine aspect of the business is what's going to kill me!

"Everyone has a computer nowadays and, therefore, companies view their employees as computer-literate and astute communicators. We, as professionals, know this isn't the case. I really thought that the total destruction of the written word and massacre of language would be tolerated by the business world for only a two- to three-year time period. However, it appears that these are now traits that are accepted and even praised by the business world and the community at large. So, with great disappointment in watching the English language be mangled and mauled, I have grudgingly accepted this as a fact of life. I still do promote editing, proofreading, and grammar and sentence structure as services for clients, but that part of my business has not grown. It's a hard sell.

"An area that is growing for me is computer and software training with clients. In this last year, I made a substantial financial and time investment and took software training courses. This has opened two new profit centers for me—client software and computer training, and high end database and spreadsheet capabilities. These are both higher dollar per hour profit centers and much more mentally rewarding.

"The other noticeable change in my business has been a decrease in tape transcription (although the past two weeks wouldn't show that!). I read an article in *Newsweek* last year about market research. It stated that the use of focus groups has decreased and researchers are now using other tools to tap the public's mind. As with everything else in life, focus groups seem to be transitioning out of style. I used to do an average of five taped interviews a week, and this past year, I believe I averaged one a week (and that could be on the high side). But now I have a deluge of work in my office, so I'm going to watch this trend. My feeling is that this is going to be a dying market.

"I do more office organization consulting now than in the past. This, again, is at a higher hourly fee. Any new profit center I enter must be at a higher hourly rate than the basic word processing. The low hourly rate is not the client I want. In fact, I recently sent one packing!

"The Internet has impacted my business positively. I now send 99% of finished tape transcripts to clients via e-mail, which means I'm no longer printing out 60- to 90-page documents! Wonderful cost and time savings. This eliminates a courier cost on the client end but with no discount in price for lack of printout on my part.

"I don't have a Web page or market on the Web. At this point, it's not my customer base. I do about zilch marketing and really grow my business on a referral basis. These are the clients that give me the biggest dollar return.

"I can't imagine, however, doing business without the Internet. Being able to make such quick contact with current clients, turn around their work, get their feedback—all immediate. I do use the Internet, too, for research for clients, which is a nice profit center."

Name: Jan Melnik

Company: Absolute Advantage (division/Comprehensive Services Plus)

Location: Durham, Connecticut

Description of Location: single-family home in rural town of 6,000 residents

Year Business Started: 1983

Primary Focus: desktop publishing, business consulting/speaking, resume/career services, and office support

Percentage Breakdown of Business: resumes 35%; desktop publishing (including book projects and *The Word Advantage* newsletter) 25%; business consulting/speaking 20%; secretarial/office support 20%

Hours Per Week Worked at Business: 35–45 hours

Start-up Cost/Investment: pay-as-I-go (reinvesting profits along way to fund future purchases . . . acquiring equipment [e.g., a transcriber] and software [e.g., PageMaker] to meet specific client needs) without incurring debt

Children at Home: 9-year-old son, twin 11-year-old sons

Biggest Challenge: Achieving balance!

What She'd Do Differently: My "learning experiences" (read: mistakes!) appear sprinkled throughout text!

Top Recommendations: My best suggestions form the basis of this entire book, of course; however, I'd strongly urge reading and rereading the top five recommendations of your peers from time to time . . . there's a huge amount of excellent advice gathered in this section culled from more than 150 years of combined professional experience in the field.

Name: Theresa Mills

Company: Mountain View Office Support

Location: Dunbarton and Concord, New Hampshire

Description of Location: single-family home in rural town of 2,000 residents

Year Business Started: 1988

Primary Focus: transcription, "although I do perform quite a bit of word processing as well as some resume work"

Percentage Breakdown of Business: transcription 85%; secretarial/office support 10%; resumes 5%

Hours Per Week Worked at Business: 30 hours

Start-up Cost/Investment: $1,000

Children at Home: Infant son, 6-year-old daughter and an 8-year-old son

Biggest Challenge: Lack of self-esteem and shyness "when it comes to networking with people. Through the business organizations that I have become involved in (i.e., ABSSI, Women Owner's Network, etc.), I have become better at interacting with people. I can't honestly say that I have completely 'overcome' this challenge, but I have more of a handle on it than I originally did."

What She'd Do Differently: "If I were to start my business over again, I would take it more seriously than I did the first time. In the beginning, I thought of it more as a hobby than a 'real' business and I'm sure that other people did, too. People seemed genuinely surprised once I began growing my business and was actually making money at it. So, start serious and stay serious!"

Top Five Recommendations:

1. Believe in your own abilities; don't underestimate your own talents.

2. Go about starting your business or growing your business at a pace that is right for you. Everyone has different circumstances that come into play, but it has to be right for you!

3. Understand up front that it won't be a walk in the park. There are going to be rough days and lonely days, especially if you've worked in a corporate atmosphere in the past. It can be pretty overwhelming to work by yourself and to have to count on your own personal efforts to make an income. For me, I still have the need to communicate with the outside, and that's where joining organizations and working with a lot of different clients can help.

4. I feel very strongly in the need to join a few business groups. It's a great way of meeting people, possibly new clients. It also does help with the isolation that someone might feel working from a home-based office.

5. Don't give up on your business if it gets off to a slower start than you anticipated. Anything worth doing takes time, and owning your own business is worth the time it takes!

1999 Update from Theresa Mills

"I would have to say that the most significant change to my business has been the addition of a satellite office located in Concord, New Hampshire. I opened the Concord office in July of 1998 because of the number of calls I was receiving from the Concord area. There seemed to be a real need for an office support business in Concord, and so I jumped on the bandwagon. The population in the city of Concord is 37,925—considerably larger than Dunbarton's 2,000! The new office is approximately 400 square feet. It wouldn't be a good location if I were to employ someone, but it works out very well for me at this time since I am still using subcontractors for transcription work. It is in a professional building rather than a storefront location because I still wanted flexibility in scheduling appointments. What I try to do is have office hours from 9:00 A.M. to 2:00 P.M. Monday through Friday. Then I work in the Dunbarton office every afternoon until 5:00 P.M. By working things out this way, I've still been able to be home for my kids, as well as do some volunteer work at the school.

"As far as the Internet is concerned, I use it to communicate with people who I've met through networking, and I do have several clients who receive their files via e-mail rather than U.S. mail. This has worked out very well because it significantly cuts down on turnaround time. I also have been contacted to be a source for transcription overflow for a company that is based in Stockholm, Sweden. It wanted to have a group in the United States that could provide transcription services on Sweden's off-hours. (There's a six-hour time difference.) I'm not sure how it will all work out, but without the Internet, the opportunity wouldn't even be possible. I do not have a Web site at this time. I guess I'm not convinced that I really need one yet; I hope to see what others are doing in this area at the next ABSSI conference.

"I did change my business name from Mountain View Secretarial Service to Mountain View Office Support. This change became effective in January of 1998. The reason for the name change was to become more updated—lose the 'secretarial' image a little bit and let potential clients know that I provide a variety of services and not only 'typing.'

"This year was the first year that I placed an ad in the Yellow Pages under 'Resume Services.' I had been very hesitant to get involved in this particular profit center in the past. However, when I researched the Yellow Pages last year, the only listing under 'Resume Services' was for Kinko's! So I got brave and placed a small ad under this heading. The new books came out in January of 1999, and I have been overwhelmed with the response that this little ad has had! So far, I have averaged approximately three to four resume calls per week, and actually booked appointments for two to three *each week*. It's been great!"

Name: Joyce Moore

Company: Moore Business Services

Location: Hendersonville, North Carolina

Description of Location: single-family home in small city of 73,800 residents ("retirement haven . . . one out of four people in Hendersonville is over age 65")

Year Business Started: 1994

Primary Focus: resumes and freelance business writing with marketing divided into three different and "almost equal segments: resumes, writing and editing, and secretarial services"

Percentage Breakdown of Business: resumes 36%; secretarial/office support 30%; freelance writing/copywriting 15%; desktop publishing 13%; transcription 5%; fax service 1%

Hours Per Week Worked at Business: about 70 hours

Start-up Cost/Investment: $12,000 (own savings and credit cards)

Children at Home: none (all four grown)

Biggest Challenge: Getting new business.

What She'd Do Differently: "I would not have quit my day job before my Yellow Pages ad came out. In fact, I would have probably kept working after it was out a few months. I used up most of my savings waiting for the ad to come out. I didn't promote myself much while I waited and lost business and opportunities. I also made the mistake of thinking my spouse was willing to take up the slack while I launched this business, and he wasn't. I'd tell everyone to have long talks about the financial side with themselves and their partners before deciding to jump in. Jumping in the way I did made my start-up much harder on me and my family than was necessary. It isn't impossible to do, but it is much more frustrating. I firmly believe I can make as much money from home as I did in the middle management position I held, but presently my monthly take is less than my weekly paycheck used to be. That is a very hard pill to swallow."

Top Five Recommendations:

1. Get a Yellow Pages ad as fast as you can.

2. Don't quit your job until that Yellow Pages ad is out.

3. Have an emergency plan for income if the business doesn't start at once or have some savings. As is commonly said, you *will* need enough to live on for six to twelve months. Or, have a spouse willing to pick up the slack while you get on your feet.

4. Learn all you can by reading and networking (on-line networking is the greatest), find out your local rules and regulations, and then take the plunge.

5. Promote, promote, promote, or starve, starve, starve. (Joyce says, "I know that from experience!" Joyce also adds, "In doing this exercise [completing the questionnaire for this book], I found that even though I'm not supporting my family, my business *is* growing! Since the first month my Yellow Pages ads have been out, total sales have more than tripled. If this trend continues, I will be making the income I need and more by year's end. Presently, the business itself is clearing enough to pay its bills. After all these months, that's an accomplishment!")

1999 Update from Joyce Moore

"Over the past three years, my business has continued to grow. In 1998, I reached my original goal of earning an amount equal to my previous corporate earnings. Based on the first quarter of 1999, this year will be equally successful. At this point, the business is supporting itself and my family.

"The biggest change in my business over the last three years has been the increase in individual clients purchasing computers. Instead of causing me to lose business, these clients have opened the way for a new profit center: computer tutoring. Word-of-mouth for computer tutoring spreads like wildfire, especially through the retirement communities.

"I have seen an increase in preparation of marketing materials, flyers, etc., as well over the last year from business start-ups. In addition, I have been in business long enough now to have increased repeat business from all areas—resumes, businesses, and individuals.

"I use the Internet to conduct business with existing clients via e-mail. It has replaced the use of faxes with many of my clients. I also use the Internet to research current trends, do job searches for clients without computers, and as a networking tool. I have a Web page under construction. Internet-specific business probably accounts for about 10% of my business at this time.

"My advice to those entering this business now is to develop a niche in what you really enjoy doing—e.g., resumes, word processing, transcription. Once you have established what you enjoy, keep your eyes open for areas in which to stretch yourself a bit. Be willing and able to diversify; don't be afraid of change!"

Name: Elizabeth (Beth) Ann Quick-Andrews

Company: Q & A Business Solutions

Location: St. Louis, Missouri

Description of Location: single-family home; my partner (spouse) and I share 750 square feet of our basement for our business. (The office has its own entrance.)

Year Business Started: 1989 (My husband and I merged our two companies in 1997.)

Primary Focus: work with associations and small business; newsletter production

Percentage Breakdown of Business: small businesses 70%; individuals 25%; large companies 5% (with desktop publishing largest single category of work)

Hours Per Week Worked at Business: 70–80 hours

Start-up Cost/Investment: minimal start-up costs; ongoing investment in equipment and software to be able to service our clients with the latest technology.

Children at Home: none

Biggest Challenge: "Staying focused on business and not getting distracted with the easy 'admin' stuff to do. Running the Quicken reports to see where I am every second of the day, etc."

What She'd Do Differently: "Specialize in something sooner. I find that the diversity can be overwhelming and makes it difficult to focus on any one thing for too long."

Top Five Recommendations:

1. Figure out what it is that you really want to do and learn everything you can about that specialty area. You can grow your business more quickly by gaining specialized skills. Those skills are more valuable to your clients.

2. Develop a solid business plan with benchmark goals for all facets of the business: marketing, financial, operations, and management. Hold regular strategic planning sessions, and involve everyone who is responsible for making that plan come to life. At the strategic planning session, take a look at what is working and what needs to be rethought.

3. Network, Network, Network. By far, this has been the best way for me to grow my business. Joining business organizations and chambers of commerce has been an excellent way to meet prospective clients and gain credibility as a professional. Networking is also great professional development because you can share your successes and learning experiences with other business owners and gain insights from their experience. I have always said, "People do business with people they know."

4. Get involved in your industry associations, and network with colleagues. This is a great way to learn about trends in the industry, new technologies, and new services being offered. It is also invaluable to be able to talk with someone who knows what you are going through when you may have a problem with a client or your software is acting up, etc. We don't have to reinvent the wheel.

5. Be creative! Be innovative! Have fun! This is a tremendous opportunity to create a company that represents your goals, your values, and your personality. Always think about how you can make things better. Do what you love and the money will follow.

1999 Update from Elizabeth Ann Quick-Andrews

"The primary focus of my business is now association management, desktop publishing, and computer consulting. The percentage breakdown of business is as follows: small businesses/organizations: 75%; large companies: 15%; individuals: 10% (with computer consulting/systems being the largest single category of work).

"I'm now working *only* 50–60 hours a week. As we continue to grow our business, my biggest challenge is transitioning my focus from being a do-er (primary production person) to a manager and delegating work to either employees or sub-contractors.

"Three years later, something I would do differently is develop a mission and vision for the company that focused on my specific skills and abilities and only take on projects that are in sync with the mission of the organization. I would develop a referral network more quickly to refer jobs to others who specialize in areas that I don't. I fell into the syndrome of 'Jack of All Trades, Master of None' for a while. A client or prospect would say 'Can you help us with . . . ?' We would say 'Sure,' and then pedal like crazy to figure out how we were going to get this done. While these can be great opportunities to expand your business, they usually end up being very costly because of unbillable learning curve time, and if you don't know what you are doing, the client will figure it out sooner or later.

"The biggest change in my business in the last three years is that my husband and I bought a house, moved my business from my parents' basement (where we shared space for my first eight years of operation), and merged our two companies into one. Jim is a computer consultant who works with small businesses to maintain systems. He is a programmer and writes custom applications for companies that need specific software to automate internal processes.

"We made the decision to merge the businesses during one of our quarterly strategic planning sessions. We were trying to determine marketing plans for two companies, and it was getting very complex and expensive. During our discussions, we came to realize the many crossover possibilities for the two companies. For example, Jim is a 'techie,' and I am better at training clients on new software packages . . . and we combine my desktop publishing skills with Jim's technical skills to design Web pages. Our decision to merge was one of the best decisions we ever made. We discovered the synergy of working together (2+2=8). Our business has more than doubled in the last two years what the two individual companies billed before the merger. We are structured with two divisions: computer systems design and development, and business services. The moral of the story is to always look for strategic partnerships that will help you grow your business.

"We have seen a significant impact of the Internet in two ways in our business. We have added Web page design to our menu of desktop publishing services. This has meant learning about a whole new medium of communication. We have had to learn how to do site development, how to register with search engines for maximum response, what types of information should be included in a Web site, etc. This has been a very lucrative profit center.

"The Internet has changed the way we communicate with our clients and prospects. We can respond more quickly to requests for information. We can send and receive data files quickly and seamlessly. We do have a Web site (www.qabs.com).

It primarily serves as an electronic brochure for our company right now. We put the Web site address on all of our marketing materials. It also serves as a sample site for prospective Web site clients to review. We do not actually 'conduct business' over the site in the form of e-commerce other than as a means of communication with clients and prospects.

"We have had the Web site up since January of 1998. We are in the planning stages of revising the information and adding to it. I would like to see us add informational articles and links to other Web sites (perhaps for a fee to make it more profitable).

"My final thoughts when thinking over the past three years and providing recommendations to new folks entering this field: Think big picture. What do you want this company to look like? What types of clients do you want to serve? What types of work do you want to do? Are your ideal clients and your specialized services in sync with each other?

"Be proactive. You have the opportunity to develop your company your way. Work only with people who will work with you and respect you. Do only those projects you enjoy doing. This will significantly reduce your chances of burnout. I mean this very sincerely. When I started, I said 'yes' to everything and then spent a tremendous amount of energy being stressed out about 'how am I going to get this done? I don't know what I am doing.' It doesn't have to be that way. I know that now. By assessing my skills, planning for what I want to do, and reviewing those plans quarterly, my business has grown tremendously, and I enjoy what I am doing—which is really the point of having your own business!"

Name: Josie Smith

Company: An Executive Assistant

Location: Chico, California

Description of Location: single-family home in a rural county of Northern California (county-wide population of 47,000)

Year Business Started: 1995

Primary Focus: word processing and desktop publishing

Percentage Breakdown of Business: secretarial/office support 50%; desktop publishing 45%; typing 5%

Hours Per Week Worked at Business: 40 hours (plus works 15–20 hours per week for part-time employer)

Start-up Cost/Investment: $7,500

Children at Home: 3-year-old son

Biggest Challenge: Helping people understand what's involved behind a home-based business ("To overcome this challenge, I've learned the fine art of just saying 'no!' ")

What She'd Do Differently: "Right now, I wouldn't do anything differently. What I have done so far has worked for me."

Top Five Recommendations:

1. Before doing anything else, do a business plan. A business plan forces you to do the research to see if your business will make it. Business plans are fun to do, particularly if it's only for yourself. It helps to focus your efforts and is invaluable because of the information it helps you uncover. I never thought I'd need one because I'm home-based and just starting out. I only did it because a seminar about them was being held and I didn't want to show up empty-handed. I'm so glad I took the time (about a week) to put one together. Every two months, I review it and make changes to it. Never do a business plan and then file it away. It's an important document meant to be used constantly.

2. Research, research, research—read, go on-line, ask around for information. When I found the message boards on AOL and read everything people had to say in them, that's when I decided to get serious and begin my own business. Before then, I was scared and clueless. After reading all the posts, I realized everyone else who starts a business is scared and clueless, so I wasn't alone.

3. Join networking groups like the chamber of commerce, but don't think your dues are going to do the job for you. You must get out there in person. You have to make the chamber (or any group) work for you. Also, join ABSSI—it is a fantastic source of information and Lynette Smith is quick to respond to your questions with encouragement.

4. Check out the competition—this was the *one* thing I hesitated to do, but what my business plan insisted I do. The dilemma facing me was how to go about it—should I call and pretend I was a potential client, or face the competition head-on. I chose the latter and was very glad I did. The responses ranged from warm and cordial (from a fellow ABSSI member) to being hung up on. It was very eye-opening.

5. Think positive, even when things aren't going your way. Business has its ups and downs. Think of every problem as a challenge that needs to be met and overcome. That's how experience is gained.

Name: Julia Tavis

Company: Got-A-Vision Graphics

Location: La Habra, California

Description of Location: changed business location from a two-bedroom townhome to an executive suite in a city of 55,000 residents

Year Business Started: 1986

Primary Focus: full-service design firm, offering complete project organization (copy-writing, editing, graphic design and layout, photography, illustration, prepress services, offset printing)

Percentage Breakdown of Business: desktop publishing: 100%

Hours Per Week Worked at Business: 40 hours (assistant also works 20 hours)

Start-up Cost/Investment: about $2,000 (borrowed from family)

Children at Home: three children, ages 5, 8, and 10

Biggest Challenge: "Balancing my time between the office, my family, and my home. Since being a work-at-home parent is a constant juggling act, *something* has to give. No one person can 'do it all.' (But I do try, and face frustration often!) I am working toward involving my children more in household chores. We're getting there . . . the older two can help with laundry, empty the dishwasher, do basic bathroom cleaning, sweep/mop the floors, vacuum, etc. (This is not to say they always do all these things . . . just that they are capable of doing them!) The youngest empties the wastebaskets and takes the dirty laundry down two flights of stairs to the laundry room. He can also help empty the dishwasher and fold towels. This continues to be a challenge for me, and because my children are growing up (as they all do!), I am having to change my strategies with their ages."

Name: Shawn Teets

Company: WordWise

Location: Indianapolis, Indiana

Description of Location: single-family home in a city of 750,000 residents

Year Business Started: 1995

Primary Focus: "I do not have a single focus at this point because I need to make money; I take every project that I can do. As soon as possible, I plan to focus on resume writing and technical writing because that is where my interest and experience lie."

Percentage Breakdown of Business: technical writing: 50%; secretarial: 25%; resumes: 25%

Hours Per Week Worked at Business: 40 hours

Start-up Cost/Investment: $3,000

Children at Home: none

Biggest Challenge: Finding enough clients to keep busy.

What She'd Do Differently: "Follow suggestions no. 1 and no. 5 below. I was getting several small clients, mostly students, while operating my business part-time (before making the jump to full-time in January 1996), so I made the assumption that the jump to full-time would be easy. It hasn't been. Second, I had much of my business plan in my head rather than on paper, so I did not have a clear idea of how to go forward."

Top Five Recommendations:

1. Be realistic about how much money you have to invest and how long you can survive without an income.

2. Be sure you have the discipline and stamina to be in business for yourself.

3. Interview some business owners in your area to see what the pros and cons really are.

4. Find a networking group to provide you with support, ideas, and referrals! Indianapolis has a great one called the Women's Home Business Network.

5. Plan! Plan! Plan! Write a preliminary business plan to remind you where you want to go and how you plan to get there.

1999 Update from Shawn Teets

"A lot has changed in the past three years! My primary focus is now providing word processing, writing, and editing services to small businesses and individuals. In terms of the percentage breakdown of business, this is what my business looks like today: editing: 50%; writing: 20%; word processing (including resumes): 15%; miscellaneous (work of a more technical nature, such as computer system analysis): 15%.

"I'm now working about 60 hours a week (if I'm lucky . . . usually, it's more!), compared with 40 hours three years ago. Currently my biggest challenge is marketing during busy times to avoid future 'dry spells.'

"I do not have a Web site, but I use e-mail for much of my business communication. Transferring files via E-mail saves me many hours and much money each month. Many projects (about 15%) only require e-mail and voice-mail communication, which allows me to work at odd hours if necessary. I also use the Internet for business research. It definitely has made me more productive and efficient."

As a prelude to your business plan writing process, imagine you are writing your *own* professional profile—just like your colleagues here—for *your* business . . . as it might read two years from now. How would you think it would read? Draw inspiration and encouragement from your colleagues!

APPENDIX

BUSINESS PLAN

One of the keys to growing your secretarial service is to have a good vision for the future. Setting goals and working toward them will not only keep your business focused but will also give you a benchmark to refer to if you feel things are starting to get out of control. A solid business plan will help you accomplish these things and more. On the eighteen pages that follow, I have included a sample plan that you can adapt to fit your own business goals.

Business Plan for

ABSOLUTE ADVANTAGE

Division / Comprehensive Services Plus

Durham, Connecticut

prepared by Jan Melnik, President

April 1997

✦ Executive Summary

Absolute Advantage, division/Comprehensive Services Plus, of Durham, Connecticut, was started as a part-time, home-based word processing/secretarial service in 1983 by Jan Melnik. Originally named "Professional Services Plus," the business was operated from the basement of the Melniks' home in Durham, Connecticut. When Ron and Jan Melnik were relocated by their employer (Digital Equipment Corporation) to North Reading, Massachusetts, in 1986, the business continued from a basement in their new home—but was renamed Comprehensive Services Plus (CSP) for better strategic placement in the Yellow Pages of area phone directories. Upon the birth of twins in 1987, Jan opted to leave her full-time position as a Project Manager with DEC and focus on building CSP into a venture generating the equivalent of her corporate salary but from a home-based location which would allow for raising her children without daycare.

In 1988, Ron accepted another relocation with Digital back to Connecticut, the Melniks sold their Massachusetts property, and they returned to their Durham, Connecticut, home (which had been leased during their two-year absence). Jan immediately re-launched CSP from the "new" location (this time, a spare bedroom on the first floor). When the birth of a third baby in 1990 forced the spare bedroom into use as a nursery, the Melniks added a 22' x 24' office to their home, complete with a separate entrance and a lavatory. The business continues to operate from this location today; however, in 1996, the company's name was again changed to better reflect the overall breadth of services and approach as well as to increase strategic alphabetical placement within the Yellow Pages. The company is now called Absolute Advantage, division/Comprehensive Services Plus; the advertising tagline is "Our name has changed, but our commitment to quality and you has not." The company's slogan is "Our Business Is Making You Look Good!"

The company has expanded from a word processing/secretarial service to providing professional desktop publishing services as well as business consulting, editorial, promotional, and complete resume/career services, taking full advantage of technological advancements over the past ten years. Nationwide, both industries in which Absolute Advantage participates (secretarial services and resume services) are well-entrenched. Absolute Advantage is one of approximately 225 secretarial services in the state of Connecticut as well as one of about 100 resume services in the state. Jan Melnik, a Certified Professional Resume Writer (CPRW) is one of less than a dozen CPRWs in the state. Nationwide, there are nearly 20,000 companies providing secretarial and professional word processing services; 6,000 firms provide resume services.

Absolute Advantage has consistently enjoyed a strong position in its marketplace by ...

- offering complete and comprehensive services to all client groups served ("one-stop shopping" service delivery concept)
- consistently generating work of a quality which exceeds exceptionally high standards
- providing rapid turnaround and sensitivity to both deadlines and confidentiality
- pricing services fairly, competitively, and profitably
- assuring equipment, software, and service upgrades and enhancements which allow for clients to maintain the competitive edge in their respective industries
- maintaining a continuing commitment to service excellence, customer satisfaction, and professionalism as evidenced by keen participation in national industry associations
- sustaining a highly visible position throughout the community through an effective, ongoing media campaign characterized by regular publicity and features in local newspapers, on radio and television programs, etc.

It should be noted that this plan was developed not as a start-up situation, but for a transition away from one business segment to another. The plan attempts to put in focus where the company has been, and where and how I want the business to be by the year 2002.

Over the next five years, Absolute Advantage will transition its operational focus from spending 85% of available time providing client-demanded services in the word processing, resume, and desktop publishing fields to around 55%. Energies will be redirected toward expansion of three key endeavors: writing/publishing, lectures/public speaking, and conducting seminars; key client accounts (requiring no more than 55% of production time) will continue to be serviced, with new accounts cultivated to replace those lost through attrition.

Based upon successes over the past four years in the areas of professional writing and publishing as well as public speaking, Jan Melnik will be pursuing these fields with concentrated focus in 1997–99. The primary challenge will be effectively transitioning and downsizing client workload, demand, and requirements, while, at the same time, successfully building up those areas identified—all without significantly impacting revenues.

✦ Company Background

Absolute Advantage, division/Comprehensive Services Plus, is operated from a home office at the Melnik residence at 432 Higganum Road, Durham, Connecticut 06422. The company was started by Jan Melnik in November 1983 and is a sole proprietorship. Jan Melnik serves as president and operator of the company (see biography in the Appendix). There is one part-time employee at present; additional services and personnel are subcontracted as necessary.

The premise under which Absolute Advantage was originally founded was to satisfy client needs for word processing. Initial clientele primarily included students (term papers, theses, and reports), individuals in need of resume and cover letter materials, and companies with a need for document preparation. Technology in 1983 allowed for document processing via word processor with letter quality printing (a Digital DECmate computer). The business operated in this fashion for nearly six years.

With technological advancements in the late 80s, Absolute Advantage progressively moved from a word processing and secretarial service into desktop publishing, business consulting, promotional, and office support services (editorial and resume services have consistently remained key aspects of the company's base over the years). Three Macintosh computers, 300 and 600 dpi laser printers, graphics capability, and page layout and design programs facilitated Absolute Advantage's strong positioning in these new fields. Clients now served include a broad cross-section of corporations, institutions, medical practices, entrepreneurs, and professional individuals. Repeat clientele and referral business accounts for the major portion of the company's current client base; new business continues to come primarily from the company's Yellow Pages advertising.

The company's emphasis has always been on achieving an extremely high level of customer service excellence; Absolute Advantage's slogan is "Our Business Is Making You Look Good!" The demand for professional services has continued to grow at an unprecedented rate with current economic factors, corporate reengineering, and outsourcing all fueling heavy demands for future services. The outlook is exceptionally strong for this industry nationwide with spiked pockets of growth even greater on both coasts.

✦ Industry

Absolute Advantage spans two basic industry classifications: the secretarial and office support services industry and the professional resume service industry.

Secretarial and Office Support Services

While secretarial services have been provided by independent companies since the advent of the typewriter, the industry really began to evolve with the introduction of computer technology and communications advancements (i.e., fax, modems, etc.). The establishment of a professional association, The National Association of Secretarial Services (NASS), in 1980 underscored the viability and magnitude of the demand for these services. NASS headquarters are in St. Petersburg, Florida. Currently, there are approximately 1,700 NASS members nationwide.

Most businesses in this industry are operated as sole proprietorship ventures, many of which are home-based. However, a number of businesses in this field operate from executive suite locations, retail storefront, and mall sites. Concrete industry data with regard to gross revenues and owner salaries is published by NASS. In *The Best Home Businesses for the 90s*, written by Paul and Sarah Edwards ("the self-employment experts") and published in 1994 (second edition), the writers project typical annual gross revenues for secretarial services at $30,000 to $45,000.

Resume Services

This industry is served by the Professional Association of Resume Writers (PARW). It was founded in 1990 by Frank Fox, the Executive Director of NASS, in St. Petersburg, Florida. There are about 1,200 members nationwide. Paul and Sarah Edwards state that typical annual gross revenues for resume writing services are $40,000 to $50,000 (*The Best Home Businesses for the 90s*). Frank Fox notes that the "income potential in the resume business can be as great as $70,000 to $90,000 per year with add-on services, such as cover letters, consultations, copies, and so on."

There is clearly a distinction between firms offering just secretarial and office support services, those offering exclusively resume services (without expanded service offerings), and those hybrids, such as Absolute Advantage, which set an industry standard for both gross business revenues and owner salary.

Industry Analysis Across Both Fields

While there are some exceptionally successful businesses in both the secretarial/office support services and resume services industries, no one company enjoys a measurable marketshare, primarily because of the regionalized aspect of each business and localized need for each service offering.

Trends impacting both industries include:

1) the continual release of newer, faster, and more efficient computer technology and document processing software (clients require the lastest-and-greatest in their documents but lack the capital, time, or expertise to handle projects in-house);

2) the ongoing practice of reengineering across this country fueling an increasingly competitive job market (clients have increased demand for professional and distinctive career search materials); and

3) the explosion of entrepreneurial ventures (start-up businesses need cost-effective yet dynamic corporate identity materials, business plans, brochures, etc.).

✦ GENERAL DESCRIPTION OF BUSINESS

Current Market Segmentation

Absolute Advantage's current business divides across the following key market areas:

- resume/career consulting and writing services for individual clients (35%)
- editorial/promotional and business consulting services for corporations and entrepreneurs (20%)
- desktop publishing services for corporations, entrepreneurs, and individual clients (20%)
- office support services (15%)
- publishing projects (10%)

Editorial/Promotional and Business Consulting Services

Services in this market segment include all stages of copy production—from research, writing, editing, and copyediting to layout and proofreading. Absolute Advantage has developed a strong reputation of "wordsmithing" and polishing communications materials. Some clients utilize Absolute Advantage to edit materials already prepared, while others prefer Absolute Advantage to create copy from scratch.

Also included in this niche of the market is development of innovative concepts and image materials for companies. Absolute Advantage specializes in helping businesses create a unique identity in their marketplace with letterhead, corporate i.d., and support materials. Absolute Advantage is recognized for creating top-notch programs that are classy, cost-effective, and produce results. These can include brochures, flyers, newsletters, business cards, and attention-capturing marketing pieces (again, most clients utilize Absolute Advantage to develop these materials completely from inception to completion).

Absolute Advantage's strategic position in this marketplace is as a business partner working with its clients to develop solutions that are successful and within budget. With regard to editorial services, Absolute Advantage postures itself as being the "professional writer/editor" on the staff of its clients … but only when they require it.

Clients served in this market include a number of small business owners/entrepreneurs (including a number in start-up mode for which service offerings also include business start-up consultation), advertising agencies, insurance brokers, medical/psychological practices, venture capital firms, companies in the financial services arena, universities, hospitals, etc.

Desktop Publishing Services

Desktop publishing projects handled for clients include simple one-page flyers and promotional coupons, multi-page newsletters and brochures, personnel manuals, catalogs, etc. Frequently, editorial services are also contracted in development of these materials.

Clients making up this market segment include small business owners/entrepreneurs, sales representatives, retailers, pharmaceutical firms, hospitals, medical/psychological practices, and multi-level marketing sales personnel.

Resume/Career Services

With resumes/curricula vitaes as the primary product in this segment, ancillary services include development of the resume documents "from scratch" (via full consultation), professional typesetting only of a client-written resume, combination packages with mini-consulting and typesetting services, cover letter creation, generation, and mass mailing services, development of distinctive introductory and leave-behind career search materials, and interview technique training services. Absolute Advantage has written more than 5,000 unique resumes for professionals in every career imaginable and at least twice that many distinctive cover letters and tools for effective career searches.

Clients served cover a wide spectrum from college graduates with baccalaureate degrees embarking on their first job search, clerical/administrative personnel, unemployed blue-collar workers, high tech, sales, financial, and management executives with Fortune-50 companies from around Connecticut and Massachusetts to displaced homemakers, individuals with military backgrounds crossing over to civilian labor pool, unskilled laborers, laid-off age 50+ middle management professionals, healthcare professionals in every field, and corporate executives.

Although a common assumption is that the stalled Northeast economy has fueled tremendous growth in this industry (and, to be sure, it has for resume services starting out in the early 90s), this business has always represented about 35% of Absolute Advantage's total product/service mix (the players and their needs simply change). In the high-growth 80s, clients were frequently job-hopping and rapidly climbing the career ladder … and needed a strong resume to position them for promotion. With the recessed 90s, clients' resume needs have changed, but remain ever-strong.

Differences in this business require maintaining cutting-edge approaches to working with clients to distinctly package their accomplishments and credentials. Formats and preferred styles change from year

to year and the successful firm must remain well-informed (clearly membership in the PARW as well as the credential of Certified Professional Resume Writer [CPRW] are key). Absolute Advantage joined the Professional Association of Resume Writers in 1994; Jan Melnik earned her CPRW in 1994, joining just a handful of professionals with this distinction in Connecticut.

Office Support Services

Included in this market segment are those services primarily associated with secretarial services: word processing, typing, invoicing, cassette and VCR transcription, photocopying, faxing, creating transparencies, generating minutes, providing mailing services, etc. On an hourly basis, services in this category are billed at the lowest rate in the tiered price structure.

The need of an individual or company for office support services is frequently what first brings a client to Absolute Advantage. Once a client, however, the full breadth of services available through Absolute Advantage are generally utilized. In the start-up years, this represented the largest market segment (ease of attracting clients through posting of notices throughout campuses of local universities brought many student term paper and thesis typing assignments). However, because of its lower hourly rate and the usual lack of creative work associated with this segment, efforts to now attract this business are minimal and only pursued when there is conversion potential (i.e., typing copy for a newsletter with the intent of taking over full production of the newsletter, which would entail both editorial and desktop publishing services). Interestingly, Absolute Advantage's second largest client (in terms of annual billing) utilizes services primarily from this segment (Revlon, Inc. of New York). The only papers typed for students now by Absolute Advantage are those for graduate students, most of whom are all professionals and have utilized Absolute Advantage for some other service initially (several of the doctors in a practice of psychologists served by Absolute Advantage have had their doctoral dissertations typeset by us). It is safe to say that this service offering is probably the backbone of any company in this industry.

Publishing Projects

A growing niche for Absolute Advantage, this segment of business represents fulfillment of several long-term personal and professional goals for Jan and also represents opportunities for greatest growth for Absolute Advantage well into the next century.

In July of 1994, Jan's first book, *"How to Open and Operate a Home-based Secretarial Services Business,"* was published by The Globe Pequot Press of Old Saybrook, CT. A trade paperback publisher with a national reputation, Globe Pequot sought Jan's expertise to author this 250-page book for their series on home-based businesses.

Sales have been very strong for this book and enhanced through Jan's reputation in the industry; she has been an invited guest on several national business radio and television programs as well as on America Online forums, she has been a keynote speaker at a number of national conventions for her industry; and she has successfully exploited the direct mail order business for her book through computer online services.

A strategic decision was made when writing the manuscript for the book during July of 1993. She included information in the appendix for readers to inquire about a resume service guide and a quarterly newsletter (neither of which had been created; she knew she had 12 months to develop these projects, the publisher's production cycle for her book). Both of these projects, as with her first 30-page typing service guide, represented long-term goals. It was anticipated that there would be demand for these additional projects.

Since July 1994 publication date of the book, hundreds of individuals have subscribed to the quarterly newsletter, *The Word Advantage* (published for people in the office support, secretarial, desktop publishing, and resume service industries as well as free-lance writers, the slogan is "Creative Ideas and Marketing Strategies for Those Who Work with Words … Keys to Success That Will Give Your Business the Advantage!)", and an equal number have plunked down $20 for her resume service guide (self-published). A contract to write a second title in the home-based business series was executed in January 1995; *How to Open and Operate a Home-based Resume Service* was published by The Globe Pequot Press in January 1996.

Equipment of Business Operation

Operated from a 528-square foot office, Absolute Advantage has the following equipment and furnishings:
- Power Macintosh PC 7100 CD-ROM
- Bernoulli 90 Transportable External Drive
- Global Teleport Gold Modem
- Hayes Modem 2400
- Macintosh IIvx
- Macintosh Powerbook 100
- NEC MultiSpin 2V CD-ROM
- Hewlett Packard LaserJet 4MPlus Printer (600 dpi)
- Macintosh Stylewriter Printer
- Sharp SF-7800 Copier (collating, auto-feed, enlarge/reduce)
- Canon 100 Fax
- Sanyo Transcriber (standard)

- Sony Transcriber (micro)
- Smith Corona 125 Electronic Typewriter
- Panasonic Answering Machine
- XL 300 Electronic Credit Card Terminal
- Dedicated business telephone line; separate dedicated fax telephone line
- Appropriate office furnishings

Suppliers/Vendors

Absolute Advantage bids out all printing work that is not handled internally; three primary vendors supply 95% of the printing services Absolute Advantage and its clients require: Young's Printing (Middletown, CT), Laser Copy & Design (Middletown, CT), and North Shore Printing (North Reading, MA).

All equipment in the office is covered under maintenance agreements; all Macintosh equipment is bundled under one contract for optimum pricing with Advanced Office Systems (Cromwell, CT). Abacus provides service and a "penny program" contract for the copier.

Specialty papers are procured through PM Resources (Oconomowoc, WI) and PaperDirect (Secaucus, NJ). Office supplies are purchased in bulk from various catalog vendors (Quill Corporation being the primary vendor); bi-monthly shopping trips to Staples office supply store round out procurement of office supplies.

Production Schedule

Industry standards typically show single operator-owners in this field who work 40 hours per week averaging 20–25 billable hours per week (with 15–20 non-billable "overhead" hours devoted to such non-income-generating tasks as invoicing, bookkeeping, marketing, selling/closing, learning new software, maintaining equipment, banking, managing supplies and inventory, business-related errands, etc.). Of the 45 hours per week typically worked by Jan (with six weeks of vacation/time off to attend professional conferences per year), an average of between 32 and 39 hours per week are billable.

Unlike many conventional businesses, however, the hours devoted to operating Absolute Advantage are not consistent with traditional "9-to-5" schedules. Instead, pockets of time are interspersed around a busy household which includes twin nine-year-olds and a seven-year-old. Client appointments are scheduled around family requirements; production work occurs "after hours."

✦ FUTURE DEVELOPMENT

Absolute Advantage anticipates making a strategic change in the direction and focus of its business sources. Demand for services in all key market areas has remained exceptionally strong for the past 14 years; Absolute Advantage has experienced growth of between 15% and 20% each year since 1988. During the past four years, a significant amount of prospective client work has been deliberately turned away as a result of achieving maximum production capacity (consistent with ability/desire to work). In a sole proprietorship business of this type, wherein there is one person handling most all of the production work as well as the financial, marketing, and administrative tasks, time limitations can ultimately impact growth beyond a certain maximum point (this, of course, varies from operator to operator based upon individual objectives and desires).

In planning for the balance of 1997, 1998, and 1999, there is every reason to support that financial growth could continue at the rate Absolute Advantage has achieved if the service offering splits remain the same; an 18% increase in gross revenues over 1996 is projected based upon an increase to hourly rates which was implemented January 1, 1997.

Absolute Advantage, however, plans a strategic shift in direction in order to address:
- professional objectives
- personal growth
- capacity as a sole proprietor

Strategic Plan 1997–2002

Over the next five years, the strategic goal will be to gradually shift away from devoting 85% of the business toward fulfilling client requirements to around 30% by the end of 2000. The balance of the business would be distributed among three endeavors: publications (30%: 15% from book publishing and 15% from newsletter publishing), lectures/public speaking (10%), and conducting seminars (30%).

Book Publishing (15%)

Simultaneous to selectively cutting back on client projects (progressively handling more and more of the top end assignments and declining work at the lower scale), publishing efforts and marketing plans for publications will be stepped up. A combination of advance monies for new book projects, royalties from existing titles, and profits from individual book sales will fuel this business growth.

In addition to the promotional/sales efforts of The Globe Pequot Press, self-promotion of the two Globe books will continue through online services, display tables at all industry conferences (three per year), direct mail, lecture, book signing engagements (first publicized book signing at a popular bookseller in Madison, CT, attracted 70 people, most of whom purchased signed copies of the book), and word-of-mouth. It is anticipated that these sales will only continue to grow based upon the trend toward home-based business development in the 90s. According to *Home Office Computing* magazine, "the number of people working from home has hit an all-time high, reaching 43.2 million," an increase of 5.1% over the last year. This number is expected to continue to rise, as companies perceive the advantages to telecommuting employees and as more and more people start their own businesses (in many cases due to companies downsizing their work force).

Jan Melnik was featured in the April 1995 issue of *Home Office Computing* (circulation 500,000), is quoted and referred to in books by Paul and Sarah Edwards as well as titles by Jay Conrad Levinson (the "Guerilla Marketing" expert), and was featured in a major profile in a summer issue of *Woman's Day* magazine (circulation 6,000,000); all publications provide information for readers to order newsletter subscriptions and copies of both books. Regular appearance and speaking on various business television programs and radio programs over the past few years also help to heighten visibility and increase book sales.

Newsletter Publishing (15%)

Quarterly publication of *The Word Advantage* will continue; a change to the original format was implemented in Fall 1995 (from eight quarterly pages, 8.5x11 in size, per quarter to 12—plus continuation of a 3–4 page supplement per issue; the newsletter is mailed first class to subscribers in envelopes to protect the publication and allow for enclosures [first renewal solicitation, second renewal reminder, ancillary attachments to articles in copy]). Staff of contributing editors is currently limited to two (in addition to Jan Melnik, Publisher/Editor); free-lance submissions are accepted for consideration; two to four are typically published in each issue.

Editorial calendar is planned one year in advance with seasonal and timely modifications to accommodate industry-breaking news as appropriate. Feedback is regularly solicited from subscriber base through ongoing survey vehicles. To date, feedback has been 100% positive and the first few campaign years for subscription renewals for charter subscribers showed nearly a 100% renewal trend.

At its inception, it was projected that the publication would be self-supporting at the year-one anniversary; this goal was achieved.

Lectures/Public Speaking (10%)

In 1994–95 and 1995–96, nearly two dozen programs/speeches were delivered. Some formats were pro bono (public library talks) at which books and newsletter subscriptions were sold.

One format was an organized bookstore book signing (again, pro bono; however, nearly 65 copies of the book were sold and the names, addresses, and telephone numbers of more than 40 people in attendance were collected as those "interested in a start-up business workshop delivered by Jan Melnik"). Because of the success of the bookstore talk/signing, this has been aggressively pursued.

Six national business radio program interviews were conducted, both pro bono, but with ample opportunities for promoting both the books and the newsletter. In fact, one radio interview was with Paul and Sarah Edwards; this led to their recommending both Jan's book and Jan's newsletter in their newly published second edition of *"The Best Home Businesses for the 90s."* This promotional vehicle will also be aggressively pursued, particularly because there is no expense involved (other than half an hour of time to be connected by telephone from the home office). Radio interviews clearly establish the author as the "expert in the industry." Business television programming has also served as an excellent forum for promotion various projects (books and newsletters).

Jan Melnik has spoken regularly before national and regional conferences of the National Association of Secretarial Services and the Professional Association of Resume Writers.

Business Start-Up Seminars (30%)

This is the area in which the most excitement for development exists and in which there is the greatest potential for significant growth, both professionally and financially. As a result of the sales of books and newsletters, one-on-one consulting to start-up entrepreneurs has been increasing steadily over the past year. There continues to be demand by telephone for follow-on consultations and initial start-up workshops.

Mini-workshop programs will be held quarterly commencing in the summer of 1997. Three hours in length, the programs will be intensive and initially offered in the home office to a maximum group size of six attendees on pre-scheduled mornings. Brochures incorporating a reply card are currently being developed presenting prospective attendees with five mornings scattered over a two-month period; with the cap of six attendees; attendance will be confirmed (with payment by credit card at the time of registration in advance) on a first-come, first-served basis.

The program cost will be $79 and will include substantive workshop materials and a sample issue of *The Word Advantage* quarterly newsletter as well as a copy of *"How to Open and Operate a Home-based Secretarial Services Business"* and a copy of *"How to Open and Operate a Home-based Resume Service."* Coffee and Danish will be supplied, but overhead costs are minimal (other than marketing materials to promote workshop, copy cost for workshop materials, and author's cost of the books).

It is anticipated that three workshops per quarter can be scheduled with five attendees each. This would generate revenues of $1,185 per quarter. If five workshops with six attendees each were achieved, this would increase to $2,370 per quarter.

Ten hours of preparation time was devoted during the spring of 1996 to fully prepare all workshop materials. Minor modifications to materials would be anticipated on a quarterly basis, but the bulk of the time (10 hours) would represent the upfront costs to developing the program.

Longer term, because of the population density in the Northeast, it would be feasible to deliver one-day workshops in strategically selected locations (using hotel conference rooms) in Connecticut, Rhode Island, Massachusetts, New Hampshire, and New York. Workshop size could be effectively increased to 20 participants. Much longer range planning could certainly take this around the country. The first pilot program was co-developed and co-facilitated with long-time colleague (and author of *"How to Open and Operate a Home-based Desktop Publishing Business"*) Louise Kursmark in the Spring of 1996 in St. Petersburg, Florida. Eighteen people attended the three-hour workshop; more registrants were wait-listed, but a cap of 18 was determined as a maximum. The workshop was rated exceptionally high by all in attendance and this programming will continue to be refined for future presentation at other national conferences.

Beyond the plans as initially described above are possibilities for integrating the workshop with other professionals in related fields. Contacts have already been established with professionals in the following industries who have expressed serious interest in collaborating to deliver joint workshop programs: personal financial planning, desktop publishing, time/stress management, entrepreneurial family issues, and human resources/executive recruiting. These avenues will all be pursued during 1997 and 1998 for possible implementation in 1998–2000.

Client Workload (30%)

Absolute Advantage hired one part-time office assistant in 1995. This person augments existing coverage of telephone inquiries and is well-trained so as to effectively quote prospective projects and schedule client appointments. In addition, this individual handles routine production work (transcription related to a client project, input of text by keyboard, proofreading, photocopying, etc.), organizes and maintains the filing system, and conducts Absolute Advantage and client marketing/mailings. Finally, this individual handles all order fulfillment tasks (with additional part-time support hired as necessary). This entails ongoing daily fulfillment of orders for books/newsletter subscriptions as well as mailing of response materials to all inquiries for information derived from online notices and major media events.

✦ MARKETING PLAN

Market Definition

Local Market

Absolute Advantage's target market includes those clients requiring professional desktop publishing services, high-end office support services, and editorial/promotional capabilities. Typical client profiles representative of this niche served encompass: entrepreneurs in nearly any field in start-up mode, solo practitioners (physicians, psychologists, accountants, attorneys, etc.), universities, hospitals, and healthcare institutions, corporations outsourcing their project work, and national sales managers with residences in Connecticut. Projects handled for this market group include: corporate identity materials, brochures, newsletters, direct mail programs, media campaigns, administrative support for special projects, and generation of industry-specific reports; inherent to all of these project requirements are high-end desktop publishing and design services as well as editorial and promotional expertise.

These clients are attracted through three means: word-of-mouth referral from existing clientele; repeat clientele (or cross-over from another service offering; i.e., handle a resume for an executive at a major pharmaceutical firm; she then contacts Absolute Advantage to handle development of a learning library for the corporation); and Yellow Pages advertising.

Absolute Advantage's other local market niche includes individuals seeking professional development of career search materials. This service includes complete development of a resume "from scratch" as well as all related cover letter, leave-behind, and follow-up pieces, consultation and editorial services, and interview training and preparation; the typical client attracted to this high-end service is a middle or upper-level executive in high tech, engineering, healthcare, bio-med, or corporate fields. Other services in this market niche encompass professional typesetting of a client's existing resume, a hybrid "mini-consultation" approach to working with clients with existing materials but in need of professional assistance (and/or incorporation of most recent position[s]), resume services for new graduates, military-to civilian clients, displaced homemakers, and outplaced middle managers and executives.

All resume clientele are attracted through the same methods previously identified (referral, repeat, or Yellow Pages).

National Market

Absolute Advantage's target audience is essentially the same as articulated for the local market. The following distinctions exist: these clients (both for resume services and for desktop publishing/office support) are attracted through word-of-mouth referrals from existing clientele; no direct advertising is conducted in national markets with the exception of highly targeted direct mail pieces.

While sales of both books and newsletter subscription do occasionally occur in the local market, the primary audience for publication efforts is a national market. Beyond word-of-mouth, the two sources of customers for these efforts are through visibility in national conferences and via online promotion and participation. For both books, The Globe Pequot Press utilizes a well-developed chain of national distributors, included Barnes & Nobles, B. Dalton, Waldenbooks, and Borders as well as numerous independents.

Competition

Absolute Advantage has closely tracked its local competition for the past seven years (since its final relocation back to Connecticut in 1988). The Yellow Pages published by the Southern New England Telephone Company serves as the primary means for obtaining critical locally competitive information on a year-to-year basis (allowing for assessment of new firms entering the field each year [based upon their presence in "the book"], those firms dropping out [again, as monitored by disappearing ads in the book], and companies expanding their advertising, maintaining their current reach, or decreasing their ads). The key marketing areas for advertising of Absolute Advantage in the Yellow Pages are served by the Middletown phone directory and the shoreline directory (Madison, Guilford, and Clinton), collectively serving 20 towns.

The second source of information used in competitive analysis is direct solicitation of pricing information and clarification of service offerings. Through informally placed telephone calls at varying intervals to all competitors servicing clients in the same market areas, strategic competitive information has been obtained. This research, collected between 1988 and 1996, has been utilized in assessing business strategies (including both service trends and pricing) of Absolute Advantage's competitors; information gleaned from these exercises has been used to "sanity-check" Absolute Advantage's market position from both a service offering and pricing perspective.

With regard to publications (both newsletter and books), there are obviously other materials available to the consumer. My objective is to obtain an ever-increasing marketshare based upon excellence in publication content and quality, position as a leader in the industry, public speaking/promotional engagements, and visibility within national industry associations. The two books are the most comprehensive texts available today for starting either a home-based secretarial service or resume service.

Pricing *(effective January 1, 1997)*

(Include copy of current Price List/Fee Schedule)

✦ AREAS OF POTENTIAL RISK

- Change in business strategy is incorrect.
- Impact on business of electronic transfer of resumes (i.e. bulletin board resumes).
- Availability of "canned" resume software programs.
- Lower unemployment rates.
- Market becomes flooded with "how-to" books and market dries up.
- Seminars are not booked.

✦ CONTINGENCY PLANS

- Redirect advertising efforts to rebuild client business (enhance Yellow Pages advertising, increase direct mail, cultivate referrals through leads programs, etc.).
- While developing new direction for business, maintain "waiting list" of prospects turned away (to re-solicit in the event this becomes necessary).
- Advise extensive network of colleagues, associates, and friends that "I'm looking for work!" (via referrals).

✦ FINANCIAL SUMMARY

This business plan was developed, as stated in the Executive Summary, to define a transition into a different segment of the business over the next five years. As such, this plan's financial focus and needs are to maintain sales and profit growth and not to request funding.

(Include financial information [actuals] for 1994, 1995, and 1996; include three-year forecast for 1997, 1998, and 1999. At a minimum, prepare Profit & Loss Statement and Balance Sheet).

✦ Appendix

Biography for Jan Melnik

Brochure and Business Card for Absolute Advantage

"Consultant Offers Advice Book for Home-based Entrepreneurs," Stacy Wong, *The Hartford Courant* (Focus on Business feature, July 21, 1994).

"How to Open and Operate a Home-based Resume Service" (book cover, published 1995, The Globe Pequot Press)

"How to Open and Operate a Home-based Secretarial Services Business" (book cover, first edition, published 1994, The Globe Pequot Press)

"Mind Your Own Biz … Go-getter from Durham pens *'How to Open and Operate a Home-based Secretarial Services Business',"* Sandi Kahn Shelton, *The New Haven Register* (cover of the Today's Woman section, September 26, 1994).

Quips & Clips (most recent issue of complimentary quarterly client newsletter).

"Secretary-Entrepreneur Speeds to Success," Patricia Seremet, *The Hartford Courant* (cover of the Business section, September 7, 1993).

The Word Advantage (quarterly subscriber newsletter, most recent issue).

Resources

Edwards, Paul and Sarah. *The Best Home Businesses for the 90s.* New York: Jeremy P. Tarcher/G.P. Putnam's Sons (1990).

Fox, Frank. Executive Director, NASS and PARW; January–February 1995 Interview.

Home Office Computing magazine. New York: Scholastic, Inc.

Levinson, Jay Conrad. *Guerilla Marketing for the Home-based Business.* Boston: Houghton Mifflin Company (1995).

National Association of Secretarial Services, 1995–96 Annual Membership Directories.

Professional Association of Resume Writers, 1995–96 Annual Membership Directories.

PERIODICALS/INFORMATION

The Word Advantage
Department GSB
P.O. Box 718
Durham, CT 06422

The Word Advantage is a quarterly newsletter published by Jan Melnik (yours truly!), author of this book and author of the popular *How to Start a Home-based Resume Service*. She is president of Absolute Advantage, division/Comprehensive Services Plus of Durham, Connecticut, founded in 1983. This 12-page quarterly newsletter (with an additional three- to eight-page supplement feature per issue) features "creative ideas and marketing strategies for those who work with words . . . keys to success that will give your business the advantage!" Contributing editors with extensive industry experience round out the professional editorial staff. *The Word Advantage* is shipped flat to all subscribers (always first-class mail) and features three-hole punching for convenient binder storage for reference purposes. Features include:

- great ideas for new profit centers

- strategies for attracting and retaining clients

- successful techniques for improving your productivity *and* profitability

- details on how to expand into broader market areas

- pricing Q & A

- sample ads, brochure copy, and marketing/promotional tips

- a forum for subscribers to exchange good ideas and tips for running a home-based business

- resume feature in each issue (considered by many to be one of the most lucrative profit centers of a secretarial service)

To subscribe, send check, money order, or complete credit card information (MasterCard, Visa, Discover/Novus, or American Express with account number and expiration date) in the amount of $40 for one-year subscription or $75 for a two-year subscription to the address above. Many back issues filled with timeless, valuable information are also available.

Resume/Personal Marketing Workshop Kit
Department GSB
P.O. Box 718
Durham, CT 06422

This complete workshop was developed and written by Jan Melnik. Take the resume portion of your business "on the road" with classes—teach! Build visibility in your community by instructing classes from your home or office, in the public library, or through an adult education or community college program. This complete package (which you can use "as is" or tailor to meet your exact needs) includes everything you'll need: the proposal letter to pitch your program along with the method for marketing to help ensure success, the materials you'll need for classes (roster, evaluation form), and a comprehensive "how-to" formula for teaching resume writing and cover letter crafting in a two-part workshop. The program is designed to educate individuals who believe they'd like to write their own resumes . . . but, in many instances, delivering the training will encourage attendees to *book appointments with you later—instead!*

   To order, send $34.95 (check, money order, or MasterCard, Visa, Discover/ Novus, or American Express information [full account number and expiration date]) to the address above.

Creative Client Communiques
Department GSB
P.O. Box 718
Durham, CT 06422

This comprehensive package was produced by Jan Melnik. It features an extensive collection (forty-plus pages) of effective and innovative communication vehicles for clients . . . from six years' worth of quarterly client newsletters (you can copy as many of these ideas/articles as you wish in your own client newsletter) to fee schedule, and from handouts for resume clients (that you may copy) to samples of actual ads and effective client follow-up correspondence, plus much more. Your creative energies will be triggered with these proven ideas that Jan has used in successfully building her business. To order the package, send $14.95 (check or money order) to the address above.

How to Start a Home-Based Resume Service (2nd ed.)
Dept. GSB
P.O. Box 718
Durham, CT 06422

This book, written by Jan Melnik, CPRW, and published by Globe Pequot Press, is considered throughout the industry as the "bible" for starting a home-based resume service. Resume services are the perfect companion profit center to an existing word processing, secretarial, or office support services business. This book details everything the entrepreneur must know to successfully start and operate this business segment. You'll read how immediate profitability can be realized with this business, how to start up with minimal expense, how to conduct a consultation and write a resume, and how to build your client base and develop a referral network. Twenty-five professional resume writers (all home-based) from around the country are profiled and provide their recommendations and salient how-to advice. In addition, scores of hiring authorities were interviewed to get "cutting-edge" information regarding what these people want to see in *your clients' resumes and cover letters* and *what the best approaches are for job-search marketing* (valuable info you can market to your clients). Finally every facet of the business operation itself—from marketing and advertising to overcoming objections in the pre-sales process and building your craft as a resume writer—is completely covered. To order, send $22.95 (check, money order, or Mastercard, Visa, Discover/Novus, or American Express information [full account number and expiration date]) to the address above.

To receive additional information about any of Jan Melnik's books or publications, please send a self-addressed, #10 business envelope with two first-class postage stamps to Dept. GSBI, P.O. Box 718, Durham, CT 06422.

Homeworking Mothers
Department JLM
Mothers' Home Business Network
P.O. Box 423
East Meadow, NY 11554
(516) 997–7394

Homeworking Mothers is a quarterly publication especially focused on home-based business pursuits for mothers with children at home. The publication provides good suggestions and ideas, lots of specific information, and support. Georganne

Fiumara, the editor, founded the Mothers' Home Business Network, a national organization with more than 5,000 members, in 1984. A freelance writer and columnist, she has written numerous articles for *Family Circle* regarding mothers who work at home. For a free, four-page brochure, a membership kit, and a sample article, send a self-addressed, stamped, #10 business envelope. You can also visit the Web site: www.homeworkingmom.com.

How to Start a Home-based Desktop Publishing Business (2nd ed.)
Department JLMS
Attn. Louise Kursmark
9847 Catalpa Woods Court
Cincinnati, OH 45242

Louise Kursmark (author, Globe Pequot Press [1999] and president, Best Impression) has compiled the best book in the industry for building a home-based business specializing in desktop publishing services. Whether you're seeking to build a business exclusively in this niche area or add this profitable profit center to your existing (or new) secretarial services business, her book details everything you need to know. As a successful hands-on business owner with her own home-based company (now seventeen years old), she knows "all the ins and outs" to help you achieve success. To order, send $22.95 (includes shipping; personal check or complete credit card information) to Louise Kursmark at the above address or you can send an e-mail to www.yourbestimpression.com.

Louise Kursmark and Kathy Keshemberg also co-produce a wonderful packet and disk for those interested in developing their own client newsletters (which, you now know, I *highly* recommend doing to build business!). Called *News You Can Use*, this package provides not only a template and recommended timetable but also actual articles you can easily import to your own newsletter format. Regular updates are available by "subscription." Contact Louise via e-mail at www.yourbestimpression.com or Kathy via e-mail at KathyKC@aol.com for additional information and ordering details.

How to Make Money by Turning Away Customers: An Information Package on Running a Successful Referral Service
Nina Feldman Connections
e-mail: Ninafel@aol.com

Nina has been brokering to other word processing/desktop publishing/computer support services since soon after she started her own word processing business in

1981. Having "invented" the type of referral arrangement she has with her service providers, Nina has been honing and revising referral methods over the years to make them as free from snags and as profitable as possible. She has compiled a complete how-to package based on her eighteen years of experience and has made it available to people interested in starting a referral service of their own.

Among the information you will receive in the how-to kit are:

- A sign-up letter Nina Feldman Connections (NFC) sends its contractors (service providers) describing fees, obligations, membership benefits

- A contract that the providers sign outlining their obligations

- A detailed questionnaire for providers to fill out outlining their skills, services, software, background, etc.

- Marketing materials NFC sends to prospective clients

- Detailed return forms for providers to account for their referrals

- A log for the providers to track NFC referrals

- A copy of NFC's Yellow Pages ad

- A sample contract for providers to use with clients to ensure that they are paid

For more information, send an e-mail to Nina at Ninafel@aol.com.

How to Run a Successful Homebased Word Processing/Desktop Publishing Service: A Resource Package
Nina Feldman Connections
e-mail: Ninafel@aol.com

Nina Feldman has been providing home-based word processing/desktop publishing and computer support referral services since 1981. Send an e-mail to Ninafel@aol.com to obtain information about the publications and services she provides as well as to request an order form.

Making Money Doing Word Processing from Home
Department JLM
109 James Drive
Troy, IL 62294
(618) 667-4666; fax (618) 667-8002

Audiotaped Interview: Home-business experts Paul and Sarah Edwards talk with *Keyboard Connection* publisher Nancy Malvin, who has owned her own home-based office support business since 1982. The interview is full of tips on start-up options, finding and keeping customers, and creating success on your own terms. The start-up worksheets take you step-by-step through developing an individualized blueprint to use in starting your own word processing business.

The set (two audiocassettes and worksheets) is available for $27.95 (send check or MasterCard/Visa information).

Resources!
Department JLMS
Computron
1615 E. Roeland, Apt. #3
Appleton, WI 54915

Kathy Keshemberg is president of Computron/A Career Advantage, a home-based business she started in Appleton, Wisconsin, in 1983. She has compiled an extensive collection of marketing pieces and operational forms designed specifically for secretarial/business support/resume services. Included are brochures, marketing letters, rate structures, policy sheet, promotional portfolio, and much more. All samples are printed on specialty papers, allowing you to make an impressive statement on a shoestring budget. Send a self-addressed, stamped #10 envelope to her at the address above for detailed information. Also refer to information provided in this Appendix under Louise Kursmark's book entry, *How to Start a Home-based Desktop Publishing Business*, for information about *News You Can Use*, a joint package that Kathy publishes with Louise.

S-O-S (Secretarial and Office Support Service) Quarterly
Department JLM
1431 Willow Brook Cove #4
St. Louis, MO 63146
(314) 567–3636

Write for complete information.

Words from Home: How to Start & Operate a Home-based
Word Processing Business
P.O. Box 1773
Pompano Beach, FL 33061

Diana Ennen, owner of her own successful business for more than ten years, has compiled a self-published guide featuring her own experiences as well as those of thirty other home-based word processing professionals. She describes everything from buying a computer to dealing with difficult clients. She states, "With more and more people wanting the good life of a successful home-based business, this book shows just how achievable it is and how profitable it can become." To order, send $28.95 (includes shipping and handling) to her at the above address.

Diana notes that over the past few years, "The biggest change I made was adding bookkeeping services into my business. One of my regular clients, whom I've had for years, asked me if I wouldn't mind keeping their books and doing their billing as well as their typing. At first I was skeptical without an accounting degree, but with Quickbooks it was easy. I've since approached several of my other clients and new businesses in the area and have found that the two go very well together, and it has added considerably to my yearly income.

"The Internet has had a big impact on my business. I now have several regular clients from other states that I've gotten from my Web site. We conduct business over the Internet almost the same as if we were right in the same town. Depending on the situation, they will either mail or e-mail me their work and I send it back as an attachment. For short documents, they usually fax it to me and I will either fax it directly out or e-mail it back to them. I've also gotten local clients from my site who just happened to come across my Web page. For one client I use PCAnywhere for their work and, therefore, I can hook right into their computer from mine at home. This allows me to do all their work and then print directly out on their printer."

PROFESSIONAL ASSOCIATIONS/ASSISTANCE

Association of Business Support Services International, Inc.

(ABSSI, Inc.)
Department JLM
22875 Savi Ranch Parkway, Suite H
Yorba Linda, CA 92887-4619
(800) 237-1462 toll-free or (714) 282-9398
Fax: (714) 282-8630

e-mail: abssi4you@aol.com
URL: www.abssi.org
Executive Director: Lynette M. Smith, CPS

ABSSI membership dues and Industry Focus subscription

- Annual *Industry Focus* subscription alone: $48

- ABSSI six-month trial membership: $75 (includes six months of *Industry Focus*)

- Annual ABSSI membership: $132 (includes *Industry Focus* subscription) Ninety-day money-back guarantee: If you're not completely satisfied with your ABSSI membership benefits, you may cancel within ninety days and receive a refund for the unused portion of your dues upon written notification and return of all association materials. (Certain restrictions apply.)

ABSSI publications (available solely through ABSSI)

Note: Add $5.00 shipping and handling to order subtotal; Californians please also add 7.75% sales tax.

- *Membership Information Packet:* Includes details on membership benefits and ABSSI publications, plus a recent sample issue of *Industry Focus* (complimentary upon request)

- *Starting a Successful Business Support Service:* Name selection, location, layout, pricing, marketing, budgeting, and best time to start (#M-114, 120 pp., $20)

- *Industry Production Standards Guide:* Apply your hourly rate to Model Operator time standards to keep money from falling between the cracks (#IPS-4, nearly 200 pp. with index tabs and three-ring binder; $64.95 nonmembers, $49.95 members)

- *Pricing Guide for Business Support Services:* How to establish profitable hourly and piece rates, and how they are affected by competitive bidding and/or business expansion (#M-109, 70 pp.; $39.95 nonmembers, $24.95 members)

- *Annual ABSSI Pricing Survey Results:* Over twenty bar charts by service type, showing range and frequency of most popular hourly or line/field rates used by ABSSI members and *Industry Focus* subscribers (#A-MAG12, $5.00, shipping and handling included)

- *Business Planning: Concept to Action:* Steps in creating a business support services plan to keep your business on track (#M-110, 150 pp.; members only, $24.95)

- *Straight Talk About Promoting Your Service:* Packed with ideas, techniques, and strategies to attack common problems with low- or no-cost solutions (#M-102, 60 pp.; $29.95 nonmembers, $20 members)

- *Fine Forms Collection + Disk:* Over twenty customizable forms from ABSSI members on billing/invoicing, client agreements, project trackers, work orders, and more; ships with form descriptions/use, blank forms, completed examples, and disk (#M-105; must specify Word 7/95, WordPerfect 7, or Word 6/Mac when ordering; members only, $28.95)

- *Successful Sales Letters, Proposals, and Literature:* Dozens of sample sales-letter paragraphs, plus guidelines for proposals, brochures, press releases, and ads (#M-111, 115 pp.; members only, $24.95)

International Association of Administrative Professionals

(For information about CPS designation [Certified Professional Secretary]; ask for copy of *The Capstone* when writing.)

10502 NW Ambassador Drive
P.O. Box 20404
Kansas City, MO 64195-0404
(816) 891-6600
Fax: (816) 894-1277
e-mail: cps@iaap-hq.org
URL: www.iaap-hq.org

Office Proficiency Assessment & Certification (OPAC)
Attn. Liza Seipel
Department JLM
Biddle & Associates, Inc.
2100 Northrop Avenue, Suite 200
Sacramento, CA 95825-3937
(916) 929-7670
(800) 999-0438, ext. 234

The OPAC System is designed to measure entry-level office skills and is used widely in both the corporate and educational markets. Home-based secretarial services that are members of the Association of Business Support Services International, Inc. can utilize this service to offer testing as a new profit center. This can be done for office staff of companies in their area through a "temporary transportable license" (in other words, they have the capability of going to a client's site to conduct prospective employee testing) *or* in their own offices using their own equipment. To offer this service, the secretarial service must be licensed through OPAC (special pricing available through ABSSI membership). Skills testing is clearly an area where there could be great opportunity for secretarial services; revenue flow is derived through both an on-site fee for the secretarial service operator to offer the service and then a "per-report" fee for scoring of each applicant tested. For complete information, write or call Liza Seipel at the contact information provided above.

The Professional Association of Resume Writers (PARW)
3637 Fourth Street North, Suite 330
St. Petersburg, FL 33704
(813) 823-3646

Contact for membership information as well as details of earning the credential of a Certified Professional Resume Writer (CPRW).

SCORE (Service Corps of Retired Executives)
c/o Small Business Development Center Headquarters
1129 Twentieth Street NW, #410
Washington, DC 20036

Contact your local SCORE chapter to arrange for a complimentary small business consultation.

INDEPENDENT SALES ORGANIZATION
(to obtain merchant account)

Discover/Novus Network
(800) 347-2000

OFFICE SUPPLY VENDORS (MAIL ORDER)

Paper Access
23 West 18th Street
New York, NY 10011
(800) PAPER 01 (727-3701)

Paper Direct
205 Chubb Avenue
Lyndhurst, NJ 07071
(800) A-PAPERS (272-7377)

Penny Wise Office Products
(offers discount to subscribers of
Homeworking Mothers)
4350 Kenilworth Avenue
Edmonston, MD 20781
(800) 942-3311

Queblo
1000 Florida Avenue
Hagerstown, MD 21741
(800) 523-9080

Quill Corporation
P.O. Box 1450
Lebanon, PA 17042-1450
(800) 789-1331

Reliable
1001 W. Van Buren Street
Chicago, IL 60607
(800) 735-4000

Streamliners
5 Pleasant View Drive
P.O. Box 480
Mechanicsburg, PA 17055
(800) 544-5779

Viking Office Products
13809 South Figueroa Street
P.O. Box 61144
Los Angeles, CA 90061
(800) 421-1222

Wholesale Supply Company
P.O. Box 23437
Nashville, TN 37202
(800) 962-9162

TIME MANAGEMENT/SCHEDULING AIDS

Franklin Covey
2200 West Parkway Boulevard
P.O. Box 25127
Salt Lake City, UT 84119
(800) 423-1492
Calendars and time planners.

BIBLIOGRAPHY

BOOKS

(Books appearing below with an * after the title are out of print; however, you are encouraged to check with www.amazon.com on the Internet for availability and special ordering information.)

Atkinson, William. *Working at Home: Is It For You?** Dow Jones-Irwin, 1985.

Belkin, Gary S. *How to Start and Run Your Own Word Processing Business.** John Wiley & Sons, 1984.

Blake, Gary. *How to Promote Your Own Business.** New American Library, 1983.

Brabec, Barbara. *Homemade Money: How to Select, Start, Manage, Market and Multiply the Profits of a Business at Home* (5th ed.). Betterway Publications, 1997.

Bradley, Marianne T. *How to Start a Successful Home-based Word Processing Business.** Vesper Publishing.

Branson, John J. *How to Start a Word Processing Business at Home.** Prentice-Hall, 1985

Brenner, Robert C. *Desktop Production Standards.* Brenner Production Group, 1996.

The Chicago Manual of Style. University of Chicago Press, 1993 (14th ed.).

Cook, Mel. *Home Business, Big Business: The Definitive Guide to Starting and Operating On-Line and Traditional Home-Based Ventures.* Macmillan General Reference, 1998.

Cornish, Clive G. *Basic Accounting for the Small Business.* International Self Council, 1992.

Davenport, Lynne. *Home Transcribing: Could You? Should You? A Practical Guide to Establishing a Professional Transcribing Service at Home.** Dalyn Press, 1984.

Dean, Sandra Linville. *How to Advertise: A Handbook for Small Business.** Enterprise Publications, 1980.

Edwards, Paul and Sarah. *Making Money With Your Computer at Home.* Putnam Publishing Group, 1997 (2nd ed.).

Edwards, Paul and Sarah. *The Best Home Businesses for the '90s: The Inside Information You Need to Know to Select a Home-Based Business That's Right for You.* J.P. Tarcher, 1995.

Edwards, Paul and Sarah. *Working From Home*. Putnam Publishing Group, 1994 (4th ed.).

Edwards, Paul and Sarah, and Douglas, Laura Clampitt. *Getting Business to Come to You*. Putnam Publishing Group, 1998 (2nd ed.).

Ferner, Jack. *Successful Time Management: A Self-teaching Guide*. John Wiley & Sons, 1995 (2nd ed.).

Glenn, Peggy. *How to Start and Run a Successful Home Typing Business.* * Pigi Publications, 1983.

Glenn, Peggy. *Word Processing Profits at Home: A Complete Business Plan for the Self-employed Word Crafter*. Aames-Allen Publishing, 1994 (2nd ed.).

Gray, Ernest A. *Profitable Methods for Small Business Advertising.* * John Wiley & Sons, 1984.

Hodson, Marcia. *Word Processing Plus: Profiles of Home-based Success.* * CountrySide Business Publications, 1991.

Holtz, Herman. *How to Start and Run a Writing and Editing Business.* * John Wiley & Sons, 1992.

Kursmark, Louise. *How to Start a Home-based Desktop Publishing Business*. Globe Pequot Press, 1999 (2nd ed.).

Levinson, Jay Conrad. *Guerrilla Marketing for the Home-Based Business*. Houghton Mifflin Co., 1995.

Levinson, Jay Conrad. *Guerrilla Marketing: Secrets for Making Big Profits from Your Small Business*. Houghton Mifflin Co., 1998 (3rd ed.).

Loftus, Michele. *How to Start and Operate a Home-based Word Processing or Desktop Publishing Business.* * Bob Adams, Inc. Publishers, 1990.

Luscher, Keith F. *Advertise! An Assessment of Fundamentals for Small Business.* * K&L Publications, 1991.

Melnik, Jan, CPRW. *How to Start a Home-based Resume Service*. Globe Pequot Press, 1997 (2nd ed.).

Morgenstern, Steve. *No-Sweat Desktop Publishing.* * AMACOM, 1992.

Mullins, Carolyn J. *The Complete Manuscript Preparation Style Guide.* * Prentice-Hall, 1982.

Parker, Yana. *The Damn Good Resume Guide: A Crash Course in Resume Writing*. Ten Speed Press, 1996 (3rd ed.).

Semon, Larry. *"Did You See My Ad?": When, Why, and How to Advertise the Small Business.* Brick House Publishing Co., 1988.

Shenson, Howard L. *The Contract and Fee Setting Guide for Consultants and Professionals.* John Wiley & Sons, 1989.

Turabian, Kate L. *A Manual for Writers of Term Papers, Theses, and Dissertations.* University of Chicago Press, 1996 (6th ed.).

Vickman, Thomas, *Home Office Tax Deductions.* Enterprise Publishing, 1992.

Wallace, Carol Wilkie. *Great Ad! Low-Cost Do-It-Yourself Advertising for Your Small Business.* Liberty Hall Press, 1990.

Will, Mimi, and Weber, Nancy. *How to Create a Successful Word Processing Business.* PPW Publishing Co., 1983.

AMERICA ONLINE (www.aol.com)

Highly recommended in a number of places throughout this book is access to one of the best business start-up arenas for support and solid business-building information, America Online's *"Business Know-How Forum."* It is a superb site for networking with colleagues, asking questions, researching common topics and problems, and gaining expertise in the secretarial services and ancillary professions. Simply select keyword "bkh" to enter the forum and, from there, click on Complete Index. Choose "DTP, WP & Office Services Forum." You'll link to industry-specific message boards, downloadable files, and chat sessions.

INTERNAL REVENUE SERVICE (www.irs.com)

Select the link *"Information On Starting And Operating A New Small Business"* on the IRS Web site (www.irs.gov) for information on the following topics: Before Starting Your Business . . . Operating Your Business . . . Employment Taxes . . . Small Business News. You can also access and order publications, forms, and instructions. Highlighted below are some IRS publications specifically of interest to home-based entrepreneurs:

Publications

Basis of Assets (#551)

Business Use of Your Home (#587)

Depreciating Property Placed in Service (#534)

Determining Whether a Worker Is an Employee (#SS-8)

Index to Tax Publications (#900)

Miscellaneous Deductions (#529)

Starting a Business and Keeping Records (#583)

Sales and Other Dispositions of Assets (#544)

Self-Employment Tax (#533)

Taxable and Nontaxable Income (#525)

Tax Guide for Small Business (#334)

Direct Sellers (#911)

Tax Withholding and Estimated Tax (#505)

Travel, Entertainment, Gift, and Car Expenses (#463)

Forms

1040 (U.S. Individual Income Tax Return)

1040-ES (Estimated Tax for Individuals)

4562 (Depreciation and Amortization)

8829 (Expenses for Business Use of Your Home)

Schedules

A (Itemized Deductions)

B (Interest and Dividend Income)

C (Profit or Loss from Business)

D (Capital Gains and Losses)

SE (Self-Employment Tax)

To request information, call the Internal Revenue Service at (800) 829–3676.

SMALL BUSINESS ADMINISTRATION

The Small Business Administration's Web site (www.sba.gov) offers links to its offices in each state in the United States and also provides information through Entrepreneurial Development and Women's Business Ownership links. From the link to your own state's SBA office, you can obtain contact information and request the *Small Business Resource Guide* or district office Start-up Kit. An on-line version of the complete Small Business Start-up Kit can be accessed through the SBA Web site. In fact, you can spend hours prowling through all the good information it offers. You'll want to check out the Online Library Reading Room. Also, be sure to visit the SBA's online classroom.

As the SBA describes itself on its own Web site, "The *Small Business Classroom* is an on-line systems resource for training and informing entrepreneurs and other students of enterprise. It is a new—easy to use—dimension in entrepreneurial training. The classroom is designed to educate and provide interactive business guidance on a variety of topics to many types of students. Besides 'traditional' small business clients, the on-line classroom will benefit high school and college students, individuals with time and travel limitations, people with disabilities, international business resources and others.

"The Small Business Classroom includes several key components: on-line courses, library, business counselors, course evaluation and comments. The Small Business Classroom is a digital strategy for reaching new *markets* and training small business clients in a changing, global environment."

INDEX

ABOUT THE AUTHOR

JAN MELNIK of Durham, Connecticut, has operated a successful home-based business since 1983. Initially naming the business Professional Services Plus when it started in Connecticut, she renamed it Comprehensive Services Plus (for better alphabetical placement in the Yellow Pages) upon her relocation to the Boston, Massachusetts, area in 1986. The name Comprehensive Services Plus (CSP) stayed when her family moved back to Connecticut in 1988 until 1996, when the name was changed to Absolute Advantage. A graduate of Bay Path College, Ms. Melnik aquired more than twelve years of professional experience with Fortune 50 corporations prior to starting her own company. She has contributed articles to a number of professional journals and industry newsletters and enjoys speaking at national conventions of ABSSI and PARW. She is a regular guest on *Money Watch* radio discussing career-related and business start-up issues. She is married to Ron Melnik and is the mother of identical twins, Daniel and Weston (born in 1987), and Stephen (born in 1990). When she isn't working or mothering, her other passions in life are reading, gardening, volunteering in her sons' classrooms, and writing children's stories.